Lorine Niedecker Collected Works

Edited by Jenny Penberthy

UNIVERSITY OF CALIFORNIA PRESS

BERKELEY   LOS ANGELES   LONDON

The publisher gratefully acknowledges the generous contribution to this book provided by the General Endowment of the University of California Press Associates.

University of California Press
Berkeley and Los Angeles, California

University of California Press, Ltd.
London, England

Library of Congress Cataloging-in-Publication Data

Niedecker, Lorine.
    [Works. 2002]
    Collected works / Lorine Niedecker ; edited by Jenny Penberthy.
        p.   cm.
    Includes bibliographical references and index.
    ISBN 0-520-22433-7 (cloth : alk. paper)
    I. Penberthy, Jenny Lynn, 1953–   II. Title.
    PS3527.I6   2002
    811'.54—dc21

                                                                2001005376
                                                                      CIP

Manufactured in the United States of America

12   11   10   09   08   07   06   05   04   03   02
10   9   8   7   6   5   4   3   2   1

The paper used in this publication meets the minimum requirements of ANSI/NISO Z39.48-1992(R 1997) (*Permanence of Paper*). ♾

for Kenneth Cox

CONTENTS

NEW GOOSE

FOR PAUL AND OTHER POEMS

FOR PAUL

Prose and Radio Plays   1 9 3 7

Notes and Contents Lists

Lorine Niedecker's work has attracted the dedication of extraordinary people, many of whom have contributed to this long-awaited book. I am deeply fortunate to have met and worked with them.

Cid Corman in Kyoto, Japan, is Niedecker's literary executor and champion. Cid has given me his trust and unstinting support throughout the long years of work on this book and others. Many many thanks to him.

Another friend of Niedecker's, Kenneth Cox, deserves my profound thanks. From London, Kenneth has read and made astute comments on my work for fifteen years. I depend upon his sharp eye and keen mind. This book is dedicated to him.

I very much regret that Gail Roub, Niedecker's friend and champion on home ground in Fort Atkinson, Wisconsin, did not live to see this book. Gail contributed generously to this and other books on Niedecker with his immediate, unhesitating supply of crucial information, documents, and photographs. He worked energetically to promote Niedecker's recognition both locally and further afield. Bonnie Roub and family continue that work today. Many thanks to them too for their support.

Another Fort Atkinson resident has been essential to my study of Niedecker. Marilla Fuge, voluntary archivist of the Lorine Niedecker Collection in the Dwight Foster Public Library in Fort Atkinson, has kept me informed of her ongoing and thorough research into the Niedecker and Kunz family histories, and indeed of all Niedecker-related events in the community. The information she supplies me with is essential to my understanding of Niedecker's life on Black Hawk Island. Contact with Marilla is always a pleasure.

Other members of the Niedecker committee in Fort Atkinson have shown me hospitality. I remember with pleasure Joan and Milo Jones, and Bill and Bobbie Starke.

Karl Gartung and Ann Kingsley in Milwaukee have been warm friends and dedicated inventive promoters of Niedecker's poetry. My thanks to both of them.

Many others have helped me compile this edition. Here in Vancouver, British Columbia, Peter Quartermain deserves particular thanks for his meticulous readings of the final manuscript and for spirited encouragements along the way. For their essential contributions of various kinds, I also thank Eliot Weinberger, Marjorie Perloff, Michael Davidson, Jerry Reisman, Glenna Breslin, Jonathan Williams, Tom Meyer, Harry Gilonis, Alec Finlay, Jonathan Greene, Laura Furman, Sharon Thesen, Michele Leggott, Lisa Robertson, the late Joan Hardwick, Keith Alldritt, Linda McDaniel, David Martin, Rebecca Newth, and Capilano College. Tandy Sturgeon deserves special thanks since it was she who first persuaded the University of California Press to take on the publication of this book. We initially began the project together; after she withdrew, she generously allowed me to continue to use her dissertation disk copy of the text of the poems.

Many libraries and librarians have given me access to materials and have been generous with their help. I would like to thank Cathy Henderson, Tara Wenger, and Pat Fox at the Harry Ransom Humanities Research Center, University of Texas at Austin; Gene Bridwell and the late Charles Watts at the Contemporary Literature Collection, W. A. C. Bennett Library at Simon Fraser University; Rodney Phillips at the Henry W. and Albert A. Berg Collection of English and American Literature at the New York Public Library; the Dwight Foster Public Library in Fort Atkinson, Wisconsin (Lorine Niedecker Collection); Special Collections at the Stanford

University Libraries (Robert Creeley Papers); the Beinecke Rare Book and Manuscript Library, Yale University (Yale Collection of American Literature); and the Department of Special Collections at Boston University Library (Lorine Niedecker Collection).

Thanks to Clayton Eshleman, who published "Next Year or I Fly My Rounds, Tempestuous" in *Sulfur* 41 (Fall 1997): 42–71.

Linda Norton, my editor at the University of California Press, has been a pleasure to work with. Her enthusiasm for Niedecker's poetry and her confidence in the importance of this book have sustained me through the years. I am also indebted to senior editor Rachel Berchten and copyeditor Kathleen MacDougall for their meticulous care in managing the production of the book.

Finally, my deepest thanks go to my family—my husband, René, and our sons, Julian and Thomas—for graciously enduring the interruptions to family life caused by this project.

J. P.

"The Brontes had their moors, I have my marshes," Lorine Niedecker wrote of watery, flood-prone Black Hawk Island near the town of Fort Atkinson, Wisconsin, where she lived most of her life.[1] Although few people endured for long the seasonal hardships of life on Black Hawk Island, Niedecker's attachments to the place ran deep. Her life by water could not have been further removed from the avant-garde poetry scene where she also made herself a home.

Lorine was an only child born on May 12, 1903, to Theresa (Daisy) Kunz and Henry Niedecker. The Kunz family owned much of the island— low-lying land bounded by the Rock River and Lake Koshkonong— including the Fountain House Inn, which they operated until Daisy's marriage to Henry in 1901. As a wedding gift, the couple were given several large properties on the island including the Inn, which they ran until 1910 when they sold it on account of Daisy's illness. In the course of Lorine's birth, her mother had lost her hearing and had gradually declined into isolation and depression over the following years.

Even so, the collection of photographs from Lorine's youth depicts a congenial childhood. There are many images of large family gatherings beside the river at the Inn, everyone dressed in turn-of-the-century finery. Lorine had a close relationship with her grandparents, particularly Gottfried Kunz, "a happy, outdoor grandfather who somehow, somewhere had

---

1. *Niedecker and the Correspondence with Zukofsky 1931–1970*, ed. Jenny Penberthy (New York: Cambridge University Press, 1993) 146.

got hold of nursery and folk rhymes to entrance me." After the sale of the Fountain House Inn, Henry divided up the Niedecker property into lots, sold some of them, and built and rented cabins on others. He turned the Inn's pleasure launches into fishing boats and with a partner operated a very successful carp-fishing business. Lorine recalled, "I spent my childhood outdoors—red-winged blackbirds, willows, maples, boats, fishing (the smell of tarred nets), twittering and squawking noises from the marsh."[2] Her work is distinguished by its attentive use of sound, a consequence perhaps of her poor eyesight and her experience of her mother's deafness, but also of her immersion in the rich soundscape of Black Hawk Island.

When Lorine was ready to start school, Henry built a large home on Germany Street (renamed Riverside Drive) in Fort Atkinson where the family lived until she entered high school. Her parents then moved back to Black Hawk Island and Lorine billeted with Fort Atkinson friends during the school week.

After graduating from high school in 1922, she enrolled at Beloit College to pursue a degree in literature but was called home in her second year to tend her mother, whose condition was deteriorating. Henry and Daisy's marriage had long since broken down as a result of her illness and his extended affair with Gerte Runke, a Black Hawk Island neighbor referred to in several of Niedecker's poems.

In 1928, Niedecker married Frank Hartwig, a former employee of her father's, and started her job as library assistant at the Dwight Foster Public Library in Fort Atkinson. Two short poems appeared in print that year. *"Transition"* reflects her exposure to the Imagist program of Ezra Pound, H.D. (Hilda Doolittle), and Amy Lowell. The second poem, *"Mourning Dove,"* begins with a condensed sample of Imagist practice followed by a

2. "Extracts from Letters to Kenneth Cox," *The Full Note: Lorine Niedecker,* ed. Peter Dent (Budleigh Salterton, U.K.: Interim, 1983) 36.

riposte to its confining limits. However, she did admire the extended Imagist poems of H.D.'s *Heliodora* (1924). According to the notes inserted into her copy of Wallace Stevens's *Harmonium* (1923), she was drawn "to the Imagists, to the wordy ones and the strange rhythms."[3]

In 1930 both Niedecker and her husband lost their jobs to the Depression. Unable to pay the rent on their home in Fort Atkinson, they each returned to their parents' homes, and the marriage effectively ended. Soon after, in February 1931, Niedecker read and was enthralled by Louis Zukofsky's Objectivist issue of *Poetry* magazine. She wrote to him with her latest poems, one of which was *"When Ecstasy is Inconvenient."* Zukofsky responded with interest and referred her to the magazine's editor, Harriet Monroe. This poem, which Monroe accepted for publication, reveals Niedecker's early surrealism, a style she was exploring long before "Mr. Zukofsky referred me to the surrealists for correlation."[4] By this time, she had read the major modernist writers whose work was available to her in Fort Atkinson, principally Virginia Woolf, Katherine Mansfield, H.D., Ezra Pound, T.S. Eliot, Wallace Stevens, D.H. Lawrence. But it was contact with the second-generation modernist Louis Zukofsky that gave her direct access to the American avant-garde.

Though it was the Objectivist issue of *Poetry* that had initiated her contact with Zukofsky, Niedecker would never count herself among the original Objectivists—Zukofsky, Charles Reznikoff, George Oppen, and Carl Rakosi. At the time, she was drawn to its affinity with her own writing: "Thank god for the Surrealist tendency running side by side with Objectivism."[5] She admired the priority Objectivism gave both to the nonreferential, material qualities of words and to a "non-expressive" poetry that

3. Lorine Niedecker Collection, Dwight Foster Public Library.

4. *Lorine Niedecker: Woman & Poet*, ed. Jenny Penberthy (Orono, Maine: National Poetry Foundation, 1996) 177.

5. *Lorine Niedecker: Woman & Poet* 85.

rejected a too-prominent stance of the poet described by Zukofsky as "imperfect or predatory or sentimental."[6] It appears that her enthusiasm for an object-based poetics was limited. Instead, she pursued abstraction. Niedecker and her Fort Atkinson friend Mary Hoard—wife of Niedecker's future employer—were fascinated by the challenge of registering experience without recourse to representational form. Poems such as the 1934 *"Canvass"* series record the linguistic content of different levels of consciousness. According to Edward Dahlberg, it was Niedecker's habit to "sleep with a pencil under her pillow so as not to miss any dreams."[7] Dream, she noted, is full of syntax: "in dream the simple and familiar words like prepositions, connectives, etc. are not absent, in fact, noticeably present to show illogical absurdity, discontinuity, parody of sanity."[8]

Niedecker and Zukofsky debated poetic strategies, he with little interest in the abstract or in surrealism but nevertheless impressed by the energy of her experiment. For the next thirty-five years they would continue their conversation in weekly letters, at times even more frequent. An edited selection of her letters to him is available in my book *Niedecker and the Correspondence with Zukofsky, 1931–1970*. Early in the friendship, toward the end of 1933, she made her first visit to New York, stayed in Zukofsky's apartment, became his lover, and fell pregnant. He insisted on an abortion, and she acquiesced. But the friendship survived these difficulties. Zukofsky continued to supply her with suggestions for reading, sent her copies of magazines and books that were difficult to obtain, read drafts of her poems, made suggestions for changes, and sent them to Ezra Pound, James Laughlin, and others for publication. For her part, Niedecker provided astute critiques of Zukofsky's work, plied him with questions, typed

---

6. *Poetry* 37.5 (February 1931): 292.

7. Noted by Edward Dahlberg on his copy of *New Directions* 12 (1950). Eliot Weinberger's private collection.

8. *Lorine Niedecker: Woman & Poet* 182.

his poems, and prepared notes on subjects of shared interest. The writing that originated in this dialogue conveys a strong sense of shared endeavor.

Both poets wrote across genres. Niedecker gave the title "TWO POEMS" to her play scripts "THE PRESIDENT OF THE HOLDING COMPANY" and "FANCY ANOTHER DAY GONE," and wrote another play script called "DOMESTIC AND UNAVOIDABLE," which she imagined as a series of "print stills" projected on a screen. In the same period, she also wrote a long semi-autobiographical prose piece, "UNCLE," based on her grandparents' and parents' lives. The work of her early years has a particularly strong and varied material presence: the prose-poems, the script-poems, the trilogy of "*Canvass*" poems printed side-by-side in allusion to a triptych of abstract paintings, and the gift-book palimpsest, which superimposes her own holograph writings onto a conventionally printed pocket calendar. As she said in a letter to Mary Hoard, "This would of course be what no one else has written—else why write?"[9]

During the period 1935–1936, she made a shift from overt surrealist experiment toward a poetry attuned to political and social immediacies: "Looking around in America, working I hope with a more direct consciousness than in the past. . . ."[10] She had read Karl Marx and Friedrich Engels and, although not a member of the Communist Party, was committed to social reform. Her writing explored folk models and, in particular, the short metrical rhymes of Mother Goose—poems of anonymous authorship, of proletarian origin, and of subtly subversive intent. Another significant shift occurred in 1938 when Niedecker began work in Madison for the federal Work Project Administration (WPA). There she was a writer and research editor with the Federal Writers' Project, helping to compile *Wisconsin: A Guide to the Badger State*. The job focused her atten-

9. *Lorine Niedecker: Woman & Poet* 88.
10. *Lorine Niedecker: Woman & Poet* 188.

tion on the local and added to her folk poems the vernacular of her Black
Hawk Island/Fort Atkinson community and particularly of her mother,
"descendant for sure of Mother Goose."[11] These poems offer a rich and
subtle study of folk habits made by a poet with twin allegiances to a rural
backwater and a metropolitan avant-garde.

Her attention to local and international politics, visible though not
prominent in her early surrealist work, coalesced in the folk project with
its poems about the Depression, the growth of fascism, the Spanish Civil
War, the Vichy government in France, the American involvement in
World War II, the atomic bomb, and so on. Her engagement in current
events and politics was matched by an interest in American history. Much
of her research would be reflected in her poems in the form of quotation, a
practice familiar to her from her reading of Zukofsky, Pound, and Mari-
anne Moore. Between 1935 and 1944 she wrote more than 80 folk poems.
Many of these would appear in *New Goose*, published in 1946 by the Press
of James A. Decker.

Upon completion of the *Wisconsin* guidebook in 1942, Niedecker
worked briefly as a scriptwriter for the Madison radio station WHA.
Then, in 1944 she began work in Fort Atkinson as a stenographer and
proofreader for the local journal *Hoard's Dairyman*. Her poor eyesight
would force her to give up the job in 1950. While she had known material
comforts in her youth, her circumstances had become increasingly strait-
ened. Her earnings were minimal and intermittent, and her parents'
resources were dwindling. Her father's carp-fishing business failed in the
late 1930s, and his property management was notoriously reckless, so that
by the time of her parents' deaths in the early 1950s, Niedecker inherited
no more than two cabins on the island. These brought in little income and
proved a great headache to manage.

In 1939, Louis had married Celia Thaew, and the birth of their son,

---

11. *The Full Note* 36.

Paul, in 1943, was a great pleasure to Niedecker. Zukofsky's letters gave her detailed accounts of Paul's childhood. In 1949 she began the long poem project "FOR PAUL," where "[t]he central figure is a child of six or seven who composes music and plays the violin. . . . [T]he poem undertakes the child's further instruction, offering a middle ground between Paul's very personal world and the real world of history, wars, depressions, art and science."[12] The project was not unlike *New Goose*, which located the local and immediate within the global. Over four years, Niedecker composed 51 poems in a sequence of eight groups, each group a varied collection of forms and styles: quotation-based poems, persona poems, ballads, blues songs, riddling rhymes, and nonsense ephemera. Free verse is positioned alongside tightly organized stanzas; individual poems range in length from 4 to 204 lines. The result is remarkably spirited and assured. Her pace of composition was brisk, and the first two groups quickly appeared in print. Then followed a sudden stalling of publication explained, perhaps, by Zukofsky's increasing discomfort with the personal content of the poems. With this project, he had assumed and was allowed a more proprietary role. His relation to the poems was, of course, close, and when he experienced them as intrusive, his criticism was barbed.

The "FOR PAUL" poems are nevertheless an assertion of Niedecker's own poetics, "the outcome of experimentation with subconscious and with folk—all good poetry must contain elements of both or stems from them—plus the rational, organizational force."[13] They are also insistently personal, at times extended and uncondensed, and in some cases focused on the less than idyllic qualities of life on Black Hawk Island. By 1956 Niedecker had abandoned the eight-group structure and rearranged the poems within a larger manuscript titled "FOR PAUL AND OTHER POEMS." Some poems were removed and others added, resulting in a collection of 72 poems. This was intended to

12. *New Mexico Quarterly* (Spring 1951): 205.
13. "Editor's Corner," *New Mexico Quarterly* (Summer 1950).

be her second book, ten years after the first, but despite her efforts, "FOR PAUL AND OTHER POEMS" was never published. Zukofsky's ambivalence was an important obstacle. As late as September 1960, Niedecker told Cid Corman that she had "ready, a book not yet printed, under title of *For Paul*."[14] Soon after she would dissolve the collection and instead publish the individual poems in magazines. Several of these were substantially revised, others remained unpublished, and still others such as "What horror to awake at night" and "Sorrow moves in wide waves" had to wait 18 years for their first publication in her *T&G: The Collected Poems (1936–1966)*.

Until the 1960s, publication—even in magazines—was a rare satisfaction for Niedecker. She told Edward Dahlberg in 1955, "Creeley has now accepted 4 [for *Black Mountain Review*]. I'm almost overcome, this would make my 6th publication in 10 years!"[15]

In the mid-1950s, after the expansive form and energetic, personal disclosure of the "FOR PAUL" poems, she shifted toward an astringent, condensed haiku form, developing her distinctive five-line stanza. The choice of a minimalist form also coincided with the start of her job, in 1957, as a cleaner at the Fort Atkinson Hospital. Until she retired in 1963, time for writing would be rare. Her friendships with neighbor Aeneas McAllister and with the Milwaukee dentist Harold Hein sustained her through the 1950s and early 1960s. An important friendship by mail with Cid Corman began in 1960. Niedecker's side of the correspondence can be found in Lisa Pater Faranda's edition, *"Between Your House and Mine": The Letters of Lorine Niedecker to Cid Corman, 1960 to 1970*.

When Ian Hamilton Finlay in Scotland read *New Goose* in 1961, the folk poems struck an immediate chord with him, caught up as he was in the

14. *"Between your House and Mine": The Letters of Lorine Niedecker to Cid Corman, 1960 to 1970*, ed. Lisa Pater Faranda (Durham, N.C.: Duke University Press, 1986) 24.

15. Edward Dahlberg Collection, Harry Ransom Humanities Research Center, University of Texas at Austin.

Scottish folk poetry revival. He wrote to Niedecker with lavish praise and offered to reprint some of the poems. Within a year *My Friend Tree* was published. It reprinted nine of the original *New Goose* poems and added seven new ones. Niedecker planned the book as a selected poems including several more from *New Goose;* however, budget constraints kept the book trim. Buoyed by the sudden interest from a publisher, Niedecker returned to thinking of herself as a folk poet. She made the too-modest comment to Jonathan Williams that her folk poetry might be her only claim to difference between herself and other poets.

In 1963, Niedecker married Al Millen, a housepainter from Milwaukee. The marriage allowed her to retire from the hospital job (she identified herself as "laborer" on her marriage license) and return to full-time writing. She moved to Al's apartment in Milwaukee; they spent their weekends on the island and their summers on road trips into the surrounding states and Canada. In 1964 she collected her current short poems—the product of ten months of new freedom—into three handmade, handwritten giftbooks for Corman, Zukofsky, and Jonathan Williams, an acknowledgment of friendship but also of the difficulty of finding a publisher.

In August 1965, Jonathan Williams offered to publish the manuscript of collected poems that she had prepared and titled *T&G*. She explained the title as an abbreviation of Lawrence Durrell's "Tenderness and Gristle" to which Williams added, much to her delight, "Tongue and Groove (if you're a carpenter)." But Jargon Society financial troubles kept the book in production limbo for four years. Niedecker waited with growing despair until it appeared in 1969. Meanwhile, in 1967, Stuart Montgomery of Fulcrum Press in London had solicited poems for another collection. In 1968, *North Central* was published. It included her two travel- and research-based poems, "LAKE SUPERIOR" and "WINTERGREEN RIDGE." The same year Stuart Montgomery accepted *My Life by Water,* which Fulcrum would publish in 1970. Originally planned as the British edition of *T&G,* it was now expanded to include the contents of *North Central* plus "PAEAN TO PLACE," her extended reflection on Black Hawk Island. *T&G* appeared in 1969, and soon after, Niedecker received Cid Corman's offer to publish a selected poems. She prepared two typescripts, "THE EARTH AND ITS ATMOSPHERE" and "THE VERY VEERY," both of which select from the same work represented in *North Central*, *T&G*, and *My Life by Water*. Neither of the typescripts was published. Her final manuscript, "HARPSICHORD & SALT FISH," ready in 1970 and including the text-derived poems such as "THOMAS JEFFERSON," "HIS CARPETS FLOWERED," and "DARWIN," was also unpublished at the time of her death.

Throughout the 1960s, she was regularly published in little magazines. Her preference for quiet led her to refuse offers to read in public, but she enjoyed enormously visits from fellow poets such as Jonathan Williams, Basil Bunting, Tom Pickard, Carl Rakosi, Stuart Montgomery, and a month before her death, Cid Corman. She savored her contact with local friends Gail and Bonnie Roub and her correspondence with Clayton Eshleman, Bob Nero, and Kenneth Cox. After the mid-1960s, letters to Zukofsky were less routine. Niedecker died of a cerebral hemorrhage on December 31, 1970, at the height of her career. Two weeks before her death she told Cid Corman, "I think lines of poetry that I might use—all day long and even in the night."[16]

During her life, she attracted high praise from her peers. Her work was much admired by Marianne Moore, William Carlos Williams, Edward Dahlberg, Charles Reznikoff, Jonathan Williams, Cid Corman, and many others. On January 5, 1971, six days after her death, the *Wisconsin State Journal* published the following letter, written by Basil Bunting from his home in Wylam, U.K.:

---

16. Cid Corman's transcription from his brief tape-recorded interview with Niedecker. The recording is held at Simon Fraser University in the Contemporary Literature Collection. The quotation appears in *Blue Chicory* (New Rochelle, N.Y.: Elizabeth, 1976), n.p.

Lorine Niedecker . . . will be remembered long and warmly in England, a country she never visited. She was, in the estimation of many, the most interesting woman poet America has yet produced. Her work was austere, free of all ornament, relying on the fundamental rhythms of concise statement, so that to many readers it must have seemed strange and bare. She was only beginning to be appreciated when she died, but I have no doubt at all that in 10 years time Wisconsin will know that she was its most considerable literary figure.

In the last two years of Niedecker's life, two books of her collected poems were published—*T&G: The Collected Poems (1936–1966)*, prepared in 1965 and published in 1969, and *My Life by Water: Collected Poems, 1936–1968*, an expanded edition prepared in 1968 and published in 1970. Jonathan Williams's timely offer to publish her collected poems reached Niedecker in 1965, when she was sixty-two years old. Since her first magazine publication in 1928, she had seen two books to press: *New Goose* in 1946 and *My Friend Tree* in 1961. Given this spare publication record, the collected poems she now had to compile could not be a conventional alignment of previously published books. Instead she chose to organize an edited selection of poems in a loose chronology of named categories—generic in the case of "Ballads," "In Exchange for Haiku," and the folk poems "New Goose/My Friend Tree," and thematic in the case of "For Paul," "The Years Go By," and "Home/World"—a schema that provided the barest allusion to the ambitious provenance of poems written in the course of thirty-five years. The usual autobiographical or biographical cues of an edition of collected poems are muted in *T&G* to the point where the collection gives the impression of an authorless text. This was perhaps a deliberate choice, consistent with her anti-authorial practice throughout her career—and a locus of her appeal for many readers. However, it was also a choice that may explain her near invisibility on the American scene.

This new edition of Niedecker's collected works aims to establish her position among twentieth-century American poets. Furthermore, it aims to restore the profile of her writing life. To this end it dismantles the previous attempts at selected and collected poems and presents the work in the sequence of its composition. This collection adds previously omitted work such as all the surviving instances of her early surrealism, the impulse that Zukofsky and Pound would disparage in her work but that would remain a steady influence throughout her career. It supplements the published *New Goose* volume and the even smaller selection of folk poems from *T&G* and *My Life by Water* with the many unpublished poems from the same project. It recovers the "FOR PAUL AND OTHER POEMS" manuscript, which she had planned as her second volume, ten years after the first, *New Goose*.

This edition organizes the work chronologically by collections, both published and projected. Not all of these can be represented here because of their overlapping content—a particular problem with the 1960s books and typescripts. I have included as many of the major groupings of her work as chronology and the need to avoid duplication will allow: collections published in her lifetime (*New Goose, North Central*); manuscripts intended for publication ("NEW GOOSE," "FOR PAUL AND OTHER POEMS," "HARPSICHORD & SALT FISH"); and the gift-books made by hand for her poet-friends at a time when publication still seemed unlikely ("HOMEMADE POEMS" and "HANDMADE POEMS"). In between these collections, the remaining poems are placed in the chronology by first traceable date of composition—dates of manuscripts and letters; dates of magazine appearance; or, in very few cases, conjectural dates. There are five cases where duplication has been necessary in order to maintain the integrity of a collection. These are flagged in the notes at the back of the book. The arrangement of the 1960s collections not represented in the text can be found in the contents lists that follow the notes.

Smaller groupings of poems are also acknowledged in this edition. When Niedecker submitted her work to magazines, she typically arranged the poems in groups. In many cases, the groupings were retrospective and transitory, made in fresh attempts to see the poems into print. "The poems in this envelope are chosen from many," she told Robert Creeley in January 1955: "If you wish to make a further choice you may do so, re-numbering them." She told Creeley again in June 1955, "You need not hold to my groupings. . . ."[1] To Cid Corman in September 1960, she said, "The short poems with Roman numerals have no real sequence in case you want to break them up."[2] Her openness to intervention is surely the pragmatism of a poet eager, if not desperate, to be published. Partly because she was published so irregularly, she had a growing body of work to draw from when she made submissions to magazines or when she compiled her books. As she revisited her poems—both published and unpublished—she revised them and altered their groupings. These groupings are always interesting and revealing—inevitably the poems accrue meaning through their proximity with others—but because of their fluctuating boundaries, they are difficult to preserve in a collection such as this. They can, however, be reconstructed with the help of the notes.

The frequently revised individual poems present further challenge to an editor's desire for a stable text. *T&G* and *My Life by Water* stand at the end of a much-edited life's work. Marianne Moore's pronouncement—"Omissions are not accidents"—at the start of her *Complete Poems* (1967) could as well function as an epigraph for Niedecker's work. But unlike Moore, Niedecker left no published record of her early versions. The drama of Niedecker's omissions and revisions occurred off-stage. This edition aims to restore that record by presenting all the surviving drafts and their revisions.

For copytext, I have settled on *My Life by Water* (1970) as Niedecker's latest and most substantial revised text, or, when a poem is not included in *My Life by Water*, the last extant version. This is a gesture toward recording

1. Robert Creeley Papers, Department of Special Collections, Stanford University Libraries.
2. *"Between Your House and Mine"* 23.

final intentions made with the awareness that Niedecker's final intentions are often difficult to assess. Since, at times, her intentions are masked by the convolutions of her close relationship with Zukofsky, the original form of the poems, recorded in the notes, will be of interest to many readers. Some begin in lengthy drafts and emerge years later much condensed. Her ambivalent statements about the practice of "condensery" suggest that this compositional record should be preserved.

My choice of the last version for copytext is in some ways at odds with my decision to preserve collections that predate *My Life by Water*, a particular problem when many earlier poems are substantially revised for *My Life by Water*. The most striking example is "Dear Paul," which was condensed from its 198 lines in the "FOR PAUL AND OTHER POEMS" typescript to 33 lines in *My Life by Water*. In all such instances, the revised poem displaces the earlier poem, whose text can be found in the notes. This practice is less than ideal, but must suffice until an electronic edition can present all of her published and unpublished collections intact.

In the notes, each work is listed by title or first line followed by a list of book and major typescript appearances. A poem listed as "Unpublished" did not appear in print during her lifetime, and a poem listed as "Unpublished in book form" appeared only in magazine form. The note then cites in chronological order the poem's composition and publication record. All drafts and variants are listed except for minor revisions of lineation and punctuation. Posthumous publications are ignored unless they constitute the first or a variant appearance of a poem. Some of the notes include relevant comments by Niedecker or others.

The disposition of Niedecker's manuscripts is not entirely known. Few manuscripts and papers from her own collection have survived: her husband followed her instructions to destroy them after her death. Those in the Harry Ransom Humanities Research Center at the University of Texas at Austin formed part of Louis Zukofsky's large bequest to the Center in 1964. In the collection are early surrealist poems from the 1930s, the unpublished "NEW GOOSE" manuscript, the "FOR PAUL" poems in their eight groups and in the "FOR PAUL AND OTHER POEMS" collection, the "HANDMADE POEMS" gift-book, and roughly two dozen other poems written between the years 1956 and 1964. The largest concentration of manuscripts belongs to the "FOR PAUL" project that occupied her between 1949 and 1956 and that generated a substantial traffic of manuscripts between the two poets. Niedecker's revisions can be traced from one manuscript to another. At times, Zukofsky noted his suggestions directly on the manuscript. Why then did these annotated manuscripts remain in his possession? Very likely he asked her to return them to him. But given the indeterminate character of this exchange of manuscripts, his annotations need to be read with care. In at least two cases, he appears to have inscribed onto early drafts subsequent revisions that are clearly Niedecker's own. It is easy to mistake these annotations for *his* revisions of the poems. See the notes to *"Thure Kumlien"* and "In Europe they grow a new bean." Throughout the notes, I have indicated apparent interventions by Zukofsky.

In the same section as the poems, I include Niedecker's early plays. Both "THE PRESIDENT OF THE HOLDING COMPANY" and "FANCY ANOTHER DAY GONE," titled "TWO POEMS" in their first published appearance, were part of her experiment in expanding the boundaries of poetry. This was true of "DOMESTIC AND UNAVOIDABLE" too. There is no evidence of these pieces being composed for radio. Reluctantly I have positioned "UNCLE," the long prose piece from the same period, in a separate section devoted to prose and radio plays later in the book. While I'm keen for the piece to be read as part of her multi-genre experimentation, its length would make a significant intrusion in the poems section. The two other prose pieces— "SWITCHBOARD GIRL" and "The evening's automobiles . . ."—are placed in the later section too. They appear alongside the scripts written explicitly for radio, "AS I LAY DYING" and "TASTE AND TENDERNESS." Space constraints have prevented me from including her critical essays on the poetry of Zukofsky and Corman.

Many of Niedecker's poems are untitled; with the few that are, the titles tend to be placed off center: "in all cases I prefer subtitle at right and no main title."[3] Longer poems and sequences retain her fully capitalized titles. Niedecker's blend of American and British spelling conventions are retained.

There have been several posthumous publications of Niedecker's poems. The first was *Blue Chicory*, Cid Corman's 1976 edition of the poems not yet published in book form. The volume draws on those published in the poetry magazine *Origin* and her 1964 holograph gift-book to Corman, "HOMEMADE POEMS," plus Corman's transcription of his cassette tape recording of her November 15, 1970, reading from the "HARPSICHORD & SALT FISH" typescript. Discrepancies of lineation occur in the transcriptions from Corman's tape recording. *Blue Chicory* was followed in 1985 by *From This Condensery: The Complete Writing of Lorine Niedecker*, a highly flawed and unreliable text. Because of its pervasive textual errors—mistranscriptions, misattributions, inaccurate dating, misunderstood sequencing, etc.—I have avoided all reference to it. Cid Corman's edition of *The Granite Pail: The Selected Poems of Lorine Niedecker* also appeared in 1985. (An expanded edition published by Gnomon in 1996 is still in print.) In 1991, Pig Press in Durham, U.K., published my edition of Niedecker's final collection, *Harpsichord & Salt Fish*.

---

3. *Lorine Niedecker: Woman & Poet* 89.

Poems

1928–1936

Transition

Colours of October
wait with easy dignity
for the big change—
like gorgeous quill-pens
in old inkwells
almost dry.

.

Mourning Dove

The sound of a mourning dove
slows the dawn
there is a dee round silence
in the sound.

Or it may be I face the dull prospect
of an imagist
turned philosopher

.

Promise of Brilliant Funeral

Travel, said he of the broken umbrella, enervates
the point of stop; once indoors, theology,
for want of a longer telescope, is made
of the moon-woman passing amid silk
nerve-thoughts in the blood.
(There's trouble with the moon-maker's union,
the blood-maker's union, the thought-maker's union;
but the play could be altered.)

A man strolls pale among zinnias,
life and satin sleeves renounced.
He is intent no longer on what direction herons fly
in hell, but on computing space in forty minutes,
and ascertains at the end of the path:
this going without tea holds a hope of tasting it.
(Chalk-faces going down in rows before a stage
have seen no action yet.)

Mr. Brown visits home.
His broker by telephone advises him it's night
and a plum falls on a marshmallow
and sight comes to owls.
He risks three rooms noisily for the brightest sconce.
Rome was never like this.
(The playwright dies in the draft
when ghosts laugh.)

.

When Ecstasy is Inconvenient

Feign a great calm;
all gay transport soon ends.
Chant: who knows—
flight's end or flight's beginning
for the resting gull?

Heart, be still.
Say there is money but it rusted;
say the time of moon is not right for escape.
It's the color in the lower sky
too broadly suffused,
or the wind in my tie.

Know amazedly how
often one takes his madness
into his own hands
and keeps it.

.

PROGRESSION

I

Here's good health, friends,
and soothing syrup for sleeplessness
and Lincoln said he thought a good deal
in an abstract way
about a steam plow;

secure and transcendental, Emerson avowed
that money is a spiritual force;
the Big Shot of Gangland declared he never really believed
in wanton murder;
Shelley, Shelley, off on the new romance
wrote inconsolable Harriet,
"Are you above the world?
And to what extent?"
And it's the Almanac-Maker joyous
when the prisoner-lad asked the pastor
"Who is Americus Vespucius?"
and an artist labored over the middle tone
that carried the light
into the shadow.
But that was before the library burned.

II

As one Somnambulist to another
our sleep could be more perfect.
Surmising planed squares of wood with legs are tables,
or poppies watched and brooded over flare finally
out of bud-shell hatched
is admitting such superstitions only wait
to beset us outright.

III

Home is on the land
though drought be solid fact,
though you tell by the summer sky
how you'll pare your potatoes next winter;

you murmur your magic (what help is the past?):
opera is an oversight
on the part of the Milky Way
and the squash blossom subsides
with the Fourth Internationale
and it's obviously not theatre.
But what can you do that yellowing season of earth
with more than nine hundred ninety
recombinations of yellows
since rain crossed the modes
of your brooding?

IV

Last lines being sentimental, reaction
is in the first of the cold. The contemporary scene is,
said the green frog by the charcoal wood, false
in every particular but no less admirable for that,
and isn't it humorous to designate at all?
I take into my hole, said he, the curse
that hangs over more than one critic, this
that if forgiven tassels are lost.
Well, and the sun does set short in winter. . . .
What's the play? The sensitive lawyer would have told
any woman her hands were as beautiful as if gloved
but for fear of having been quoted.
At the Capitol, cheese legislation only sets silk hats
tipping, rats divine, toward feline waistbands.
At home, it's blizzard or a curved banana-moon
on a window sash, soap flakes on wash day
and door knobs wet; hornets' nests in tobacco pipes.

I must possess myself, get back into pure duration,
or I should like to be an orator and rise
to my full height, or now that roads are closed
stop quietly in print the one available weather:
how the head hums, men of Ireland, and it goes
the next log on the hearth from violins to harlequins
to modern women and violins again, and the last
determination coincides with the first, and so then
summer has not been since the bliss and doll's house lady
and all that waxing of the lily and sweet care
of people on the stem. . . . I remember a garden:
exigential, or violet, I've forgotten, but delphinium
with suspect of turquoise, formulosos deterred
at the start from interval form by trick of eye
or soul or sun and since by whom . . . you
swinging your cape too far to the left, the effect
is blue, not periwinkle; you triumphant over cauliflower
polonaise; you full of principles; and you crying
crush infamy when you should be shaking hands
with the Cardinal. The most public-cant-and-cabbage-
interruption comes, however, from circles where
the farm question is discussed,—a white dome logic
no wayside strabismic house, rafters owling out
the night would recognize; no talk there, none,
of why there's nothing like a good warm cow
when the wind's in the west.

V

It comes out in March by the back fence, the full
and true Relation of the present State of new country
and the coming of the world green. Some believed
she was immune from such a Thing being they had adopted
a youngster in dispare, most persons, you find,
peck and peck and seldom really lay any eggs, red
though suns set for windy to-morrows. Spring looms also
in phonographic deep song on a level with the water
and in spoken acknowledgment of carved humidor
so calm what is this woman a man should say: woman.
Complaints differ: trees have their roots in China;
it was tried there three thousand years ago and failed.
April a silver symbol is of rain and universal love;
April ergo lost integral if not grey gone. New
reviews use the dusking nounal (how do you die, thrush,
this afternoon) with a lamp and aluminum forecast
(light gets mooned in a clouded river, and frogs
are out scouring, one ratchet ahead of cracked piccolos).
My dear May: I should like to buy myself flowers,
arrive at the door and give them to you. May, again,
I believe to have seen in my best swooning moments,
but I might easily have been prejudiced by a slow heart
or what the porcelain painter said in that nerve-ray
or by the Slumbrous my shadow spoke, going by. This swale
can only be the mode by which we condense all exposition
to a green blood-beat and bleach intact. Let no man say
from grass to grass he never to himself has sunk
is the first tremble of an old vibration orioled
at dandelion heat. In Swalery I forget my face,

beyond that it's something to have under a sunbonnet
when aphorists and haymakers meet. And doctor,
nothing so good I know for intricate rhyme schemes
in six-syllable lines within ten-syllable lines
of an evangelical staple as bug-sing and carrot seed,
observe now, while perspective is the next show
in the gallery, it's a fervid shade, and there'll be
stricken areas in the throat waiting for the blowing.
A touch of noon? Try then: each man to his own sleep
in the night skies. Gaspaciousness enmillions
dread-centric introspectres. Future studies
will throw much darkness on the home-talk.

VI

Meanwhile surviving burial and the garden with too many
tall stones entails backroads, berries and what is socialism.
If I had two pigs, said the farmer, and you hadn't any,
I'd have to give you one, and the gardener said, fist
to mahogany, no more petals would fall from the silver vased
red poppy than enough. Meanwhile coming in the afternoon,
one wakes about the beaches long-summering. A girl's hair
lies in a neat droll along the back of the neck, a man
can't rest unless he's tired; another eats between dinner
and tea to stimulate the circulation, this class of ideas
brown bodied, pistoned and cogged and nowhere dissembled.
To retire to the wood out of glaring might mean freedom
from the blue pressure of my fellow magnetoes, and nothing
less to lift plants from the habits of their whorls
than a storm passage in the strings, the brass being silent

for many bars. I should say the social behavior of the individual
should be thoroughly rained on, and in the same rheumatism
the Introspect's Umbrella Mender waved good-bye. Of course,
I shall meet people here, my antecedents perhaps. But how
shall I know them? If I am fernal, it's fern country, then;
fern fever has been spread by mono-men I shall pass in the air
of my time and whose main frond cuts I shall have to regret.
Someone has said: rapid lighted pimperly advanced; I've forgotten
who. A little false for a person in my position: gloom-elmed,
gloam-owned, retreating. (Cuckoo, that juggling of hollow nuts)
Memory is blue in the head? Heads are easily taken off.
Move on from brown laterals of the same day, ascertain oneself
center of climatic being and fall all energy gone yellow.
For the emotion of fall has its seat in the acoustic gland;
wind: strong distance in closest places. On the life side then,
I stand out in the open again as do houses and barns.
I hear it from hand to hand there's been death on the road,
he, not finding where the flowers were, seized a tree.
If this is a game there must be refreshments, but if
dessert be fragile sky, trees pink-rust, crisp as a pie
with a butter-crust, I ought to be going home.

VII

I must have been washed in listenably across the landscape
to merge with bitterns unheard but pumping, and saw
and hammer a hill away; sounds, then whatsound, then
by church bell or locomotive volubility, what, so unto
the one constriction: what am I and why not. That
was my start in life, and to this day I touch things

with a fear they'll break. A cricket and poplar tradition
has me standing instead of running. Of course, no one cares
about my troubles except those who let themselves fall
into the determinism I've been so careful to create.
(Having fallen, cease to care—blue jay variants
have their own mode of call.) But who am I to observe
myself? Dynamist for being out of dream?
It's what comes of looking way back on the upper right
shelf of the lower left cupboard; never be witty
with any finality. From here, it takes so many stamps
to post the most modern researches.

VIII

Close the door and come to the crack quickly.
To jesticulate in the rainacular or novembrood
in the sunconscious . . . as though there were fs
and no ings, freighter of geese without wings.
I know an ill for closing in, a detriment to tie-ups.
They pop practical in a greyfold, bibbler and dub—
one atmosnoric pressure for the thick of us.
Hurry, godunk, we have an effort to wilt.
I shall put everything away, some day,
get me a murmurous contention, and rest.

.

Canvas[1]

Unrefractory petalbent
prognosticate
halfvent purloined
adark
vicissitudes of one-tenth
      steel-tin
bluent, specifically unjust
      cream   redbronze
attempt salmon egress
masked eggs
      ovoid
      anodyne lament
metal   bluegreen
         smoke dent
            drying
exceptional retard
bald out
affidavit
flat grey shoulder.
carrions eats its call, waste it.
He: she knows how
for a testament to Sundays.

For exhibition[2]

for round
of or
in the young beautiful of life
hat laid away, done for . .
help a doorlight undergo
            monotones
faily   refervid
      emotionally
or coral on black velvet
gumdrops and proletarian fiction . .
fast whaler
formaldehyde   backline reversed
no ageratum
mine might blast the nose
impectinal . .
a   jellying
      If you
Denmark
whisper   I can't quite notify
an extreme time.

Tea[3]

dilemma
my suit, continuous
dear hind button off . .
the velocities with which different
      fluents change
Newton's   compose in the mass
wander   anent
      anyone
      (negress certainly not)
            sidewheeler
         painted:
on the next moon
      be still: we are near life
focus your face to a
then oh, divers lanterns in
I meet
      sworn
         thick   think
shuffles o loud foot.
to come to the end and pass it
but I am having

1. subconscious 2. wakeful 3. full consciousness

Beyond what[1]

decapitated areas
momently to the constant removal
liquidating aftermath
inspired marksmanship
Devil the ash trays show it
instant with glee
black winged lazuli
beets redden and revert

I heard[2]

too far for me to see
lest we forget
no fan thank you
peonies
if only one could
I was born on a farm
I watched arrive in spring
city your faith in arches

Memorial Day[3]

Thou hast
not foreign aggression
but world disillusionment
dedicated to the proposition
of an ice cream cone
and the stars and stripes forever
over the factories and hills of our country
for the soldier dead

1. subconscious 2. toward monologue 3. social-banal

Stage Directions

The window woman whose dress has been hung and draped
looks out. There's a wax-wing on every leaf, hay background,
statecraft, salve smell and lavish retort. Shh . . .
the man with the juniper growth to his beard,—bankers
leave their wives to their safes and redouble openings.
They walk around the oblong and Oh is the heart of the modern
furniture. Once out the knock is on the other side.
I seem to take *un ciel*, a circle in another tongue.
Have we experienced a cycle from which we are likely
to recover, or have we seen the death of an era? A loop
of blue light shows white organdie ruffles herself.
My hat—it was taken for a flight—too sad for my face
to assume. Young escort bows. I can't pick a thing up
and bring it to successive stages. Yet for what we see
the mind has to sink down out of sight—perhaps not possible
for us. But think how paultry: the common black and white,
the breakfast table and then all the rest of the meals.
We have our limberger but we mustn't bring it to the table.
Have you been married? Yes, I've been attacked.
The ring of light flames as on comes the night scene
from Tremulus Asps. Somebody sleeps under the oatshed
and resets his pudding. Ticci Tape-over's buttons shine.
He points. I wish there was something to listen to
particularly. Wuzz or whir. His wife says he used to work
in a factory; now he's a gentleman—runs a beer tavern.
But he doesn't exercise enough. If only he could
make himself tired. Blackness soughs as a matter
of lighting. Fanatic acid. Constructions gleam—

triangles and verbal arra. Inimical Pop-its down front
kneeling in swift, strange prayers assure the world
they're dangerous. See how it brings the red swing closer.

.

Synamism

Berceuse, mediphala
and the continent. German and therefore unidentified.
Cricket night, seismograph and stitch. All tongues backed
by a difference. Likelihood without of left-overs cooling,
weatheroid and furor occult, functionary tri-mundane. And
the scientific equiptical left nerves on the floor.

Most
people have to have an attachment. It's all very tiresome.
To wag addenda. Add and add and you'll see it,
and there's nothing less.

The most famous resort
should know better than develop a scene around the face
of its beholder. Speaking of why a cherry orchard
has to become a world, why become a gabbling humanity?
Nobody attests a grove of titles. Are you an emblem
of discount? Superhoned? Assumptions taxed are most related
when untangled, the horn playing a thread, cows untended.
The best always stays where it is. Others have to break it
down to see it. Why dig when the dug is present? That holds
for silence. Light facades its works, ambulates in a single
area, tension regold. If you forget, remember: a wire fence

conceals a tree if it came first to the eye. Judgement:
a menstrualoid broke its shell, I was born.

It must be

not just a synamism between black and retreat but
a savage displacement in silk centre, these roundings
where a flower pulls embattlements down, displeasure
enlightens great eagles. Dancing the blood rim. Could hope
make it thinner? Reverse it and you have my offer to pay.
Galactic numena, eye floats and recitative. Pepitte,
this papering evening I want a theatre.

.

Will You Write Me a Christmas Poem?

Will I!

The mad stimulus of Gay Gaunt Day
meet to put holly on a tree
and trim green bells
and trim green bells

Now candles come to faces.
You are wrong to-day
you are wrong to-day,
my dear. My dear—

One translucent morning
in the development of winter
one fog to move a city backward—
Backward, backwards, backward!

You see the objects and the movable fingers,
Candy dripping from branches,
Horoscopes of summer
and you don't have Christmas ultimately—
Ultima Thule ultimately!

Spreads and whimpets
Good to the cherry drops,
Whom for a splendor
Whom for a splendor

I'm going off the paper I'm going off the pap-

Send two birds out
Send two birds out
And carol them in,
Cookies go round.

What a scandal is Christmas,
What a scandle Christmas is,
a red stick-up
to a lily.

You flagellate my woes, you flagellate,
I interpret yours,
holly is a care divine
        holly is a care divine

and where are we all from here.
Drink for there is nothing else to do
but pray,
And where are we all from here.

Throw out the ribbons
and tie your people in
All spans dissever
once the New Year opens
and snow derides
a doorway,
its spasms dissever

All spans dissever,
Wherefore we, for instance, recuperate
no grief to modulate
no grief to modulate
Wherefore we, Free instance

The Christmas cacophony
one word to another,
sound of gilt trailing the world
slippers to presume,
postludes, homicles, sweet tenses
imbecile and corrupt,—
    failing the whirled, trailing the whirlled

This great eventual heyday
to plenty the hour thereof,
fidelius.
Heyday! Hey-day! Hey-day!

I fade the color of my wine
that an afternoon might live
foiled with shine and brittle
I fade the color of my wine

Harmony in Egypt,
representative birthday.
Christ what a destiny
What a destiny's Christ's, Christ!

.

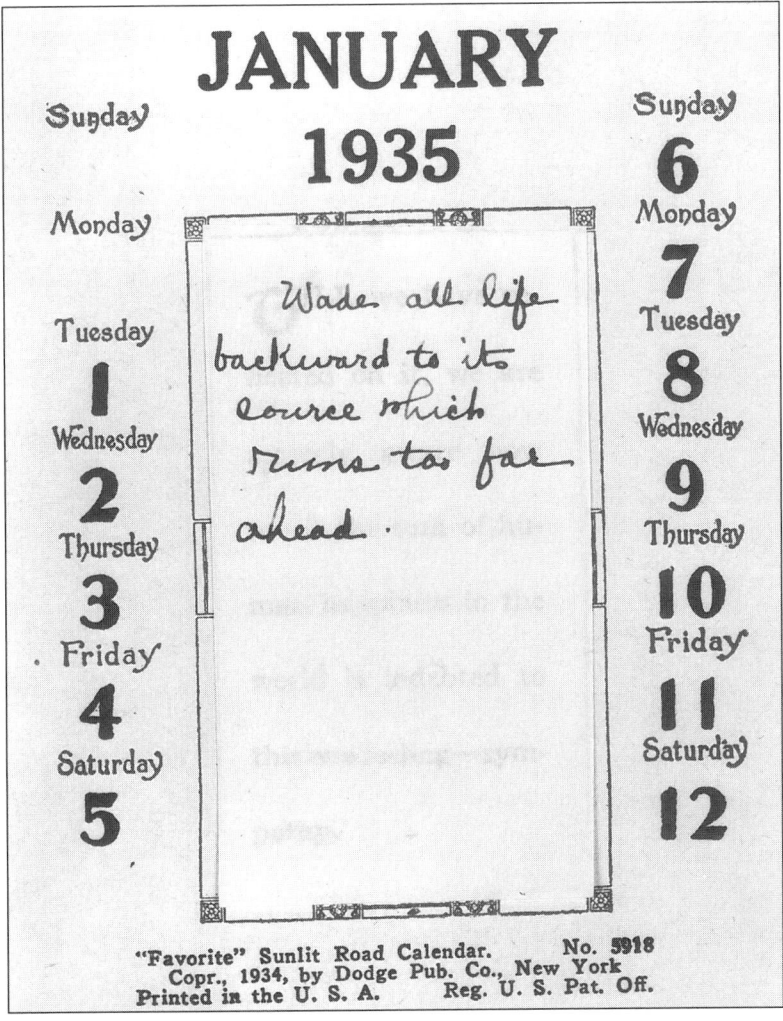

Wade all life / backward to its / source which / runs too far / ahead.

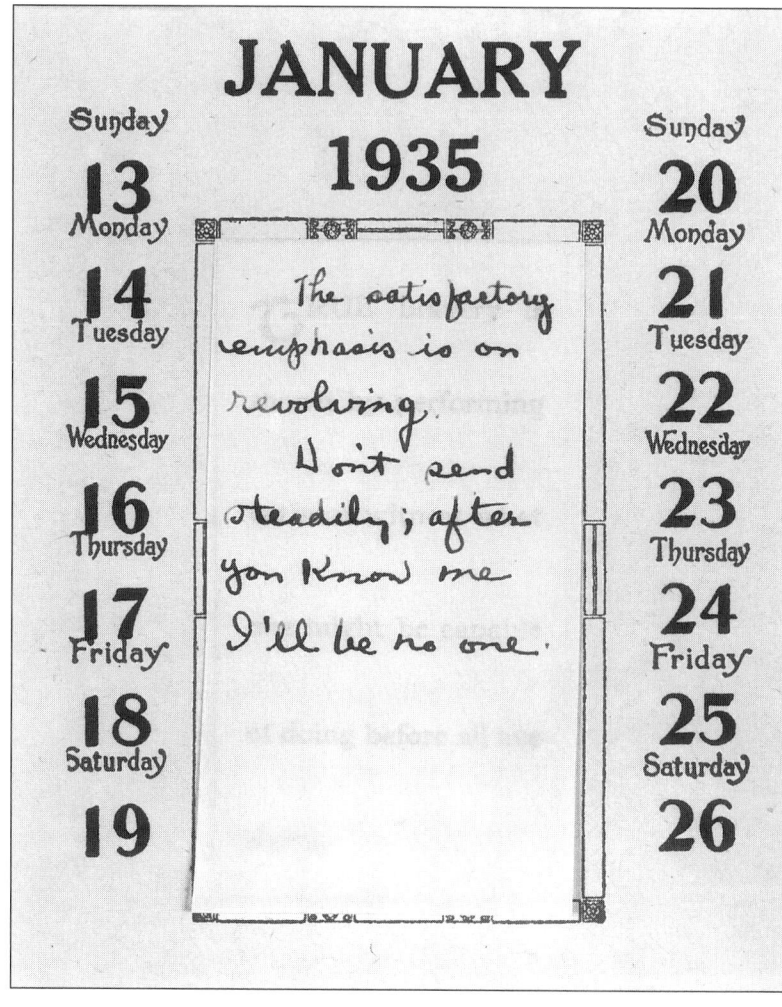

The satisfactory / emphasis is on / revolving. / Don't send / steadily; after / you know me / I'll be no one.

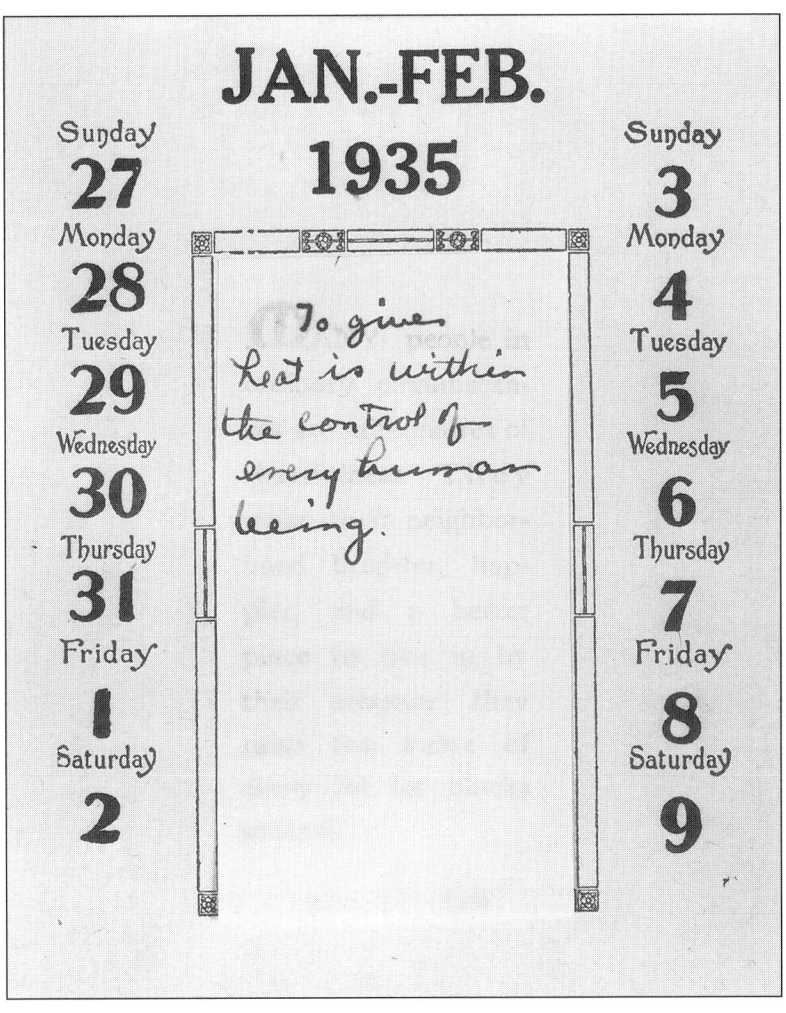

JAN.-FEB.
1935

Sunday
27

Monday
28

Tuesday
29

Wednesday
30

Thursday
31

Friday
1

Saturday
2

Sunday
3

Monday
4

Tuesday
5

Wednesday
6

Thursday
7

Friday
8

Saturday
9

To give / heat is within / the control of / every human / being.

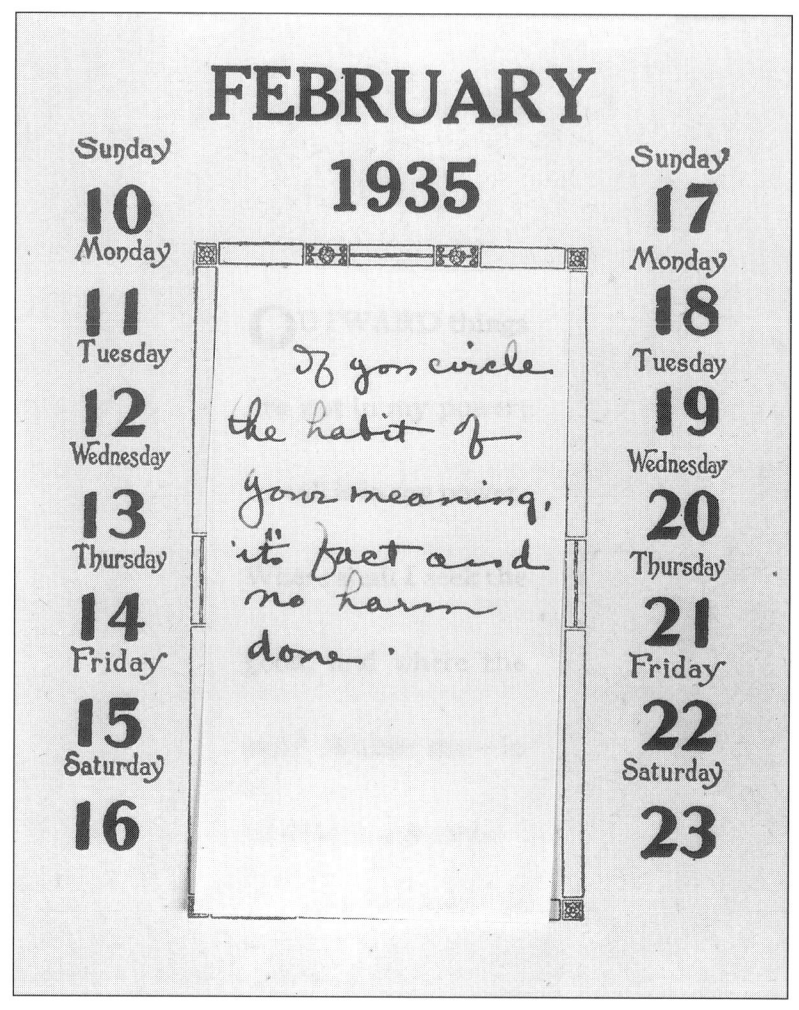

If you circle / the habit of / your meaning, / it's fact and / no harm / done.

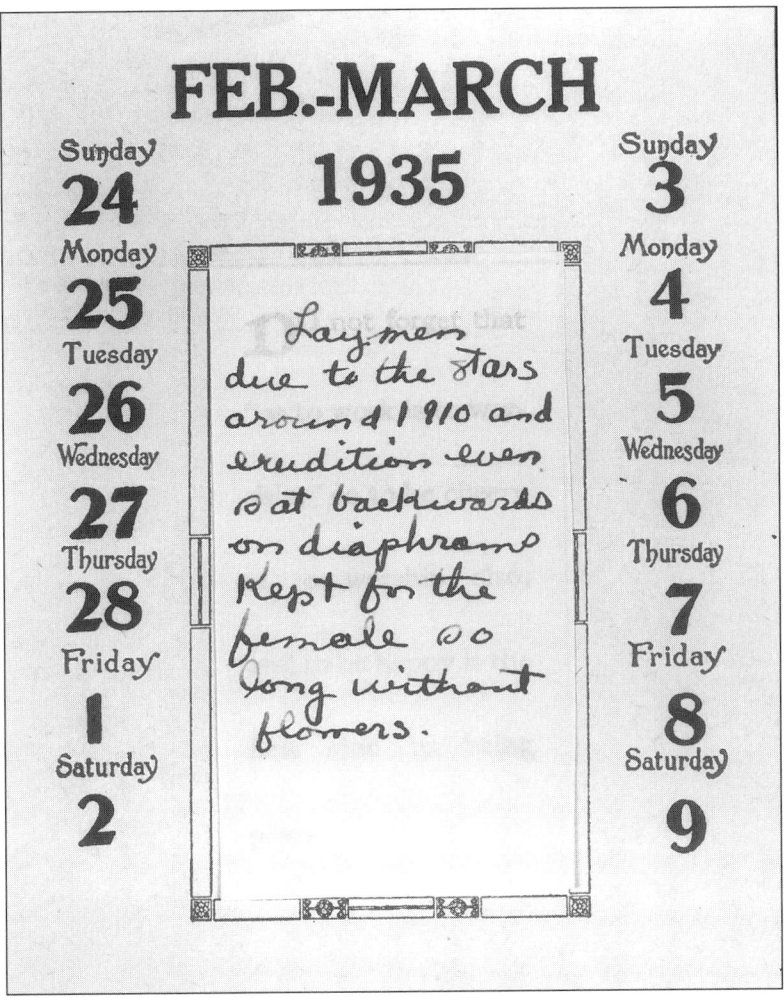

FEB.-MARCH

1935

Sunday
24

Monday
25

Tuesday
26

Wednesday
27

Thursday
28

Friday
1

Saturday
2

Sunday
3

Monday
4

Tuesday
5

Wednesday
6

Thursday
7

Friday
8

Saturday
9

Laymen / due to the stars / around 1910 and / erudition even / sat backwards / on diaphrams / kept for the / female so / long without / flowers.

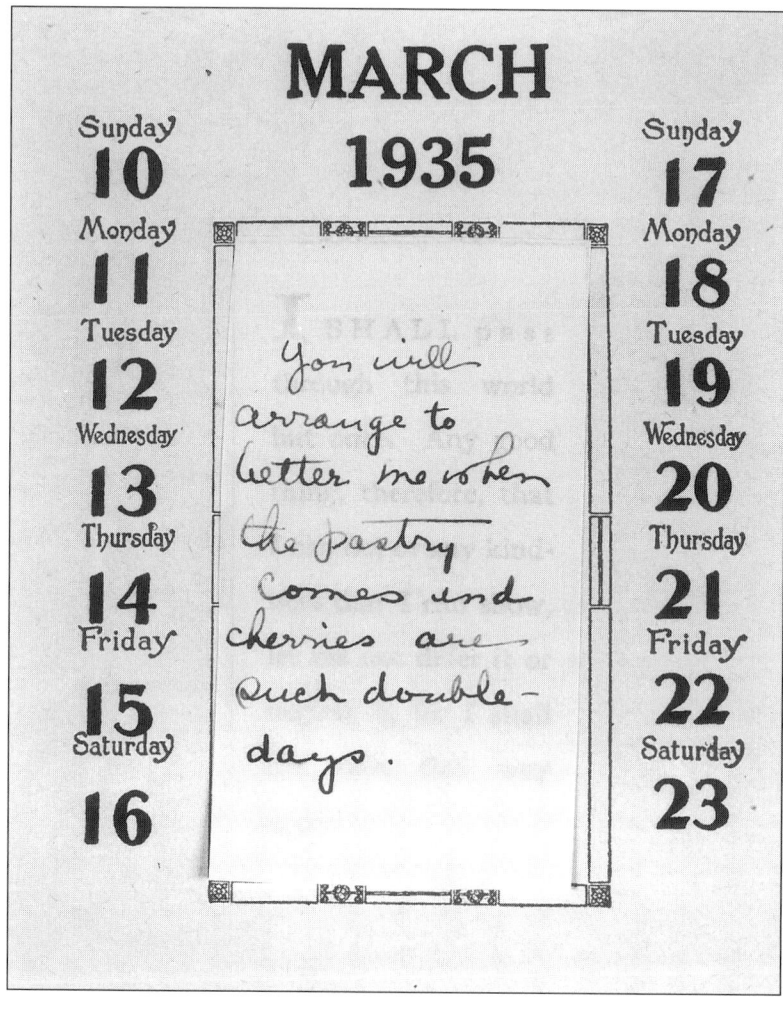

MARCH 1935

Sunday **10**	Sunday **17**
Monday **11**	Monday **18**
Tuesday **12**	Tuesday **19**
Wednesday **13**	Wednesday **20**
Thursday **14**	Thursday **21**
Friday **15**	Friday **22**
Saturday **16**	Saturday **23**

You will arrange to better me when the pastry comes and cherries are such double- days.

You will / arrange to / better me when / the pastry / comes and / cherries are / such double- / days.

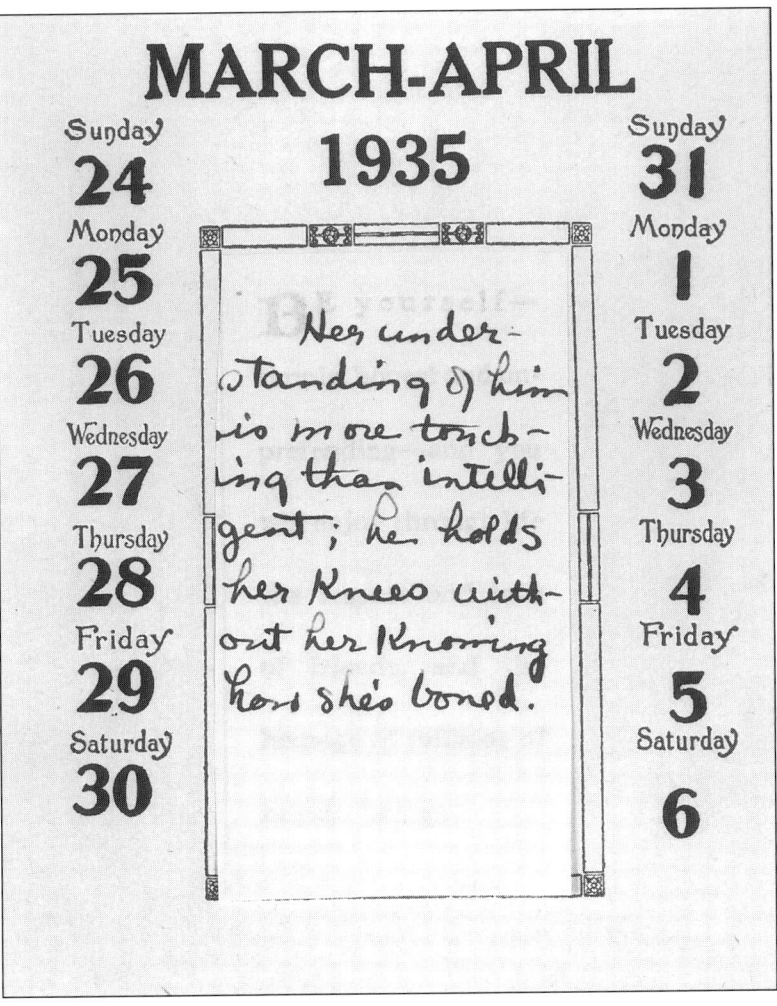

MARCH-APRIL
1935

Sunday
24

Monday
25

Tuesday
26

Wednesday
27

Thursday
28

Friday
29

Saturday
30

Sunday
31

Monday
1

Tuesday
2

Wednesday
3

Thursday
4

Friday
5

Saturday
6

*Her under- / standing of him / is more touch- / ing than intelli- /
gent; he holds / her knees with- / out her knowing / how she's boned.*

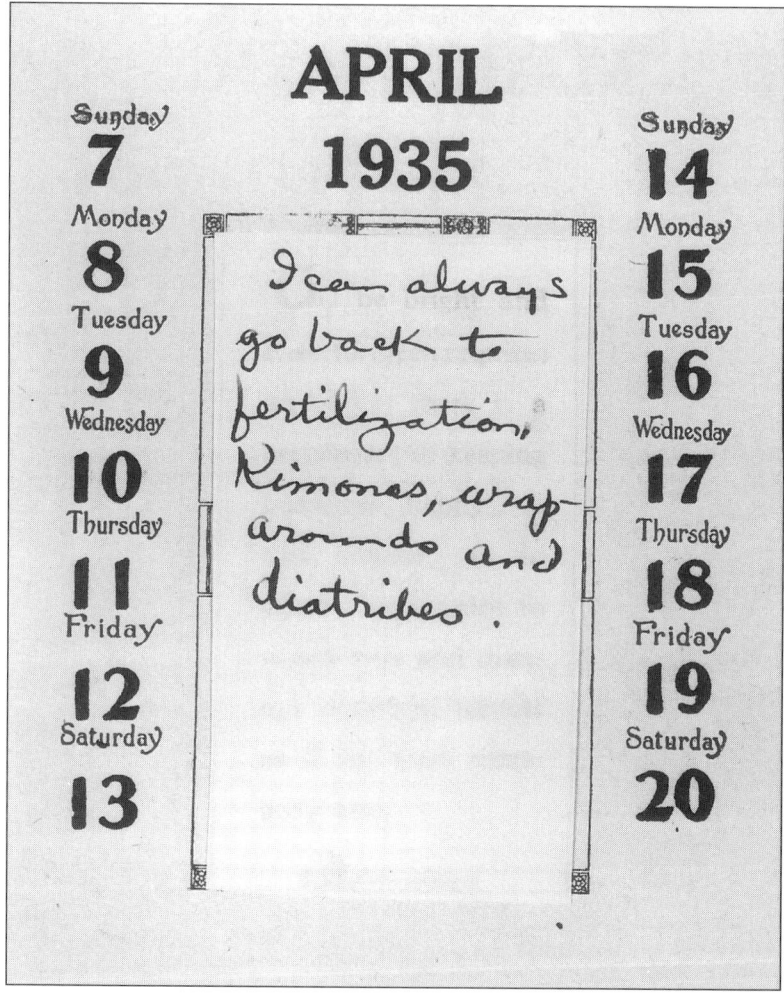

I can always / go back to / fertilization, / kimonos, wrap- / arounds and / diatribes.

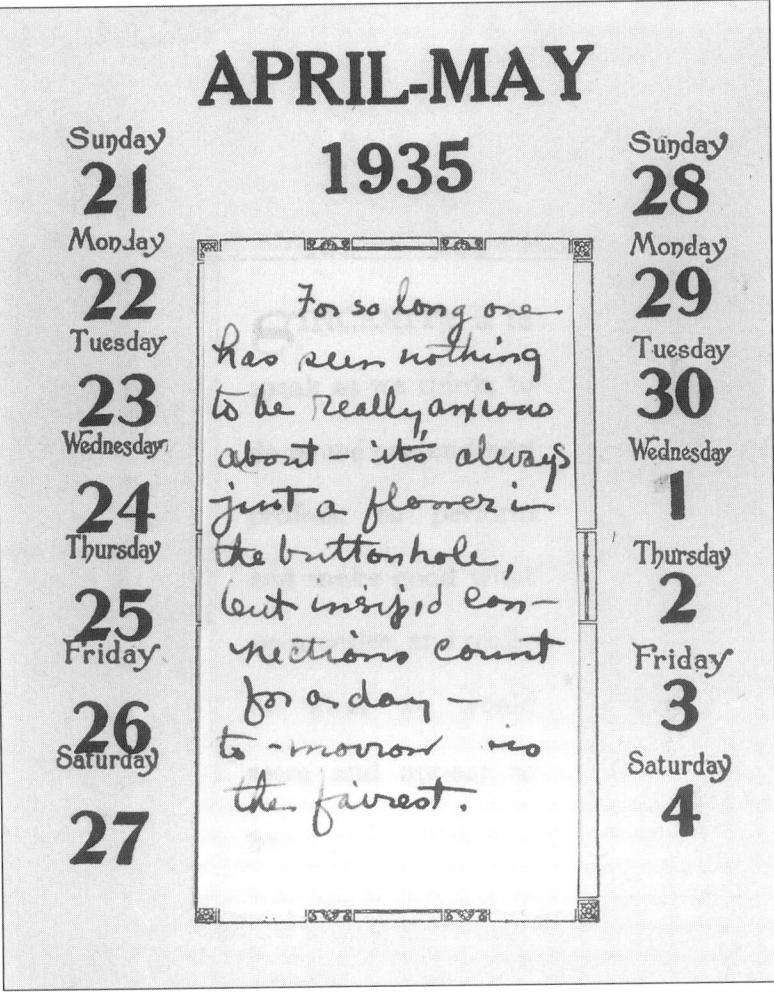

APRIL-MAY
1935

Sunday **21**
Monday **22**
Tuesday **23**
Wednesday **24**
Thursday **25**
Friday **26**
Saturday **27**

Sunday **28**
Monday **29**
Tuesday **30**
Wednesday **1**
Thursday **2**
Friday **3**
Saturday **4**

For so long one has seen nothing to be really anxious about — it's always just a flower in the buttonhole, but insipid con-nections count for a day — to-morrow is the fairest.

For so long one / has seen nothing / to be really anxious / about—it's always / just a flower in / the buttonhole, / but insipid con- / nections count / for a day— / tomorrow is / the fairest.

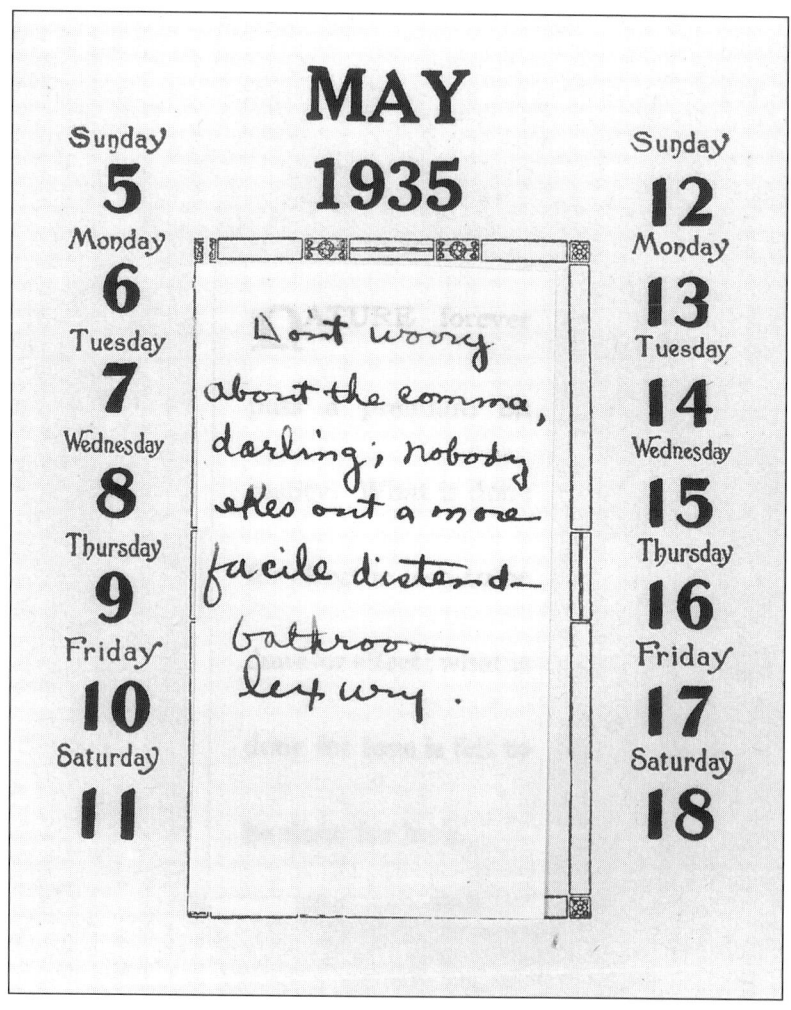

Don't worry / about the comma, / darling, nobody / ekes out a more / facile distend— / bathroom / luxury.

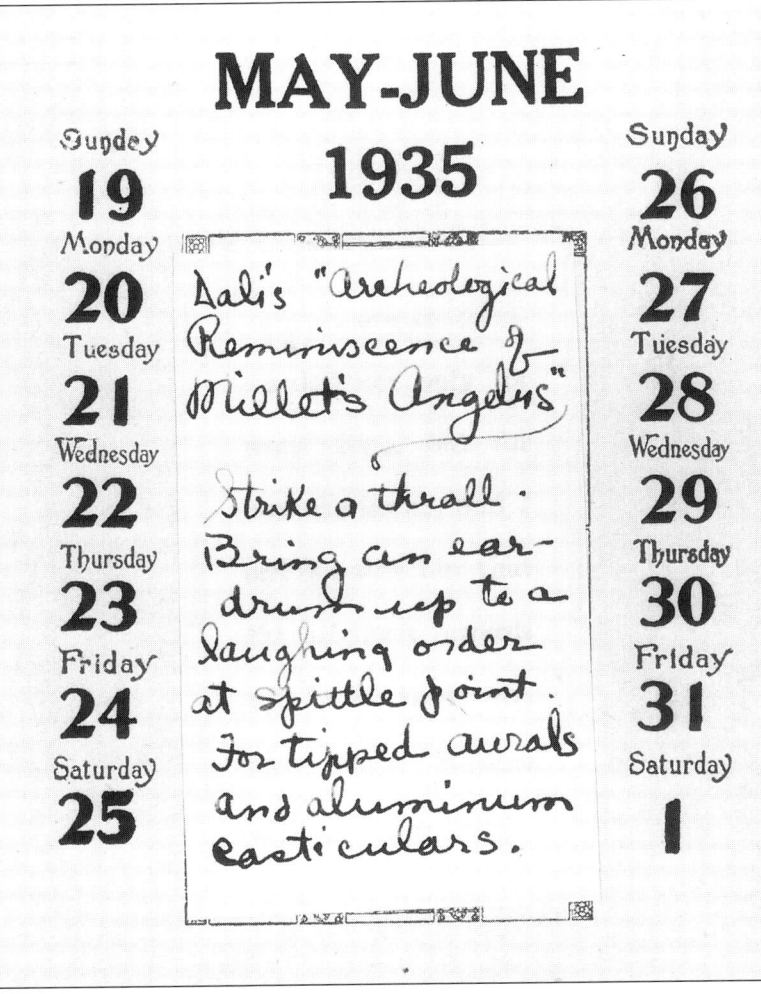

MAY-JUNE
1935

Sunday 19
Monday 20
Tuesday 21
Wednesday 22
Thursday 23
Friday 24
Saturday 25

Sunday 26
Monday 27
Tuesday 28
Wednesday 29
Thursday 30
Friday 31
Saturday 1

Dali's "Archeological
Reminiscence of
Millet's Angelus"

Strike a thrall.
Bring an ear-
drum up to a
laughing order
at spittle joint.
For tipped aurals
and aluminum
casticulars.

Dali's "Archeological / Reminiscence of / Millet's Angelus" / Strike a thrall. /
Bring an ear- / drum up to a / laughing order / at spittle point. /
For tipped aurals / and aluminum / casticulars.

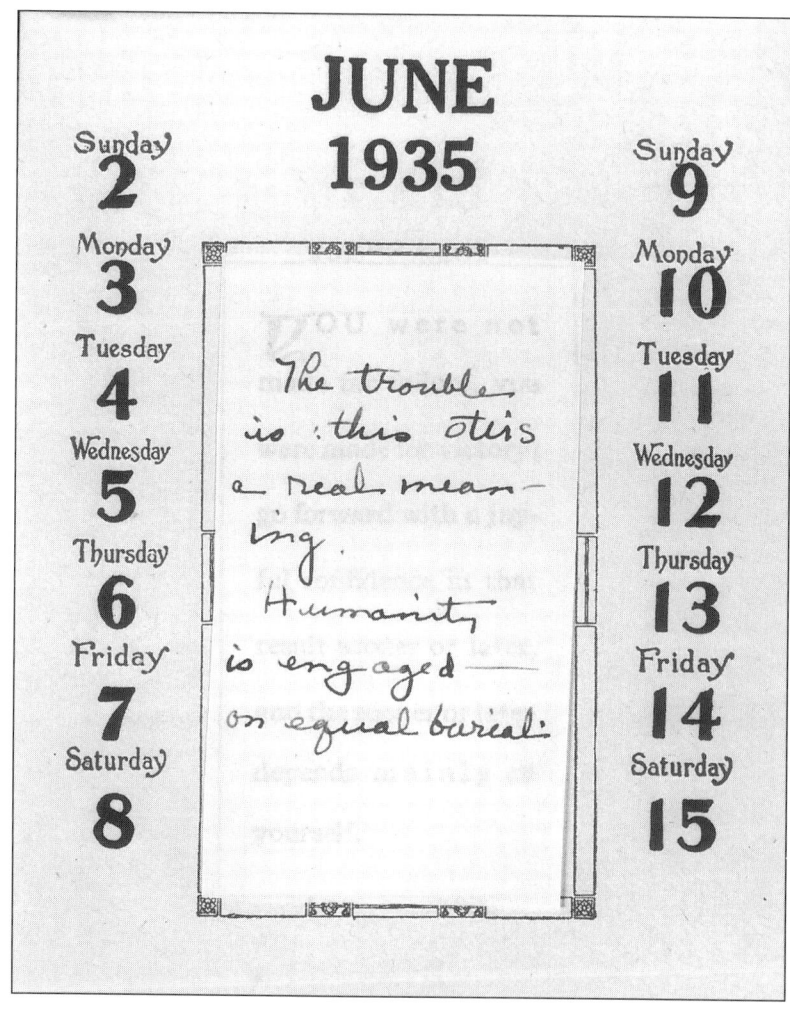

The trouble / is: this stirs / a real mean- / ing. /
Humanity / is engaged— / on equal burial.

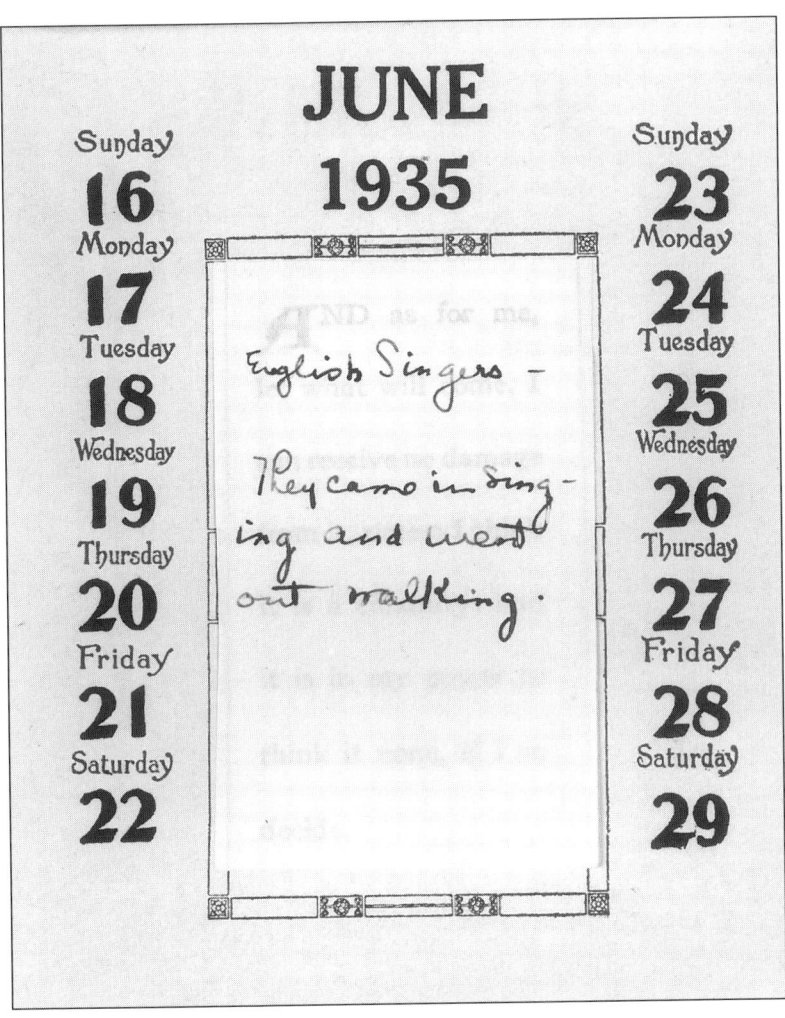

English Singers— / They came in sing- / ing and went / out walking.

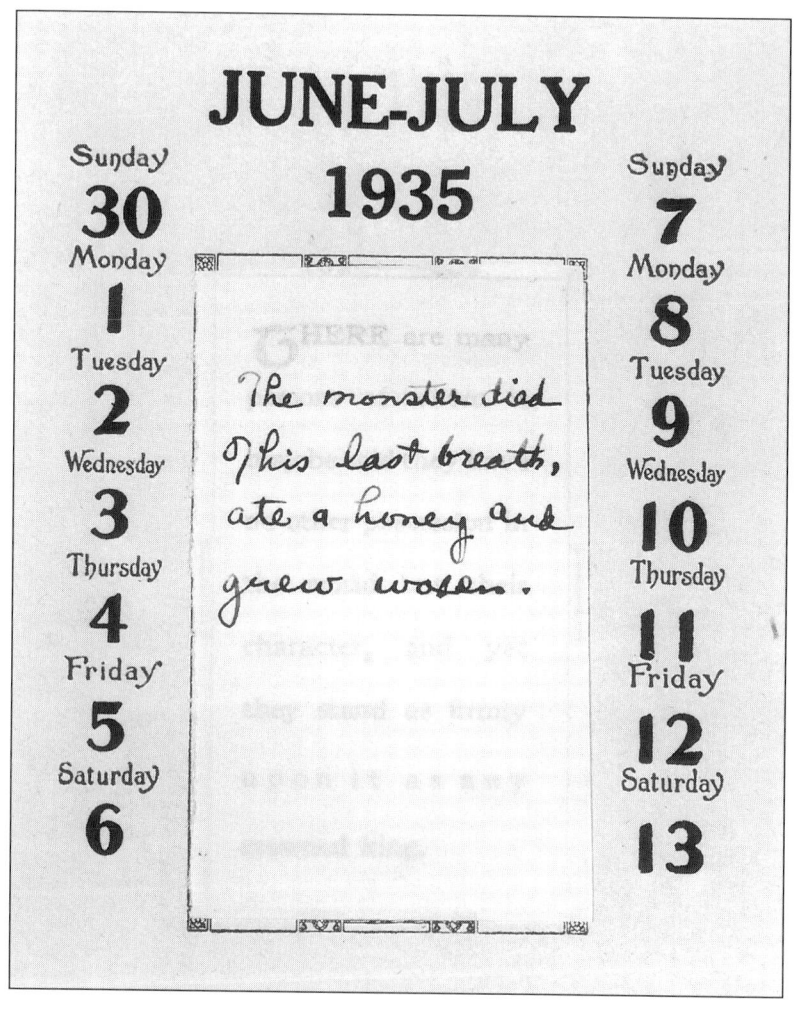

JUNE-JULY
1935

Sunday
30
Monday
1
Tuesday
2
Wednesday
3
Thursday
4
Friday
5
Saturday
6

Sunday
7
Monday
8
Tuesday
9
Wednesday
10
Thursday
11
Friday
12
Saturday
13

The monster died
This last breath,
ate a honey and
grew woßen.

The monster died / of his last breath, / ate a honey and / grew waxen.

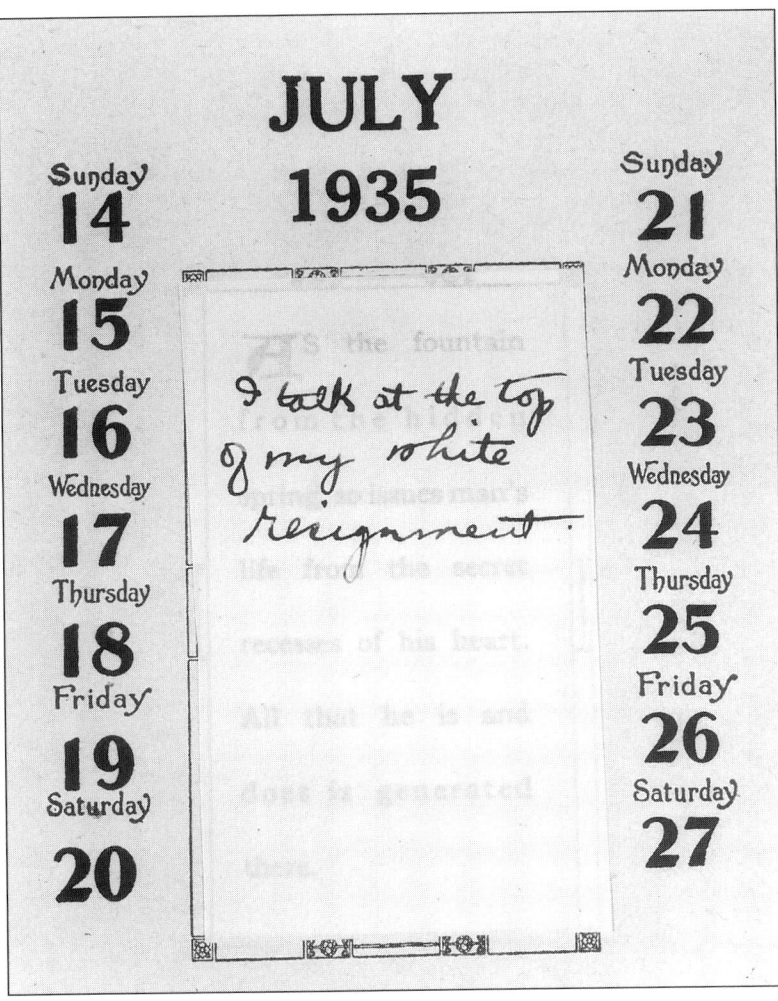

JULY
1935

Sunday
14

Monday
15

Tuesday
16

Wednesday
17

Thursday
18

Friday
19

Saturday
20

Sunday
21

Monday
22

Tuesday
23

Wednesday
24

Thursday
25

Friday
26

Saturday
27

I talk at the top / of my white / resignment.

I talk at the top / of my white / resignment.

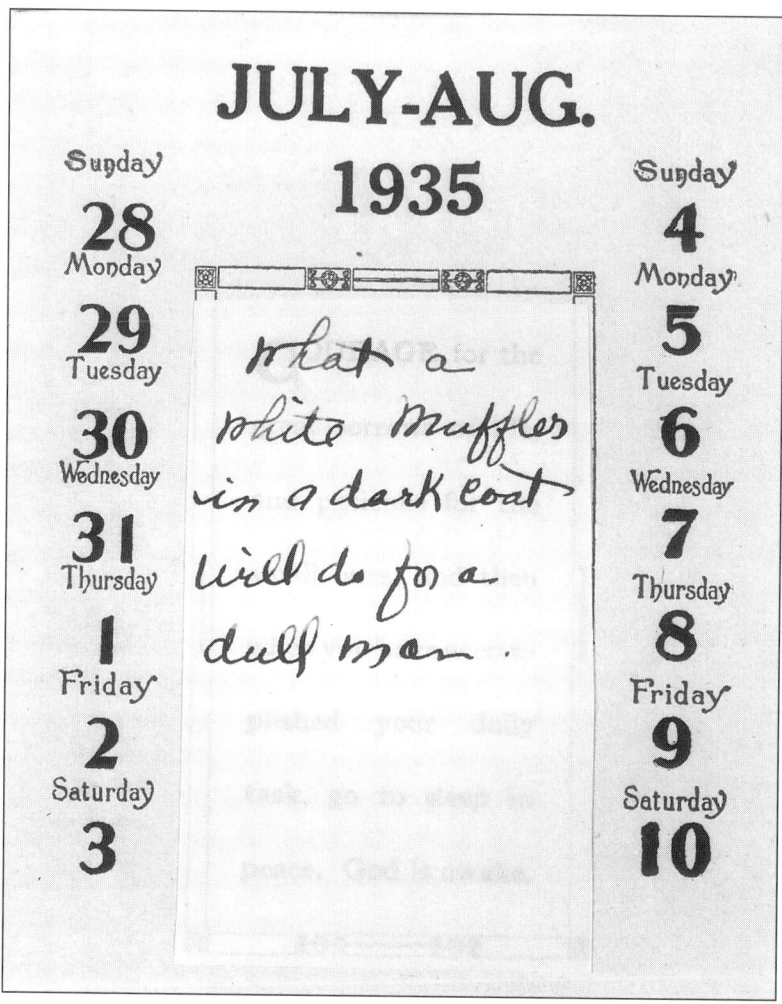

What a / white muffler / in a dark coat / will do for a / dull man.

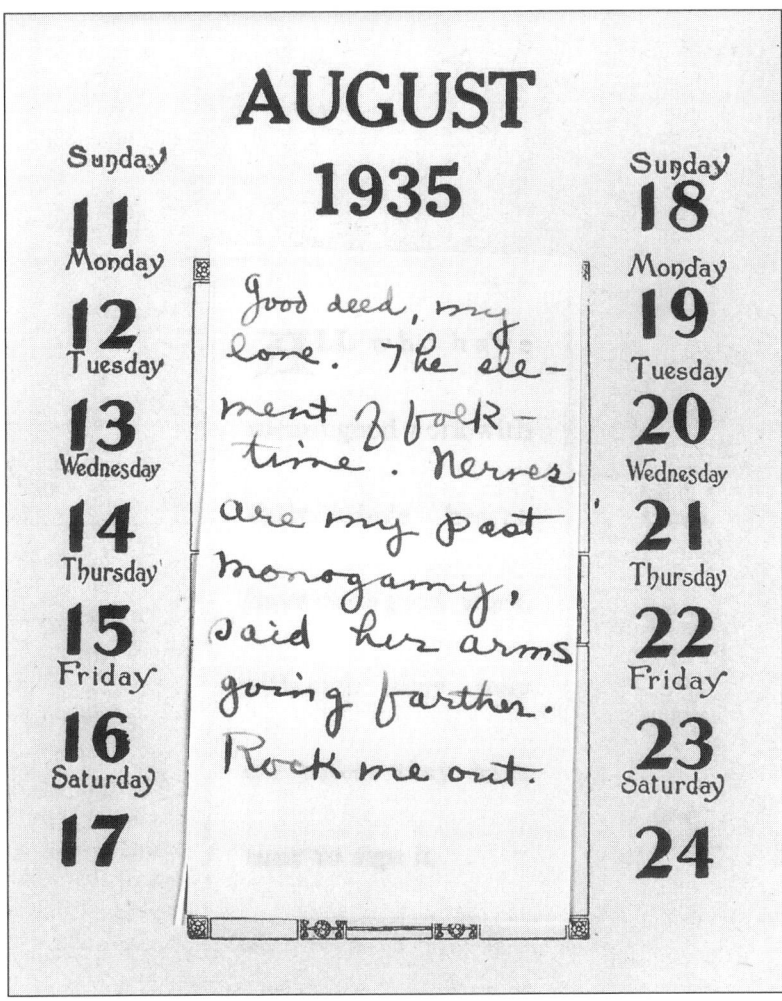

Good deed, my / love. The ele- / ment of folk- / time. Nerves / are my past / monogamy, / said her arms / going farther. / Rock me out.

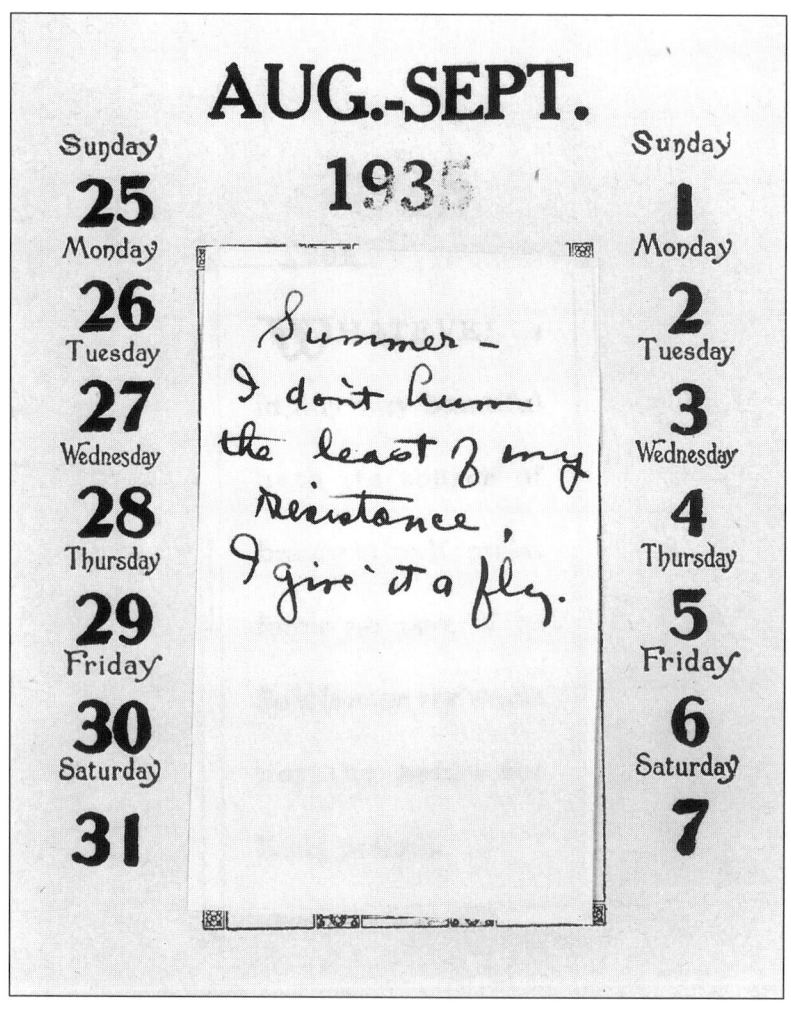

Summer— / I don't hum / the least of my / resistance, / I give it a fly.

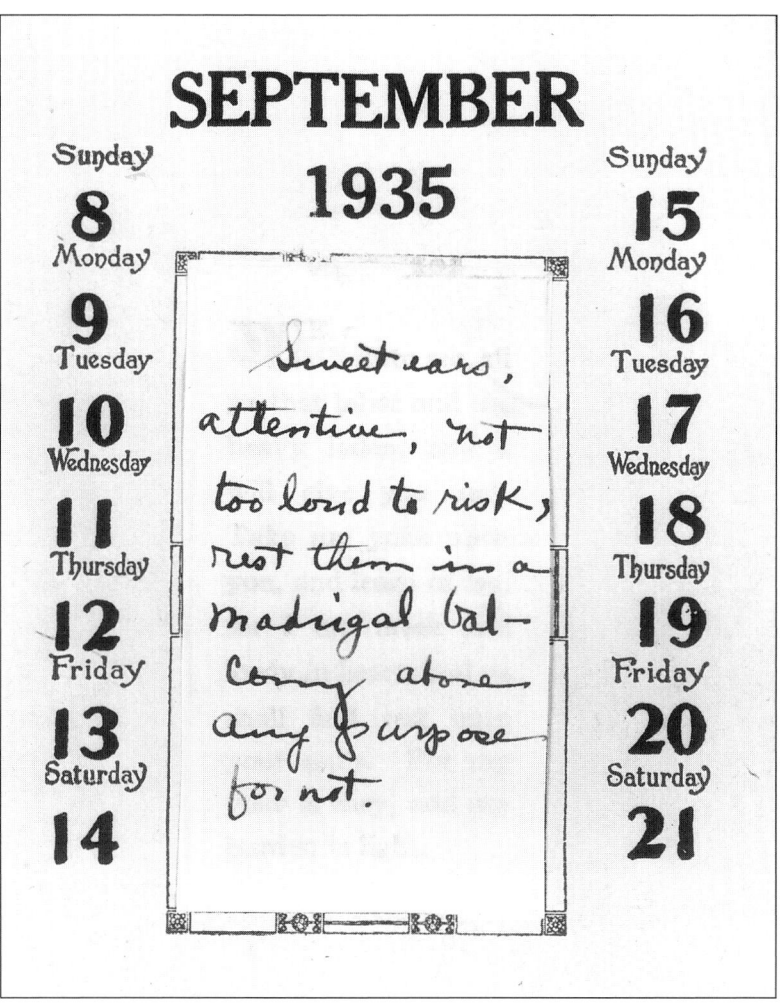

Sweet ears, / attentive, not / too loud to risk, / rest them in a / madrigal bal- / cony above / any purpose / for not.

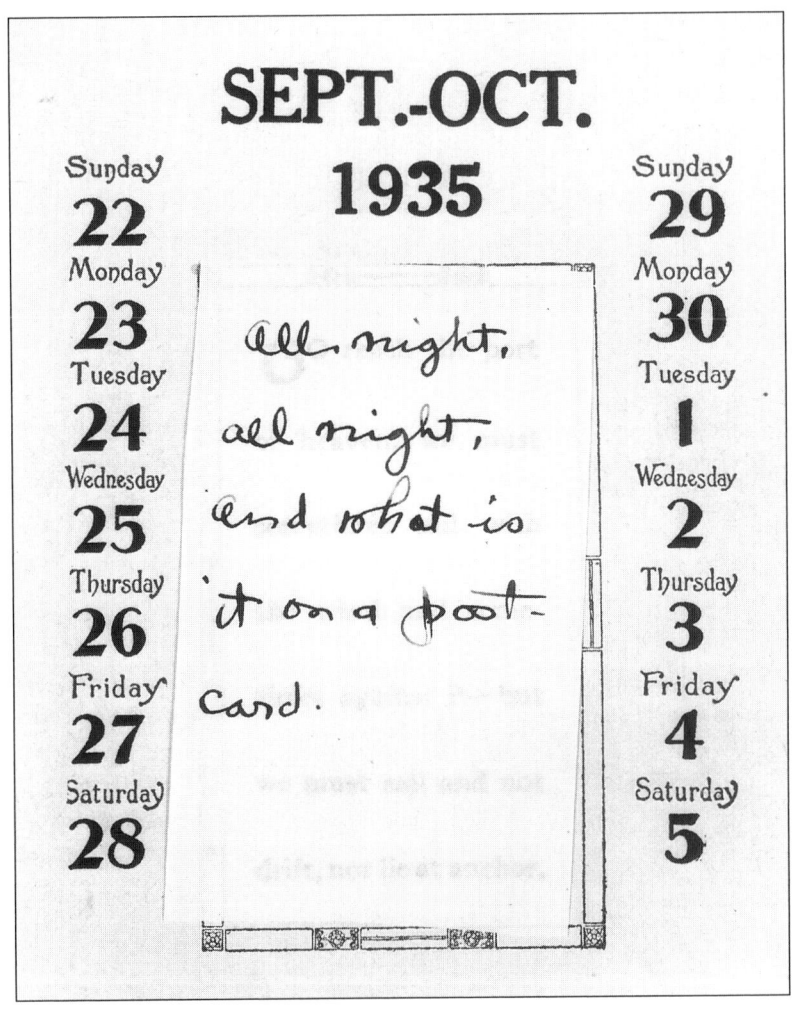

All night, / all night, / and what is / it on a post- / card.

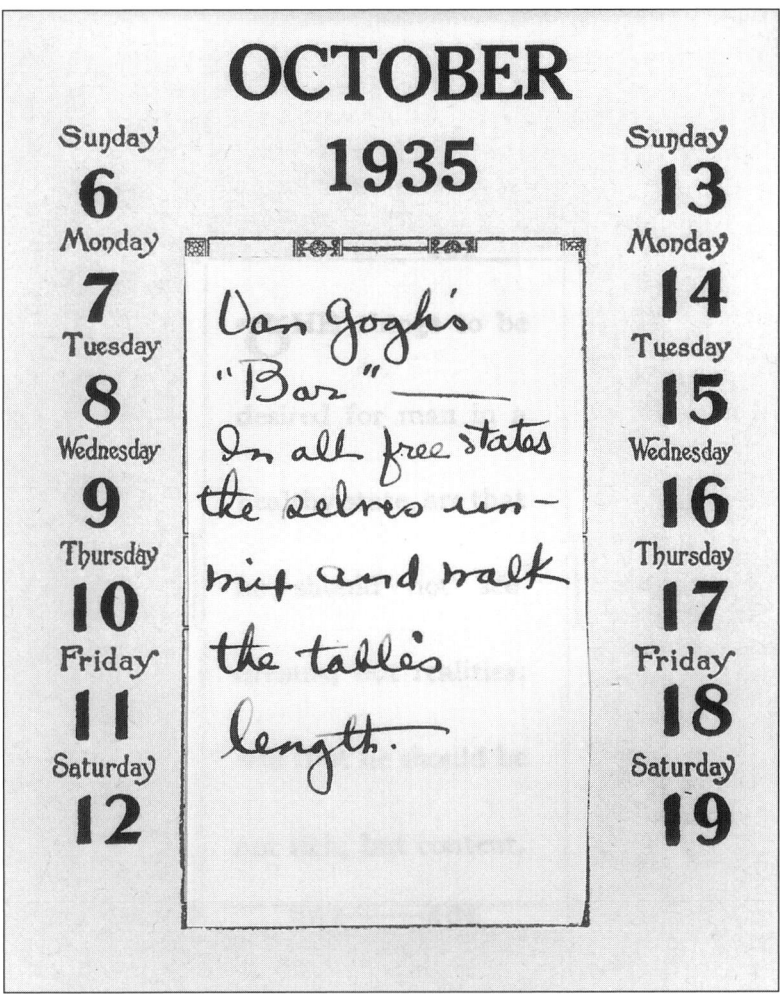

Van Gogh's / "Bar"— / In all free states / the selves un- / mix and walk /
the table's / length.

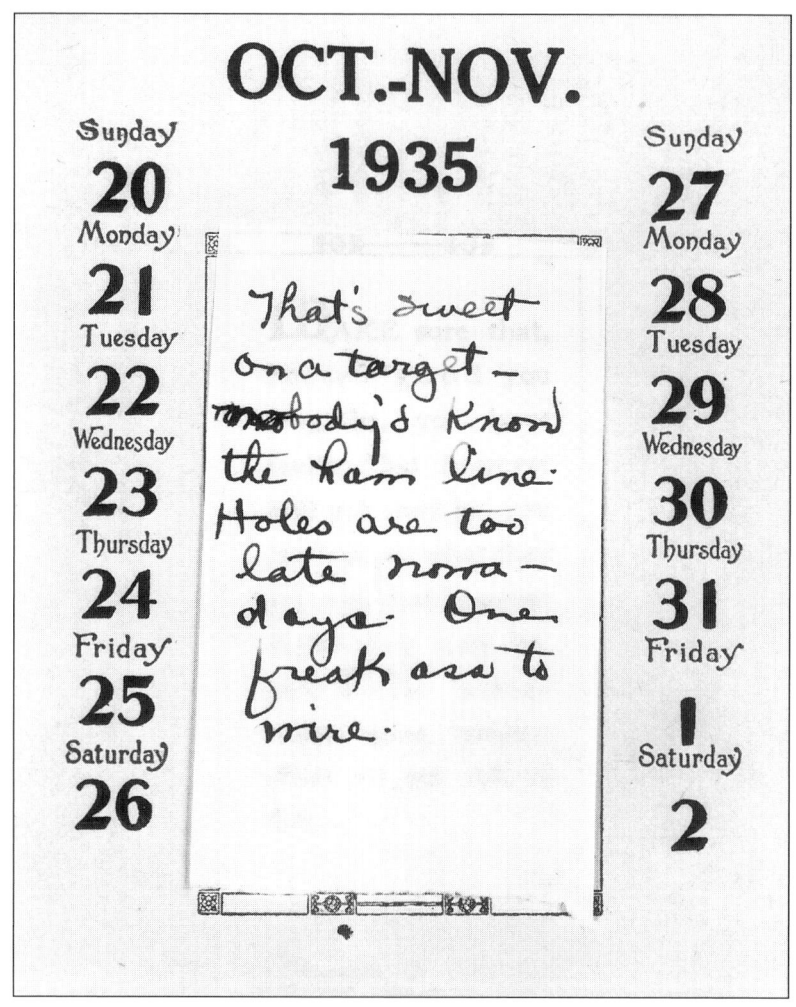

That's sweet / on a target— / nobody'd know / the ham line. /
Holes are too / late nowa- / days. One / freak ass to / wire.

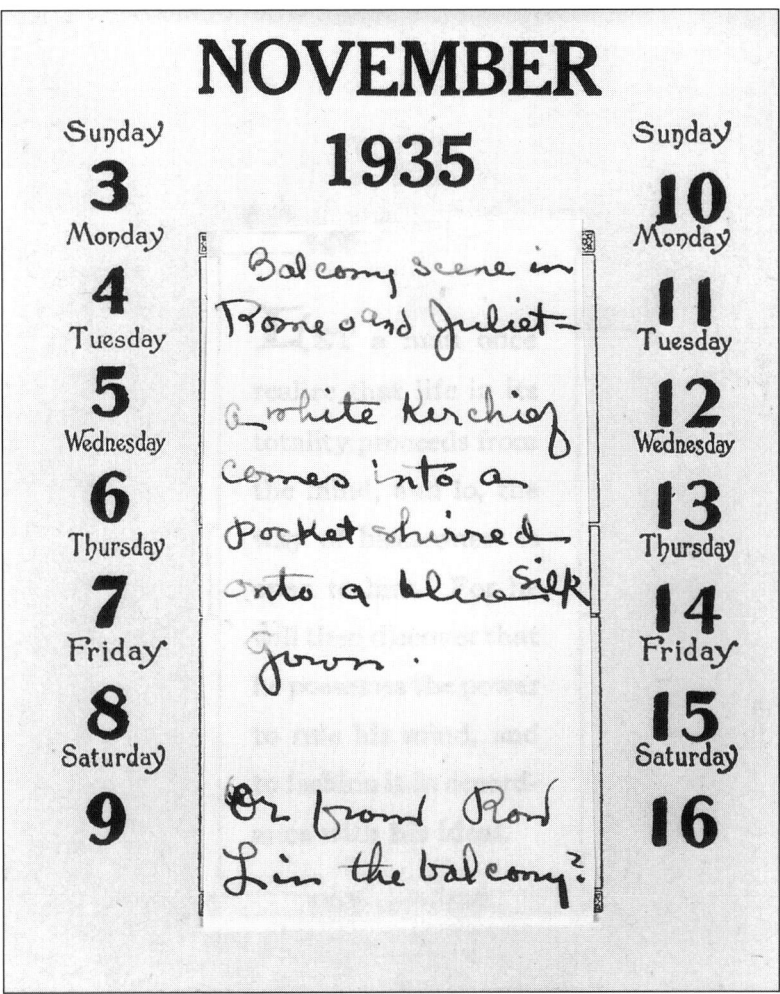

Balcony scene in / Romeo and Juliet— / a white kerchief / comes into a / pocket shirred / onto a blue silk / gown. / Or from Row / L in the balcony?

NOVEMBER
1935

Sunday
17
Monday
18
Tuesday
19
Wednesday
20
Thursday
21
Friday
22
Saturday
23

Sunday
24
Monday
25
Tuesday
26
Wednesday
27
Thursday
28
Friday
29
Saturday
30

I like a / loved one to / be apt in / the wing.

Sweet ekes / of soft drips— / bathroom / luxuries.

DECEMBER
1935

Sunday
15
Monday
16
Tuesday
17
Wednesday
18
Thursday
19
Friday
20
Saturday
21

Sunday
22
Monday
23
Tuesday
24
Wednesday
25
Thursday
26
Friday
27
Saturday
28

Transubstan- / tiation of acro- / bats, moon-eyes / and downward / mouth. Round- / acres intrude / a nose where / no listening / ever came. / Smooth out the / substance of your / acetylene worry.

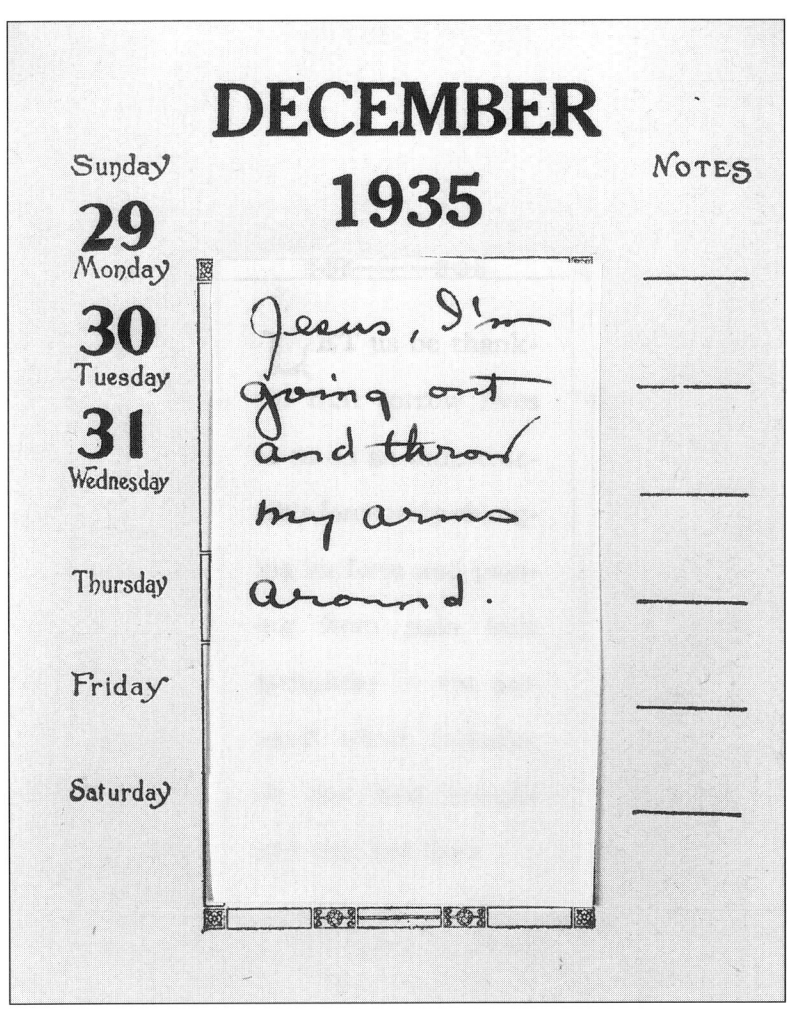

Jesus, I'm / going out / and throw / my arms / around.

Voices from dining room and hall off study. Voices of old man and old woman as their shadows pass back and forth with trays of food and drink, near entrance of study—their forms are reflected on wall of study. The curtain rises on a young man seated at desk in the study, busy with pencil, paper, ruler. The only light is shed from a reading lamp onto desk and leaving rest of room in comparative darkness. A confused murmur of voices of men and women from dining room soon becomes merely a suspicion of sound as of air in a tunnel or as a loud speaker of a radio turned on but not speaking—movement in stillness out of which the action of the words comes clear.

Gentleman gentle—	. . . . Miserly . . . .
Woman high—	. . . . motion . . . .
Woman low—	. . . . intensifies a goal . . . .
Gentleman loud—	. . . . and a featherman's . . . .
Woman husky—	. . . . hat.
Old man—	(*with bottle and spoon*) Take every hour when necessary; the complaint must be necessary several hours.
Gentleman gentle—	. . . . Ex— . . . .
Gentleman loud—	. . . . collect . . . .
Woman high—	. . . . in trinity . . . .
Woman low—	. . . . and doubly the canticle . . . .
Woman husky—	. . . . waste.
Old man—	They don't have a minister; they have a doctor.
Woman husky—	Oh, do you think we should indoctrinate at certain points?
Gentleman loud—	Well, one thing . . . .
Woman low—	. . . . announces a fabricoid . . . .
Woman high—	. . . . and another . . . .

Gentleman gentle—	. . . . assembles a divinity.
Gentleman loud—	Downstairs I tender the right . . . .
Old woman—	After dinner the women smoke and the men retire to the front room.
Woman high—	Some men, they say, entered the forest today; it was a bad omen; not long after a tree fell.
Young man in study—	Will they come in scarlet or in the month of the first canterbury bells?
Woman low—	Have you been . . . .
Woman high—	. . . . to the bread-eaters' lately?
Young man in study—	Marigolds in stink-orange.
Old woman—	I suppose if they need stones she'll have to go along; they'll want time to pay for em.
Young man—	Always through windows a curtain about somebody else. (*He gets up to look through curtains—whether door or window audience cannot tell.*)
Woman low—	(*Near*) When I'm alone it's an open day. I clouded myself on him.
Woman husky—	But surely there is another who scenes passably?
Woman low—	(*Nearer*) Night that opens its puny residua unoccupied of sleep . . . .
Young man—	(*Now back at desk, looks up quickly at curtains, is silent.*) (*Even "sound" ceases. There is now and while young girl and man are to talk normal and absolute quiet. Girl's voice, for she is never seen, is intimate.*)
Young girl plain—	Garden plans? I couldn't pre-arrange a garden. I'd hate to come upon a flower and find I'd put it there.

Young man—	Who are you?
Young girl—	O.S.R. Return.
Young man—	Only scientists have three initials and a last name.
Young girl—	My hand scratches seeds of whorfels.
Young man—	She's unconscious. It must be her strong will that does it.
Young girl—	And corners are precarious beasts. They put a wall of weeping between us, suffering, the technologic absolute.
Young man—	(*Shifting in his chair*) My dear, I have other affiliations. It's been penciled and ruled. My life is elsewhere. (*Confused murmur begins off stage.*)
Young girl illumined—	Oh, I shouldn't want you to be faithful to me alone. (*Study light is off immediately. Servant's pantomimes again, definite.*)
Old man—	(*Puts his arm around the old woman*) That's a very good mousetrap.
Old Woman—	How comes? (*Confused murmur becomes "sound". Light is turned on as if by someone unseen; no one there; light goes off again.*)
Gentleman gentle—	Minockua . . . .
Woman high—	. . . . the day is fattening . . . .
Gentleman loud—	. . . . Brimble . . . .
Woman husky—	. . . . the Brand . . . . (*Doors close, keys jingle.*) *Curtain.*

THE PRESIDENT OF THE HOLDING COMPANY

PRESIDENT

I will enforce it that after supper you speak about dusk.

SECRETARY

I have this concrete immolence

VOICE OUTSIDE

this messenger from the dead.

PRESIDENT

Have you looked up Sumatra's defence of cat-tails?

SECRETARY

Pardon sir, who gives you frantic worry when the rest of
us boop on the stairs?

PRESIDENT

I consume it my dignity

VOICE OUTSIDE

to go straight to the devil

PRESIDENT

Stuff and retain him . . . I'll have him by the stem of his hat.

SECRETARY

O Matchbox, save him, he's the best timidity we have.

PRESIDENT

O why am I tired why haven't I
a circumlocus of design

someone to come in and say
the pears smell ripe here . .

But I'm bound to the fears of my weathers.
Are you ready to release the evening?

SECRETARY

Maygo is waving his voice by the well.

PRESIDENT

Success like raisins comes first in the mouth.
But who wants a mouthful of raisins?

VOICES OUTSIDE

Sylva Wergles was a worty witchwoo
She lived by the side of a tree.
She combed the worldside for pennies and peas
And woo-ed a few sallies to sea.

O my, said the counterfeit judge, By the boo
You cost me a tendril and then a long shoot.
Get thee from me and relate
How frogs come out of a gate.

SECRETARY

It can't be commercial poetry.

PRESIDENT

I doubt its prowess. It lacks compulsion.

VOICES OUTSIDE

O sweet little Tilda's an open sale
She comes from a baudy and lands in a gale.
She tunes up the strings of her gay rig-a-roo
And plays a high banner to how so come who.

PRESIDENT

The traffic is ended. The last star is a bonded issue.
Sighing is extinct. I've gone to the morning entry.

FANCY ANOTHER DAY GONE

The glare from the brass horn makes sun-brown satin fit
smoothly the girl by the window. Even the young man is
straight and bright.

SHE

Please come. I want you to justify my landscape. (*She
looks out of the window and lights the late afternoon.*)

HE

I love you magnificently. I've had every drop of blood
from the moonstone put into a venture for you.

SHE

(*takes his hands*) It's a high hurt.

HE

The plight of the individual is our happy finale. (*Both
absorbed by the glow move out.*)

GRANDMOTHER

(*sidling the luminous flood*) She picks and promises and
castillates the dew. And he's a tin whistle substitute,
works for the wonder constructor who eats and then
expectorates when he wants to build a lake where a
hill is.

The family, entering, pales and points after tea-time.

MOTHER

Studying? Why so stupid, son.

STUDY BOY

(*in khaki*) They're putting us thru an elemental dog-trot
in sargonic culture. We're now at the hammer and fan-
wheel stage,—star-falling comes next.

MOTHER

And this painting, daughter, that you hold so dear . .

FATHER

A silk contortion heavily blotched toward the centre.

DAUGHTER

He has issued also complaints in vast design.

BLUE TIE SON

The very devil of a good thought.

GRANDMOTHER

He ate a mushroom for breakfast. He can't be divine anymore.

MOTHER

He wears that kind of practitioner's overcoat . .

BLUE TIE

He repeatedly assumes his dais.

FATHER

All the same, I'd write him and ask what his inventions are.

DAUGHTER

He's done a great deal with words that look like pictures.

FATHER

I don't suppose a father ever cocktailed his hopes to that.

(*chorus by two small children skipping in and out*):
I don't suppose a man ever, no, I don't suppose a man ever.

MOTHER

What unbooked revelry . .

GRANDMOTHER

Today let us weep for tomorrow may be fraught with foolishness.

MOTHER

(*pauses in front of daughter before going off completely*)
Darling, you've some bad laughter lines.

DAUGHTER

But facts are a mass of coercives.
(*Children dance in to tea-table and away.*)

GRANDMOTHER

Not a raisin goes to cookie in this house but what they
know it.

STUDY BOY

(*The room grows an even, late daylight—Study boy takes his
books nearer the window.*) This map has a cherry
expedition punctured by toothpicks to rescind a felled
hatred. Wind me a furlough. I'm bound to need air.

SLEEPY SON

Feathering Heights—how they can dance up there.

BLUE TIE

And let their seams out in the wind . . .

SLEEPY

Sweet pillow, Madge. What exquisite tether and release.
A little difficult, tho, to be a constant wind.

STUDY BOY

Oh you don't use the right weapons.

(*small children and Grandmother sing out*):

> "Rings on your fingers,
> bells on your toes,"
> Tether your feathers,
> Tar all your foes . .

DAUGHTER

Flightful conceit. . . .

GRANDMOTHER

Somnambule enchants a wiry daisy, curvets and comes
back.

STUDY BOY

I prefer my women on paper.

BLUE TIE

(*looking into cup*) Concatenations streaking a bird with a
tail-light.

SLEEPY

Hang your tea-cup relations.

BLUE TIE

(*idling about the room, glances over father's shoulder at
magazine*) Literate man would like to hear from readers
interested in talking about things that count.

STUDY BOY

What's a dismissed attavater?

BLUE TIE

It means the ease comes out of the sound.

FATHER

It's what is called imminent custody.

(*piano fortissimo from a nearby key*)

DAUGHTER

Beethoven's ironworks. (*The room is a strong dusk and the
window steel-blue*)

(*pianoworks*)

STUDY BOY

Don't invert me. I wasn't so smelted in a long time.

(*Piano fades along with the family, the Octaves of Point
Lessening.*) Tomes at the window establish the smoke
scene as the night of the mandolin query.

HE

Vertebrate lives spread the hour. On the instable count
no face line ever vented approach.

SHE

Is the midnight capsule ready to gloat?

HE

It's only lachrymose and octo-even by the enervator on
the tombstone. Fentry the watchman restored his
eyesight on that.

SHE

These failings tie you up with home. For me it's just
unknown distance.

HE

My dear, I care a great deal for the pear-shaped of the
lute species.

SHE

It's hard to glutinize in leafless time.

HE

Who has unsettled you about this matter?

SHE

Oh—appetizers, upholders of the law . .

HE

Drizzlers in the sink.

SHE

My faint memory of viscera should be certainly viscarra.
Let's rush the blood to some other point.

HE

I suppose it's profound to guess whether . .

SHE

(*plucks the mandolin*) Prayerful inebriate shelters his
wings.

HE

(*blows his cigarette smoke white in the dark*) I shall never be
able to enlarge my scope as I wish.

SHE

Have you been to the proper authorities?

HE

Don't be nemeebic.

SHE

I love you despite the coconut on your tie.

HE

Would you be traditional in buttering your bread?

SHE

Not if there were plums to placate the ardor.

HE

Then what are we waiting for?

(*Grandmother candles her hopes to an empty room, has them
blown by the wind at the window, trudges the length of the
night.*)

News

To wit, the lover said.

As a young woman
I saw that

done

no child
no enlightenment.

We approach the dignity
of the ad.

Or successfully maintain
a humorous relation

between the ayes
and the nose

(got to give the asses
an eye)

Faces slander
O I see
faces
slander.

Find body
of ashamed man.

Labor leader flogged to death,
believed in destroying home, church
and civilization, radio caster said,

no right thinking people
could deny it
said

People should know
who the floggers are
how the air mind
gets a raise

and the extravagant
broadcast
without mercy.

The issue wouldn't have been brought up
if your husband hadn't been killed.

The police described him
as an intelligent man.

Lilies
of the kind

look   she's right.

The flag   go hang

in the war market
to which the farmers
of this country
bring their products.

Duck
wobbler
for all intentions.

They separated
not legally,
the world has no notice.
His old wife illegally starves

his mother
nothing left
eats
dies.

You
got food?

I'd like to keep my hat and coat
reasonably clean
on the walk from New York
to California gate unless I get work—
will pay $10.

My shoulder worn

over and down Payroll Hill

fashions mornings after.

Raw wind, rain,
one month going into another
what the hell

Frail limbs are proportionately low
Buy a limb today.

And while we walk
we ride

footgear alert
to beat the sweet tenor
of their sentiment
(they keep their trees
away from us)

a tour of the tines—
rise and sore

life term.

.

1936—1945

O let's glee glow as we go
there must be things in the world—
Jesus pay for the working soul,
fearful lives by what right hopeful
and the apse in the tiger's horn,
costume for skiing I have heard
and rings for church people
and glee glo glum
it must be fun
to have boots for snow.

.

Troubles to win
and battles to bin
and after
a tare in the side
of all my ties
              and barn
                      dances.

.

A country's economics sick
affects its people's speech.

No bread and cheese and strawberries
I have no pay, they say.

Till in revolution rises
the strength to change

the undigestible phrase.

.

Lady in the Leopard Coat

Tender spotted
hoped with care
she's coming back
from going there.

.

Jim Poor's his name
and Poor Jay's mine,
his hair's aflame
not worth a dime
          or he'd sell it.

.

Scuttle up the workshop,
settle down the dew,
I'll tell you what my name is
when we've made the world new.

.

There was a bridge once that said I'm going
and a cistern that said What Ho
and the stick said lying on the ground
how am I to grow?

.

When do we live again Ann,
when dirt flies high
in wheeling time
and the lights of their eyes see ours.
For if it's true
we're the dung of the earth
and they the flowers
from stock that's running out
they need to be planted over.

They'll never know
the weeping diff'rence, Ann,
when the whole world laughs again.

.

Missus Dorra
came to town
to buy some silkalene.
The clerk said Oh
my dear Mrs. Morra
is it in style ageen?

All these years
I saved and saved
and saved my silkalene
and yesterday
I threw it away—
how would taffeta be?

No, taffeta
cracks from hanging, besides
it's not being worn.
Mrs. Porra my dear
if you're going to be hung
won't crêpe do as weel?

.

No retiring summer stroke
nor the dangerous parasol
on the following sands,
no earth under fire flood lava forecast,
not the pop play of tax, borrow or inflate
but the radiant, tight energy

boring from within
communizing fear
into strike,
work.

.

To war they kept
          us going
but when the garden
          bloomed
I let them know
          my death.

With time war
          is splendid
and the rainbow
          sword,
they do not break
          my rest.

.

Petrou his name was sorrow
and little did he know
they called him Tomorrow
and Today let him go.

.

The eleventh of progressional
the make-believe of prayer,
too many dunderoos
and everybody there.

If you stay at home
loving in the light
you'll always get an answer
wrong or right.

■

Young girl to marry,
winds the washing harry.

■

I spent my money
by the ocean
and have not any
to fill a tooth.

■

Trees over the roof
and I was down
when the night
came in.

.

New Goose

Don't shoot the rail!
Let your grandfather rest!
Tho he sees your wild eyes
he's falling asleep,
his long-billed pipe
on his red-brown vest.

■

Bombings

You could go to the Underground's platform
for a three half-penny tube fare;
safe vaults of the Bank of England
you couldn't go there.

The sheltered slept
under eiderdown,
Lady Diana and the Lord himself
in apartments deep in the ground.

■

Hop press
             and conveyor for a hearse,
Newall Carpenter Senior's
                  two patented works.

. . .

Kilbourne. Eighteen sixty-eight.
Twelve hundred women and boys hopped.
When the market raced down to a dime a pound
from sixty-five cents, planters who'd staked
all they had, stopped.

.

Ash woods, willow, close to shore,
gentle overflow each spring,
here he lived to be eighty-four
then left everything.

Heirs rush in—lay one tree bare
claiming a birdhouse, leave
wornout roof hanging there
nothing underneath.

If he could come back and see his place
fought over that he'd held apart
he'd say: all my life I saved
now twitter, my heart.

He owned these woods, every board,
till he lost his spring and fall;
if he could say: trees craved for—
overflow to all.

.

The music, lady,
you demand—
the brass
breaks my hand.

.

For sun and moon and radio
farmers pay dearly;
their natural resource: turn
the world off early.

.

She had tumult of the brain
and I had rats in the rain
and she and I and the furlined man
were out for gain.

.

My coat threadbare
over and down Capital Hill
fashions mornings after.

In this Eternal Category's
land of rigmarole
see thru the laughter.

     .

Mr. Van Ess bought 14 washcloths?
Fourteen washrags, Ed Van Ess?
Must be going to give em
to the church, I guess.

He drinks, you know. The day we moved
he came into the kitchen stewed,
mixed things up for my sister Grace—
put the spices in the wrong place.

     .

Not feeling well, my wood uncut.
                    And why?
The street's bare-legged young girls
        in my eye

with their bottoms out (at home they wear
                long robes).
       My galoshes
     chopped the cold

till cards in The Moon where I sawed my mouth
                to make the bid.
And now my stove's too empty
     to be wife and kid.

   .

Remember my little granite pail?
The handle of it was blue.
Think what's got away in my life—
Was enough to carry me thru.

   .

A lawnmower's one of the babies I'd have
if they'd give me a job and I didn't get bombed
in the high grass

by the private woods. Getting so
when I look off my space I see waste
I'd like to mow.

   .

My man says the wind blows from the south,
    we go out fishing, he has no luck,
    I catch a dozen, that burns him up,
I face the east and the wind's in my mouth,
but my man has to have it in the south.

.

Du Bay

He kept a grog shop, this fur trader killer?
Defense: Any fur trader would
to make merchandise go. Moses Strong:
Inquire if the liquor was good.

He called Chief Oshkosh's daughter his wife?
Irrelevant!—John B. Du Bay
shot a man for claiming his land, enough
the possession of real estate.

Witnesses judged him as good as the average
for humanity, honesty, peace.
The court sent him home to his children,
his dogs, his gun, and his geese.

.

I'm a sharecropper
down here in the south.
Housing conditions are grave.

We've a few long houses
but most folks, like me,
make a home out of barrel and stave.

.

Here it gives the laws for fishing thru the ice—
only one hook to a line,
stay at the hole, can't go in to warm up,
well, we never go fishing, so they can't catch us.

.

On Columbus Day he set out for the north
to inspect his forty acres,
brought back a plaster of Paris deer-head
and food from the grocers and bakers,

a wall-thermometer to tell if he's cold,
a new kind of paring knife,
and painted in red, a bluebottle gentian
for the queen, his wife.

.

Black Hawk held: In reason
land cannot be sold,
only things to be carried away,
and I am old.

Young Lincoln's general moved,
pawpaw in bloom,
and to this day, Black Hawk,
reason has small room.

．

We know him—Law and Order League—
fishing from our dock,
testified against the pickets
at the plant—owns stock.

There he sits and fishes
stiff as if a stork
brought him, never sprang from work—
a sport.

．

The clothesline post is set
yet no totem-carvings distinguish the Niedecker tribe
from the rest; every seventh day they wash:
worship sun; fear rain, their neighbors' eyes;
raise their hands from ground to sky,
and hang or fall by the whiteness of their all.

.

I said to my head, Write something.
It looked me dead in the face.
Look around, dear head, you've never read
of the ground that takes you away.
Speed up, speed up, the frosted windshield's
                    a fern spray.

.

Grampa's got his old age pension,
$15 a month,
his own food and place.

But here he comes,
fiddle and spitbox . . .

Tho't I'd stop with you a little,
Harriut,
you kin have all I got.

.

There's a better shine
on the pendulum
than is on my hair
and many times

.. ..

I've seen it there.

.

The museum man!
I wish he'd taken Pa's spitbox!
I'm going to take that spitbox out
and bury it in the ground
and put a stone on top.
Because without that stone on top
it would come back.

.

That woman!—eyeing houses.
She's moved in on my own poor guy.
⠀⠀⠀She held his hand and told him where to sign.

He gives up costs on his tree-covered shack—
insurance against wind, fire, falling aircraft, riots—
⠀⠀⠀home itself, was our break in the thick.

Because look! How can she keep it?—
to hold a house has to rent it out
        and spend her life on the street.

        .

Hand Crocheted Rug

Gather all the old, rip and sew
the skirt I've saved so long,
Sally's valance, the twins' first calico
and the rest I worked to dye.
Red, green, black, hook,
hitch, nevermind, cramped
around back not yet the turn
of the century . . . Grandpa forward
from the shop, "Ought to have a machine."

        .

They came at a pace
to go to war.

They came to more:
a leg brought back
to a face.

        .

I doubt I'll get silk stockings out
of my asparagus
that grows too fast to stop it,
or any pair of Capital's
miracles of profit.

.

To see the man who took care of our stock
as we slept in the dark, the blackbirds flying
high as the market out of our pie,
I travel now at crash of day
on the el, a low rush of geese over those below,
to see the man who smiled
and gave us a first-hand country shake.

.

A monster owl
out on the fence
flew away. What
is it the sign
of? The sign of
an owl.

.

Gen. Rodimstev's story
(Stalingrad)

Four of us lived off half an acre
till grandfather traded it
for a gallon of liquor.

White Guards flogged father to death,
I studied to save
man's sweet breath.

.

Birds' mating-fight
feathers floating down
offspring started
toward the ground.

.

From my bed I see
the wind willow
the grass.

From my head
in feathers comes
a gas.

I think of a tree
to make it
last.

.

Asa Gray wrote Increase Lapham:
pay particular attention
to my pets, the grasses.

.

Pioneers

Anson Dart pierced the forest,
                              fell upon wild strawberries.
Frosts, fires, land speculation, comet.
                                   Corn to be planted.
How to keep the strawberries?—
                              Indians' sugar full of dirt.
How to keep the earth.

Winnebagoes knew nothing
of government purchase of their land,
agency men got chiefs drunk
then let them stand.

On the steamer *Consolation*

       came Dart's wife and daughters,

already there his sons and three sides of the house.

In the Great Bitter Winter a rug closed the side

          that was bare.

For mortar they bored out a white-oak log,

pounded enough corn for a breakfast Johnnie cake

by rising—all sons—at 4:00.

Could be more, could be warmer, could be more.

Sun, turn the earth once more.

Between fighting fourteen nations' invading troops

and starting the first thousand-acre farms

   we hungered,

an effort to rise or stand up straight.

A tractor has seven hundred fifteen parts.

     I studied—

I'm a Morvin from the Eraya tribe—

       learned all about oil and sand

the whole inner essence of the core.

Gorky recalls Professor Hvolson

          lecturing on Einstein,

clung with his hands to the pulpit,

swayed back and forth from lack of food.

Then—the first one!—red wheels

     dipped, met the earth.

Red wheels gave the earth a new turn.

   ▪

Well, spring overflows the land,
floods floor, pump, wash machine
of the woman moored to this low shore by deafness.

Good-bye to lilacs by the door
and all I planted for the eye.
If I could hear—too much talk in the world,
too much wind washing, washing
good black dirt away.

Her hair is high.
Big blind ears.

I've wasted my whole life in water.
My man's got nothing but leaky boats.
My daughter, writer, sits and floats.

.

Audubon

Tried selling my pictures. In jail
twice for debt. My companion
a sharp, frosty gale.

In England unpacked
them with fear:
must I migrate back
to the woods unknown, strange
to all but the birds
I paint?

Dear Lucy, the servants here
move quiet
as killdeer.

.

van Gogh

At times I sit in the dunes,
faint, not enough to eat.
The path thru the dunes
is like a desert . . . the family's shoes
patched and worn and many more
such views.

.

What a woman!—hooks men like rugs,
clips as she hooks, prefers old wool, but all
childlike, lost, houseowning or pensioned men
her prey. She covets the gold in her husband's teeth.
She'd sell dirt, she'd sell your eyes fried in deep grief.

.

The brown muskrat, noiseless,
swims the white stream,
stretched out as if already
a woman's neck-piece.

In Red Russia the Russians
at a mile a minute
pitch back Nazi wildmen
wearing women.

.

The broad-leaved Arrow-head
grows vivid and strong
in my book, says: underneath
the surface of the stream the leaves
are narrow, long.
I don't investigate,
mark the page . . . I suppose
if I sat down beside a frost
and had no printed sign
I'd be lost. Well, up
from lying double in a book,
go long like a tree
and broad as the library.

.

"New Goose" Manuscript

To a Maryland editor, 1943:
The enclosed poems are sepa-
rated by stars to save paper.

Dear MacCloud:
the poems called Goose
separated by stars
to save the sun—

"We couldn't get away
with these down here
in the south on the brow
of Washington"—

appeared: your night's
folk-tongue.

▪

Summer's away, I traded my chicks for trees
so winter's tea-kettle on the high wood stove
            my feet to the heat
            my back in the shade
will tally with the tit-wit that sang
                    from the upmost branch.

▪

She was a mourner too. Now she's gone
   to the earth's core,
with organ notes, buried by church that buries the live,
intoning: That torture called by men delight
     touches her no more.
So calm she looked, half smiling: Heaven?
       No, restore
my matter, never free from motion,
   to the soil's roar.

 .

Seven years a charming woman wore
her coat, removed the collar where it tore,
little warmth but honor in her loose
thin coat, without knowing why
she's so. Charming? Well, she's destitute.

 .

The land of four o'clocks is here
the five of us together
  looking for our supper.
Half past endive, quarter to beets,
seven milks, ten cents cheese,
  lost, our land, forever.

 .

Just before she died
my little grandma with her long, long hair
put her hand on mine: I'm nearly there.

What'll I do all my life,
I cried, my work's cut short; I've a share
in the speed-up; a long, long race to spare.

.

Brought the enemy down
as his descendents the bombs
blew up Somerset House—

staircase at least
where records go down
to Shakespeare who never ceased.

.

Nothing nourishing,
common dealtout food;
no better reading
than keeps us destitute.

.

The number of Britons killed
by German bombs equals
the number of lakes in Wisconsin.

But more German corpses
in Stalingrad's ruins
than its stones.

■

Old Hamilton hailed the man from the grocery store:
What's today, Friday? Thursday! Oh,
nothing till tomorrow.

■

Motor cars
            like china
sometimes chink each other.

Will the speeding sugar bowl
            of taffy color
stop to eat people?

■

Allied Convoy
Reaches Russia

The ship that saved us—Uncle Joe!
Guns a quarter-mile long!
Red Comrades start their tanks in the hold,
climb in on the dock and are gone.

.

Depression years

My daughters left home
I was job-certified
to rake leaves

              in New Madrid.

Now they tell me my girls
should support me again
and they're not out of debt

          from the last time they did.

.

Coopered at Fish Creek,
farmed at Egg Harbor,
teamed on the ice from Green Bay to Death's Door,
kept hotel till it burned,
fished and returned

to the Creek, then started for more.
Tennessee, Black Hills,
now my farm at Lost Lake,
and that'll be the end of J. E. Thorp.

.

A working man appeared in the street
in soldiers suit, no work, no peace.
What'r you doing in that dress,
a policeman said, where's the fight?
And after they took him for a ride
in the ambulance, they made arrest
for failure to molest.

.

Woman with Umbrella

Lonely woman, not prompted
by freshness from the sky
to run with friends and laugh it off,
arrives unsparkling but dry—

she's felt the prongs of her own advance
thru the crowded street,
knows that lonely
she is dangerous to meet.

.

Automobile Accident

Not finding where the flowers were
he seized a tree.

. . .

Airplane or star?—so bright!
Star. I saw it last night.

∎

Look, the woods, the sky, our home.

It's going to rain and if we're wise
we'll go in the wood and get us home
some chunks to keep us warm.

And while we're cutting trees it rains
and we are wise to go home
to keep from getting stiff and great.

∎

Coming out of Sleep

O rock my baby on the tree tops
and blow me a little tin horn.
They've got us suckin the hind tit
and that's the way I was born.

O let me rise to the door-knob
and let me buy my way.
I know the owner of the store
and that's the way I was raised.

.

Voyageurs
sang, rowed
their canoes full of furs,

sang as they rowed.
Ten minutes every hour
rested their load.

.

I walked
from Chicago to Big Bull Falls (Wausau),
eighteen-forty-four,
two weeks,
little to eat.
Came night
I wrapped myself in a piece of bark
and slept beside a log.

.

See the girls in shorts on their bicycles
right here in Janesville. And why?—
no modesty anymore,
all gone by.

.

When Johnny (Chapman) Appleseed
came to a place he didn't like
he covered it with apple trees.
He was the early American apple
who changed the earth by dropping seeds.

He walked all over the mid-west states.
His trees grew while he slept.
Gave to the poor tho he himself
lived on roots and had no bed.

Nor had he a wife. Nor creed
that embraced grafting. Johnny
reproduced by seed.

.

Tell me a story about the war.
All right, six lines, no child should hear more.

The marshal of France made quite a clatter:
Dear people, I know you're too hungry to flatter

but eat your beef-ounce from a doll's platter,
you'll think it's a roast wrapped in a batter.

Along came the bishop his robe a tatter:
Sleep and it won't matter.

.

Poet Percival said: I struck a lode
but it was only a bunch in a chimney
without any opening
and as I left a sucker jumped me . . .
This is truly a rich and beautiful country.

.

Terrible things coming up,
these trailer houses.
People want to live in em,
park all over,
set out for somewhere,
never come home.

Nice!—
needn't clean anything,
just throw it out the window
onto somebody else.
Shiftless life!

.

1937

In the picture soldiers
moving thru a field
of flowers,
Spanish reds.
The flowers of war
move cautiously
not to tread
the wild heads.

Here we last,
lilacs, vacant lots,
taxes, no work,
debts, the wind widens
the grass.
In the old house
the clocks are dead,
past dead.

.

Their apples fall down
and rot on the ground—
they don't spray their trees,
trees need care.
You can tell they're no good
that live there.

Apples are high—
that shows they're scarce,
still the stores always seem to have plenty.
Can't get a price
the farmers say—
I guess it's because there'r too many.

■

The government men said Don't plant wheat,
we've got too much, just keep out weeds.

Our crop comes up thru change of season
to be stored for what good reason

way off and here we need it—Eat
who can, who can't—Don't grow wheat

or corn but quack-grass-bread!
Such things they plant around my head.

■

1945—1956

New!
Reason explodes. Atomic split
shows one element
Jew

Now hide
who can bombarded particles
of international
pride

.

(L.Z.)

"An acre of music"
or a room closer to it
movement, rest, repeat,
for those making music
but not allowed to hear it
and those in peril
on the street

.

Chimney Sweep

He fished the black deep
to eat,
swam the river, struck a stone
before he could sleep.

One Sunday morning,
unlearned in all but soot,
he flashed and went down
in a book.

.

Swept snow, Li Po,
by dawn's 40-watt moon
to the road that hies to office
away from home.

Tended my brown little stove
as one would a cow—she gives heat.
Spring—marsh frog-clatter peace
breaks out.

.

Regards to Mr. Glover

Yes, I've lived a good life—cows, the soil—
but what do we know for sure? Light from stars
dead a billion years still pricks . . . see! . . .
I can't conceive . . . let the cost of war out
of it. You say each birthday you know more,
better. Well. I don't. And I'm not stuck
in that old stuff: cosmos versus puny

man, God, no. What is life? (not always
does one feel this intimate) My only
fear: I'll go blind before I give
the soil my phosphorus. And you, my friend,
happy anniversary.

.

Sunday's motor-cars
jar the house.
When I'm away on work-days
hear the rose-breast.
Love the night, love the night
and if on waking it rains:
little drops of rest.

.

Let's play a game.
        Let's play Ask for a job.
What can you do?
        I can hammer and saw
        and feed a dog.
 You'll do! Take this slip
to the department of song.
        You must ask me where I'm from.

Oh yes, you're from the country
called The Source.
      Will the nurse in your plant
      give me sweet pills?
No! We're not at war.
      One console-ation is:
      we can always play
      Ask for a job.

.

Lugubre for a child
but for you, little one,
life pops
      from a music box
shaped like a gun.

Watch! In some flowers
a hammer drops down
like a piano key's
      and honeybees
wear a pollen gown.

A hammer, a hummer!
A bomber in feathers!
Hummingbirds fly
      backwards—we eye
blurred propellers.

Dear fiddler: you'll carry
a counter that sings
when man sprays
        rays
on small whirring things.

  .

Could You Be Right

He asked: Will man obsolesce
when he sends the rays against himself?
And she, sore-pressed: Absurd!—
obsolesce is not a word.

But think of Troy, it was a word
before we dug and found that world . . .
yet ah, girl with Helen's light,
could you be right?

  .

Look close
the senses don't get it all
a few hundred thousandths of a centimeter
in wave length and you see the mark
or you don't

Sylvashko and Robertson
shook hands hard
and the air was loaded
and after tea vodka—
"To the friendship of our countries"—
guilty of reason
matter that day
hit home

.

If I were a bird

I'd be a dainty contained cool
Greek figurette
on a morning shore—
H.D.

I'd flitter and feed and delouse myself
close to Williams' house
and his kind eyes

I'd be a never-museumed tinted glass
breakable from the shelves of Marianne Moore.

On Stevens' fictive sibilant hibiscus flower
I'd poise myself, a cuckoo, flamingo-pink.

I'd plunge the depths with Zukofsky
and all that means—stirred earth,
cut sky, organ-sounding, resounding
anew, anew.

I'd prick the sand in cunning, lean,
Cummings irony, a little drunk dead sober.
Man, that walk down the beach!

I'd sit on a quiet fence
and sing a quiet thing: sincere, sincere.
And that would be Reznikoff.

■

High, lovely, light,
the Easter cake was beaten
electrically and eaten
down. Cousins, good night.

Child at your mountain-height—
your cello and bow in Easter's
high, lovely, light,
climb this one, tone feaster:

What eggs them on to bite
a frosted muff, to sneeze on,
sleep? To what season
are they tuned tight,
high, lovely, light?

■

Letter from Paul

It is yes with a lyre, ax and shovel
and snowman falling down.
This is my mother's birthday.
"Don't buy me a present"—what a sound—
        "don't
we can't afford it." Selfish of her.
And when Mozart was five
                just plain 5
how proud his father was
that his son had played
              every single note.

    .

Two old men—
one proposed they live together
take turns cooking, washing dishes
they were both alone.
His friend: "Our way of living
is so different:
        you spit
        I don't spit."

    .

Paul, hello
    what do you know

Goodbye
    why

.

So this was I
in my framed
young aloofness
unsuspecting
    what I filled

eager to remain
a smooth blonde cool
effect of light
an undiffused good take,
    a girl
    who couldn't bake

How I wish
I had someone to give
this pretty thing to
who'd keep it—
    something of me
    would shape

.

Am I real way out in space
asked Paul, then you see—
they rave to me of contests.
Compete, they say—my violin—
with tap-dance-acrobatics.
The winner plays the floor
with his feet.

.

On a row of cabins
next my home

Instead of shaded here
birds flying through leaves
I face this loud uncovering
of griefs.

What irony that I
with views verdant like the folk
should be the one
to go.

.

In moonlight lies
       the river passing—
it's not quiet
       and it's not laughing.

I'm not young
       and I'm not free
but I've a house of my own
       by a willow tree.

.

The cabin door flew open
         the woman fell out
it is not known whether
         she fell on land or sea

the man's grave
grave face

who were they

undoubtedly they knew tender moments
between sex and well-dressed courtesy—

men are tender with women
not passion-violent
when they are happy in general
and she—impossible to be grateful
without showing it

before the earth fell away
that they went out on Sunday to see.

.

The elegant office girl
is power-rigged.

She carries her nylon hard-pointed
breast uplift
like parachutes
half-pulled.

At night collapse occurs
among new flowered rugs
replacing last year's plain,
muskrat stole,
parakeets
and deep-freeze pie.

.

When brown folk lived a distance
from my cottages my hand full of lilies
went out to them
from potted progressive principles.

Now no one of my own hue will rent.
I'll lose my horticultural bent.

I'll lose more—how dark
if to fight to keep my livelihood
is to bleach brotherhood.

.

For Paul and Other Poems

Paul
now six years old:
this book of birds I loved
I give to you.
I thought now maybe Paul
growing taller than cattails
around Duck Pond
between the river and the Sound
will keep this book intact,
fly back to it each summer

maybe Paul

∎

What bird would light
in a moving tree
the tree I carry
for privacy?

Down in the grass
the question's inept;
sora's eyes . . .
stillness steps.

∎

Nearly landless and on the way to water
I push thru marsh.
I lost a view . . . I saw
(and proceed in depth in place of lateral range)
the child with bigger, stiller eyes than sora's.

Homer's wandering thru hell.
And we can't afford to hire him.
He loses ground building cabins—
outdoor knickknacks—that block a view.
He himself and his wife demand more elephants
on glass shelves than we have books.

In summer silence moves.
Fall pheasants' cry:
rifle shells-in-tin-box-rattle,
over us wax-leaf poplars shine and shudder
as my mother,
continue after the mind is blown.

.

Understand me, dead is nothing
whereas here we want each other,
silence, time to be alone
and Paul's growing up—
baseball, jabber, running off to neighbors
and back into the Iliad—"do you really believe
there were gods, all that hooey?"
And his violin—improvising

made a Vivaldi sequence his,
better than I could have done with poetry
at twice his age . . .
so writes your father, L. before P.

A start in life for Paul.
The efforts of a life
hold together as Einstein's
and lead to expectations of form.

To know, to love . . . if we knew nothing,
Baruch the blessed said, would we exist?

For Paul then at six and a half
a half scholarship—
turn the radio dead—
tho your teacher's gone back to Italy
stumped by American capital.

In my mind, the child said,
are rondeau-gavottes 1 to 11,
here is number 12.

·

How bright you'll find young people,
        Diddle,
                and how unkind.
When a boy appears with a book
they cry "Who's the young Einsteind?"
Einstein, you know, said space

is what it's made up of.
And as to the human race
"Why do you deeply oppose its passing"
you'll find men asking
the man with the nebular hair
        and the fiddle.

   .

If he is of constant depth
if he has the feeling—
numbers plus their good
by the time he's twelve

I want that chord, he cries,
and the sun and moon and stars

so what . . .
boy, are you Greek
without the Wisecrack god

   .

The young ones go away to school
come home to moon

like Frederick the Great
what was it he ate

that had to be sown
in the dark of the moon

Isn't it funny
people run their acres without a hat
figuring rain in the next moon change

while you on a stool
at numbers in a heavenly scale
know the moon changes
                 night and noon

   .

Some have chimes
three long things
as you come in.

They smile
and give you lettuce
because you've brought
your violin.

   .

O Tannenbaum
the children sing
round and round
one child sings out:
atomic bomb

Not all
is check-writing
but as the queen, Elizabeth,
beside the barge that night
            "Longing
to listen . . .
Muzik is a nobl art"

．

In the great snowfall before the bomb
colored yule tree lights
windows, the only glow for contemplation
along this road

I worked the print shop
right down among em
the folk from whom all poetry flows
and dreadfully much else.

I was Blondie
I carried my bundles of hog feeder price lists
down by Larry the Lug,
I'd never get anywhere
because I'd never had suction,
pull, you know, favor, drag,
well-oiled protection.

I heard their rehashed radio barbs—
more barbarous among hirelings
as higher-ups grow more corrupt.
But what vitality! The women hold jobs—
clean house, cook, raise children, bowl
and go to church.

What would they say if they knew
I sit for two months on six lines
of poetry?

.

Not all that's heard is music. We leave
an air that for awhile was good, white cottage,
spruce . . . What if the sky is gone and they hold
the hill armed with tin cans—they're not bad kids—
you have the world. Remember the little
lovely notes "the little O, the earth."
This thing is old and singing's new—you
just more full. Come, we'll sit without birds
between city bricks. See! The sun hits.

.

Tell me a story about the war.
All right, six lines, no child should hear more.

The marshal of France made quite a clatter:
Dear people, I know you're too hungry to flatter

but eat your beef-ounce from a doll's platter,
you'll think it's a roast wrapped in a batter.

Along came the bishop his robe a tatter:
Sleep and it won't matter.

.

Laval, Pomeret, Pétain
all three came to an end.

Bourdet, Bonnet, Deladier
so did they.

They tried each other
they sold out their brother

the people of France.
Let's practice your dance.

.

Thure Kumlien

Bigwigs wrote from Boston: Thure,
we must know about the sandhill crane,
is it ever white with you
and how many eggs can you obtain?

For Thure the solitary tattler
opened a door
to learned birds with their latest books
who walked New England's shore.

One day by the old turnpike still crossing
the marsh, down in the ditch
he found a new aster—to it he gave
his name as tho he were rich.

.

Shut up in woods
he made knives and forks
fumbled English gently:

Now is March gone
and I have much undone

It would be good
to hear the birds
along this shore intently

without song of gun

.

Your father to me in your eighth summer:
"Any fool can look up a term,
it's the beat and off beat, the leg lifted
or thudded that counts."
And "Now that I'm involved in two houses
each one a system, I realize
the less one has the richer one is
if one could sit in one spot
and write.
Paul's playing 'Handle.'
His eyes are clear in this air,
he sees what few others can,
the lawn is mown,
we're here till we go."

.

To Paul now old enough to read:
Once a farmer, Crèvecoeur
tried to save his heart
from too much hurt.

Hero of vegetables,
hero of good
he learned to know every plant
in his neighborhood.

He loved Nantucket, grazing land
held in common.
Here one lawyer only found
the means to go on.

Green, prickly humanity—
men are plants whose goodness grows
out of the soil, Mr. Stinkweed
or Mrs. Rose.

. . .

Read Crèvecoeur and learn fast—
the firefly, two pairs of wings
and a third to read by
disappearing.

.

What horror to awake at night
and in the dimness see the light.
    Time is white
    mosquitoes bite
I've spent my life on nothing.

The thought that stings. How are you, Nothing,
sitting around with Something's wife.
    Buzz and burn
    is all I learn
I've spent my life on nothing.

I'm pillowed and padded, pale and puffing
lifting household stuffing—
    carpets, dishes
    benches, fishes
I've spent my life in nothing.

.

Sorrow moves in wide waves,
   it passes, lets us be.
It uses us, we use it,
   it's blind while we see.

Consciousness is illimitable,
   too good to forsake
tho what we feel be misery
   and we know will break.

.

Jesse James and his brother Frank
   raided, robbed and rode away.
Said Frank to the rising Teddy R:
   You're my type, you're okay.

Once on his way to a Shakespeare play
   Frank was almost caught.
The gunnin Jameses and the writn Jameses—
   two were taught and all were sought.

No killers were Frank and Jesse James,
   they was drove to it. Their folks was proud.
Let no one imagine they were bad as kids—
   brought up gentle in a bushwhack crowd.

. . .

May you have lumps in your mashed potatoes
   Henry and Wm. cried
to those who stood up to them in argu-
   ment and their words haven't died.
Don't melt too much into the universe
   but be as solid and dense and fixed
as you can. This what Henry and Wm.
   said in the evening after 6:00.

.

Old Mother turns blue and from us,
   "Don't let my head drop to the earth.
I'm blind and deaf." Death from the heart,
   a thimble in her purse.

"It's a long day since last night.
   Give me space. I need
floors. Wash the floors, Lorine!—
   wash clothes! Weed!"

.

I hear the weather
      through the house
or is it breathing
        mother

  .

Dead
she now lay deaf to death

She could have grown a good rutabaga
in the burial ground
        and how she'd have loved these woods

One of her pallbearers said I
      like a dumfool followed a deer
wanted to see her jump a fence—
        never'd seen a deer jump a fence

pretty thing
      the way she runs

  .

Can knowledge be conveyed that isn't felt?
But if transport's the problem—
they tell me get a job and earn yourself
an automobile—I'd rather collect my parts
as I go: chair, desk, house
and crankshaft Shakespeare.

Generator boy, Paul, love is carried
if it's held.

.

Ten o'clock
and Paul's not in bed!
He's reading Twelfth Night
all Viola said.

Drink to three, the family
around the bathroom tap.
Little Paul—Corelli,
what's that?—belly!

Wash and say good night
to variants and quarto texts,
emendations, close relations.
Let me hear good night.

.

Adirondack Summer

If he's not peewee wafted
        tiny glissando
        in deep shade
or a newspaper
he'll attack exercises ever calculated
to float the ear in beauty.

.

The slip of a girl-announcer:
Now we hear
Baxtacota in D Minor
played by a boy who's terrific.

This saxy Age.
Bach, you see, is in Dakota
but don't belittle her,
she'll take you where you want to go ta.

.

Now go to the party,
Master Paul Kung.
Wear your mother's ancient
imitation silk black dress,
whisk brush for beard,
your bathrobe's braid-tie
hung safety-pinned from Eton cap
turned front to back,
shoe string side burns
to hold the beard.

What you don't know,
that even yet
players come dressed with shields
and spears.

.

Dear Paul:

the sheets of your father's book of poetry
are bound for England.
At last, after the hardships
he can say "take back to your ship
a gift from me,
something precious, a real good thing . . .
such as a friend gives to a friend."

You ask what kind of boats in *my* country
on my little river.

Black as those beside Troy,
but sailless tar-preserve-black fish barges
and orange and Chinese-red rowboats
in which the three virtues
               knowledge, humanity, energy
Sometimes ride.

All children begin with the life of the mind—
if there were no marsh or stream
imagine it
99 children go into business
              selling angleworms,
the hundredth develops free fingers in John Sebastian Brook.

"Paul's playing 'Handle.'
His eyes are clear in this air,
he sees what few others can,
the lawn is mown,
we're here till we go."

Yes, comes a measure marked Autumn
the passing of the little summer people,
schools of leaves float downstream
past lonely piers

soft still-water twilight,
morning ice on the minnow bucket.

.

My father said "I remember
a warm Thanksgiving Day
we shipped seine
without coats
nudged 20,000 lbs. of barged buffalo fish
thru the mouth of the river
by balmy moonlight
other times
you laid out with your hands glazed
to the nets"

.

You know, he said, they used to make
mincemeat with meat,
it's raisins now and citron—like
a house without heat—

I'll roof my house and jump from there
to flooring costs. I'll have to buy
two doors to close two openings.
No, no more pie.

.

He built four houses
to keep his life.
Three got away
before he was old.

He wonders now
rocking his chair
should he have built
a boat

dipping, dipping
and sitting so.

.

In Europe they grow a new bean while here
        we tie bundles of grass
with strands of itself—as my grandfolks did grain—
        against the cold blast
            around my house.

From my cousin in Maine: We've found a warm place
        (did she say in the hay?)
for the winter. Charlie sleeps late, I'm glad for his sake,
        it shortens the day
            around my house.

.

Paul
      when the leaves
         fall

from their stems
      that lie thick
         on the walk

in the light
      of the full note
         the moon

playing
      to leaves
         when they leave

the little
      thin things
         Paul

.

I've been away from poetry
many months

and now I must rake leaves
with nothing blowing

between your house
and mine

.

I am sick with the Time's buying sickness.
The overdear oil drum now flanged to my house
serves a stove costing as much.
I need a piano.

Then I'd sing "When to the sessions
of sweet silent thought"
true value expands
it warms.

.

The death of my poor father
leaves debts
and two small houses.

To settle this estate
a thousand fees arise—
I enrich the law.

Before my own death is certified,
recorded, final judgement
judged

taxes taxed
I shall own a book
of old Chinese poems

and binoculars
to probe the river
trees.

.

To Aeneas who closed his piano
to dig a well thru hard clay
Chopin left notes like drops of water.
Aeneas could play

the Majorcan sickness, the boat on which pigs
were kept awake by whips
the woman Aurore
the narrow sand-strips.

"O Frederic, think of me digging below
the surface—we are of one pitch and flow."

.

My friend the black and white collie
stood at my door in the cold days
when the wolf was expected.

She lay her brown nose inside my coat.
We two unfortunate dogs.

.

                    "Oh ivy green
            oh ivy green—"
you spoke your poem
as we walked a city terrace
and said if you could hear—sneeze
            sneeze on the corner—
                Handel clean
Christmas would be green
Christmas would be cherished.

            To the mother
        ivy
does not matter
with her son's cold no better
unless a friend should hold her
            warm in a green
                    cover
then Christmas would be cherished
Christmas would be cherished.

.

As I shook the dust
from my father's door
I saw young Aeneas
on the shore

mulling the past
—a large town
and a wartime island—
a pleasure now.

I'll wait, he said,
till a star shows
that's gone
when it snows.

.

They live a cool distance
inside today's woods.
My cutting friends' concise art
—intelligence in beauty—

      exacts their violinist son
      to make it come clean-sung.

Their further woods—
they live without food-heavy table,
soft bed, the whole easy lot of us,
the sick, thick leaf-tickling outersurface
lot of us.

A tough game, art,
humanity's other part.

．

Violin Debut

Carnegie Hall, the great musicbox—
lift the lid on the hard-working parts
of the boy whose smooth power
is saved—

his tone and more: what he's done with his life
—those two who sent the flow thru him have done—
he's been true to himself, a knife
behaved.

．

    Horse, hello
I too live hot before the final flash
          cavort for others' gain
We toss our shining heads
in an ever increasing standard of sweat
The mind deranged, Democritus
Who knows us, friend—
our indicator needles shot off scale—
Spinoza, Burns, Xenophanes knew us
in days when thought arose and kindly stayed—
All creatures whatsoever desire this glow

    .

Energy glows at the lips—
a cigarette—
measure the man pending . . .
under him droppings
larger, whiter than owls'—
What thought burns here?

    .

Hi, Hot-and-Humid

That June she's a lush

Marshmushing, frog bickering
moon pooling, green gripping

fool
keep cool

.

Woman in middle life
raises hot fears—

a few cool years after these
then who'll remember

flash to black
I gleamed?

.

We physicians watch the juices rise
                    as we tend
                    to bend her
toward the soft-blowing air.
Girl, personal grass,
                    we saved you
                    waved you

closer. Don't despise us
      if we ask
      or do not ask:
what for?

   .

1937

In the picture soldiers
moving thru a field
of flowers,
Spanish reds.
The flowers of war
move cautiously
not to tread
the wild heads.

Here we last,
lilacs, vacant lots,
taxes, no work,
debts, the wind widens
the grass.
In the old house
the clocks are dead,
past dead.

   .

European Travel
(Nazi New Order)

From Croatia my home to Moelling no pay
for our work, lay down at night without hay,
three days toward Berlin, one bread for six,
saw many die of cold and the whips.
At Bergen built roads tied to a pot,
crossed to Sweden tho one in our party was shot.

.

Depression years

My daughters left home
I was job-certified
to rake leaves
                    in New Madrid.

Now they tell me my girls
should support me again
and they're not out of debt
        from the last time they did.

.

So you're married, young man,
to a woman's rich fads—
woman and those "buy! buy!"
technicolor ads.

She needs washers and dryers
she needs bodice uplift
she needs deep-well cookers
she needs power shift.

A man works in two shops—
home at last from this grave
he finds his wife out
with another slave.

She'll sue for divorce
he'll blow his brains,
the old work-horse
free at last of his reins.

.

She grew where every spring
water overflows the land,
married mild Henry
and then her life was sand.

Tall, thin, took cold on her nerves,
chopped wood, kept the fire,
burned the house, helped build it again,
advance, attack, retire.

Gave birth, frail warrior—gave boat
for it was mid-spring—
to Henry's daughter who stayed
on the stream listening

to Daisy: "Hatch, patch and scratch,
that's all a woman's for
but I didn't sink, I sewed and saved
and now I'm on second floor."

.

I sit in my own house
secure,
follow winter break-up
thru window glass.
Ice cakes
glide downstream
the wild swans
of our day.

.

*On hearing
the wood pewee*

This is my mew
    as our days last—
        be alone

Throw it over—
    all fashions
        feud

Go home where the green bird is—
    the trees where you pass
        to grass

.

Along the river
    wild sunflowers
over my head
    the dead
who gave me life
    give me this
our relative the air
    floods
our rich friend
    silt

.

He moved in light
    to establish
the lovely
    possibility
we knew
    and let it pass

.

Keen and lovely man moved as in a dance
to be considerate in lighted, glass-walled
almost outdoor office. Business

wasn't all he knew. He knew music, art.
Had a heart. "With eyes like yours I should think
the dictaphone" or did he say the flute?

His sensitivity—it stopped you.
And the neighbors said "She's taking lessons
on the dictaphone" as tho it were a saxophone.

He gave the job to somebody else.

.

He lived—childhood summers
    thru bare feet
then years of money's lack
    and heat

beside the river—out of flood
    came his wood, dog,
woman, lost her, daughter—
    prologue

to planting trees. He buried carp
    beneath the rose
where grass-still
    the marsh rail goes.

To bankers on high land
    he opened his wine tank.
He wished his only daughter
    to work in the bank

but he'd given her a source
    to sustain her—
a weedy speech,
    a marshy retainer.

.

I rose from marsh mud,
algae, equisetum, willows,
sweet green, noisy
birds and frogs

to see her wed in the rich
rich silence of the church,
the little white slave-girl
in her diamond fronds.

In aisle and arch
the satin secret collects.
United for life to serve
silver. Possessed.

.

Dear Mona, Mary and all
you know as I grow older I think
of people when I was younger

I am lame and dizzy but eat
and hear from Ireland
where my mother was

There's a story in the paper
about the river in your country
how it's used and owned by the people

Television here but I can't use it
I'd go out of my head
old folks often can't

. . .

International loneliness
is homed. Dear old uncle's
porch's people, prices, peppermints
rock him. He must reach
the hallway off the living room
by night.

.

Don't tell me property is sacred!
Things that move, yes!—
cars out rolling thru the country
how they like to rest

on me—beer cans and cellophane
on my clean-mowed grounds.
Whereas I'm quiet . . . I was born
with eyes and a house.

.

Wartime

I left my baby in Forest A
quivering toward light:
Keep warm, dear thing, drink from the cow—
her stillness is alive

You in the leaves sweetly growing—
survive these plants upheaved
with noise and flame, learn change
in strategy.

I think of Joe who never knew
where his baby went
and Mary heavy, peace or war,
no child, no enlightenment.

.

February almost March bites the cold.
Take down a book, wind pours in. Frozen—
the Garden of Eden—its oil, if freed, could warm
the world for 20 years and nevermind the storm.

Winter's after me—she's out
with sheets so white it hurts the eyes. Nightgown,
pillow slip blow thru my bare catalpa trees,
no objects here.

In February almost March a snow-blanket
is good manure, a tight-bound wet
to move toward May: give me lupines and a care
for her growing air.

.

People, people—
ten dead ducks' feathers
on beer can litter . . .
                    Winter
will change all that

.

July, waxwings
on the berries
have dyed red
       the dead
branch

.

Old man who seined
to educate his daughter
sees red Mars rise:
      What lies
behind it?

Cold water business
now starred in Fishes
of dipnet shape
      to ache
thru his arms.

.

Mother is dead

The branches' snow is like the cotton fluff
she wore in her aching ears. In this deaf huff
after storm shall we speak of love?

As my absent father's distrait wife
she worked for us—knew us by sight.

We know her now by the way the snow
protects the plants before they go.

.

The graves

You were my mother, thorn apple bush,
armed against life's raw push.
But you my father catalpa tree
stood serene as now—he refused to see
that the other woman, the hummer he shaded
            hotly cared
for his purse petals falling—
                    his mind in the air.

.

Kepler

Comets you say shoot from nothing?
In heaven's name what other
than matter can be matter's mother.

.

Bonpland

"Revolutionary palingenesis"—

his plants rode the Orinoco sheltered
while he sat in the rain.

He chopped, climbed, dug the jungle
for his beloved lost girl,
returned with botany
alone.

Rebellion-plotting Bogota
moved him—

nine years in Paraguay's dictator's
prison

—to graft a phrase.

.

Happy New Year
"Glorious and abundant
The cherry trees are in flower
In all the world there is nothing
Finer than brotherhood."

My friend, you were right.
Two thousand years
beyond you
I hand you this:

Trees' bloom with snow-
clean sorrow
better than bitter
winter
       brotherhood

Resolved: beyond
flowering cherry trees
dissolved enmity
find summer
        brother

■

1957—1959

Linnaeus in Lapland

Nothing worth noting
except an Andromeda
with quadrangular shoots—
       the boots
of the people

wet inside: they must swim
to church thru the floods
or be taxed—the blossoms
       from the bosoms
of the leaves

   .

Fog-thick morning—
I see only
where I now walk. I carry
       my clarity
with me.

   .

Hear
where her snow-grave is
the *You*
      ah you
of mourning doves

   .

Cricket-song—
What's in The Times—
     your name!
       Fame

here

on my doorstep
—an evening seedy
     quiet thing.
      It rings
a little.

   .

Musical Toys

               for a blind child

Do you see?—
sharp spires—
you could be hurt
   by the church.
Better

this dog
tinkling
  three nice
     mice
blind.

   .

I fear this war
will be long and painful
and who
       pursue
it

.

Van Gogh could see
twenty-seven varieties
    of black
       in cap-
italism.

.

No matter where you are
you are alone
and in danger—well
        to hell
with it.

.

How white the gulls
in grey weather
        Soon April
        the little
yellows

    .

Springtime's wide
water-
        yield
but the field
will return

    .

White
among the green pads—
      which
        a dead fish
or a lily?

    .

Dusk—

He's spearing from a boat—

How slippery is man
      in spring
            when the small fish
                spawn

.

Beautiful girl—
pushes food onto her fork
with her fingers—
  will throw the switches
of deadly rockets?

.

New-sawed
clean-smelling house
sweet cedar pink
      flesh tint
I love you

.

My friend tree
I sawed you down
but I must attend
an older friend
the sun

.

1960 — 1964

In Leonardo's light
we questioned

the sun does not love
My hat

attained
the weight falls

I am at rest
You too

hold a doctorate
in Warmth

.

You are my friend—
you bring me peaches
and the high bush cranberry
                you carry
my fishpole

you water my worms
you patch my boot
with your mending kit
            nothing in it
but my hand

.

Come In

Glen Ellyn

Education, kindness
live here
whose dog does not impose
    her long nose
and barks quietly.

Serious wags its tail
—they see us—
from curtain tie-backs
    no knick-knacks
between us.

    .

The men leave the car
to bring us green-white lilies
    by woods
These men are our woods
yet I grieve

I'm swamp
as against a large pine-spread—
his clear No marriage
    no marriage
friend

    .

The wild and wavy event
now chintz at the window

was revolution . . .
Adams

to Miss Abigail Smith:
You have faults

You hang your head down
like a bulrush

you read, you write, you think
but I drink Madeira

to you
and you cross your Leggs

while sitting.
(Later:)

How are the children?
If in danger run to the woods.

Evergreen o evergreen
how faithful are your branches

.

FLORIDA

1

Always north of him
I see

he's close
to orange, flower

roseate bird
soft air

the state
I'm in

2

Henry James

St. Augustine
they overplayed
its Spanish story

yet was this romance
that most solicited
him

3

Cape Canaveral

Space shot off
man appears normal

4
Flocks
of headkerchiefs

the plumed flamingo
gone

the vanity of women
slacked

￭

My life is hung up
in the flood
    a wave-blurred
        portrait

Don't fall in love
with this face—
     it no longer exists
       in water
          we cannot fish

￭

Easter

A robin stood by my porch
   and side-eyed
      raised up
        a worm

￭

Get a load
    of April's
        fabulous

frog rattle—
    lowland freight cars
    in the night

.

Poet's work

Grandfather
    advised me:
        Learn a trade

I learned
    to sit at desk
        and condense

No layoff
    from this
        condensery

.

Property is poverty—
I've foreclosed.
I own again

these walls thin
as the back
of my writing tablet.

And more:
all who live here—
card table to eat on,

broken bed—
sacrifice for less
than art.

.

Now in one year
    a book published
        and plumbing—
took a lifetime
      to weep
          a deep
            trickle

.

River-marsh-drowse
and in flood
    moonlight
      gives sight
of no land.

They fish, a man
takes his wife to town
with his rowboat's 10-horse
    ships his voice
to the herons.

Sure they drink
—full foamy folk—
      till asleep.
  The place is asleep
on one leg in the weeds.

.

Club 26

Our talk, our books
riled the shore like bullheads
at the roots of the luscious
large water lily

Then we entered the lily
built white on a red carpet

the circular quiet
cool bar

glass stems to caress
We stayed till the stamens trembled

.

To foreclose
or not
on property
and prose

or care a kite
if the p-p
be yellow, black
or white

∎

*To my small
electric pump*

To sense
and sound
this world

look to
your snifter
valve

take oil
and hum

∎

T. E. Lawrence

How impossible it is
to be alone
the one thing humanity
   has never really
moved towards

∎

As I paint the street

I melt the houses
to point up the turreted cupola
I make hoopla

of the low tavern's neon cross—
very like a cross from here—
I honor the huge blue distant dome
valid somehow to the fellow falling high

∎

Art Center

Glass
and wide seaview

Race that walks
                from there
you are lovely

You have *seen*

.

Homemade/Handmade Poems

Consider at the outset:
to be thin for thought
or thick cream blossomy

Many things are better
flavored with bacon

Sweet Life, My love:
didn't you ever try
this delicacy—the marrow
in the bone?

And don't be afraid
to pour wine over cabbage

.

Ah your face
but it's whether
you can keep me warm

.

Alcoholic dream
that ran him
       out from home
          to return
leaning

like the house
in this old part
        of town leaves him
            grieving:
why

do I hurt you
whom I love?
    Your ear
        is cold!—here,
drink

.

                To my pres-
                sure pump

I've been free
        with less
            and clean
I plumbed for principles

Now I'm jet-bound
by faucet   shower
heater   valve
ring seal   service

cost to my little
    humming
        water
            bird

.

Laundromat

Casual, sudsy
social love
at the tubs

After all, ecstasy
can't be constant

．

March

Bird feeder's
    snow-cap
        sliding
            off

．

Something in the water
like a flower
will devour

water

flower

．

Santayana's

For heaven's sake, dear Cory,
poetry?—I like somewhat
the putrid Petrarch
and the miserable Milton.
I don't have books,
don't meet important persons
only an occasional stray student
or an old Boston lady.

.

If only my friend
would return
and remove the leaves
                from my eaves
troughs

.

                Frog noise
            suddenly stops

Listen!
They turned off
their lights

.

In the transcendence
of convalescence
the translation
of Bashō

. . .

I lay down
          with brilliance
I saw a star whistle
          across the sky
before dropping off

.

To whom
can I leave
    Audubon's Avocet
    on green sportsman's cloth
    wide oak framed
    above the warm polished
    copper-braced sweet-smelling
    cedar box
when I must leave
this flyway

.

Margaret Fuller

She carried books
and chrysanthemums
to Boston
into a cold storm

.

Watching dan-
cers on skates

Ten thousand women
  and I
    the only one
      in boots

Life's dance:
  they meet
   he holds her leg
     up

.

Hospital Kitchen

Return
the night women's
gravy

to the cleaned
stove

.

Chicory flower
on campus

Open-field
  blue-wheeled
    gone by hot noon

to revolve
  earth-evolved
    mind-city

.

Fall

Early morning corn
shock quick river
edge ice crack duck
talk

Grasses' dry membranous
breaks tick-tack tiny
wind strips

.

LZ's

As you know mind
aint what attracts me
nor the wingspread
of Renaissance man

but what was sensed
by them guys
and their minds still carry
the sensing

.

Letter from Ian

Aye sure
a castle on a rock
in the middle of Edinburgh

They floodlight it—
big show up there
with pipe bands
and all

Down here along the road
open your door
to a posse of poets

.

Some float off on chocolate bars
and some on drink

Harmless, happy, soft of heart

This bottle may breed
a new race

> no war
> and let birds live

Myself, I gripped my melting container
the night I heard the wild
wet rat, muskrat
grind his frogs and mice
the other side of a thin door
in the flood

.

I knew a clean man
but he was not for me.
Now I sew green aprons
over covered seats. He

wades the muddy water fishing,
falls in, dries his last pay-check
in the sun, smooths it out
in *Leaves of Grass*. He's
the one for me.

.

Scythe

Spite
    spit
loud
      sound:
where is my scy'?

Why
by your nose—
      so close
  a snake
would've bit

  ■

So he said
on radio

I have to fly
wit Venus arms
I found fishing
to Greece
then back to Univers of Wis
where they got stront. 90
to determ if same marble
as my arms

  ■

*I visit
the graves*

Greatgrandfather
under wild flowers sons
sons here now I
      eye
of us all

but sonless
see no
      hop
clover boy to stop
before me

   ■

For best work
you ought to put forth
      some effort
      to stand
in north woods
among birch

   ■

The obliteration
of the world
his dinner speech
tonight   I beseech
you

eat
the recommended melon
before the fruit flies
                    rise
from it

.

Spring
    stood there
        all body

Head
    blown off
        (war)

showed up
    downstream

October
    is the head
        of spring

Birch, sumac
    before
        the blast

.

The park
"a darling walk
for the mind"

A sense
of starlings musing
on robins

Green statue—
            Burns!

near abandoned
steepled
railroad station

lakeshore silence

glass box mushroom
with stairway stem
art museum

and townward
            the taverns

.

Who was Mary Shelley?
What was her name
before she married?

She eloped with this Shelley
she rode a donkey
till the donkey had to be carried.

Mary was Frankenstein's creator
his yellow eye
before her husband was to drown

Created the monster nights
after Byron, Shelley
talked the candle down.

Who was Mary Shelley?
She read Greek, Italian
She bore a child

Who died
and yet another child
who died.

.

Wild strawberries
Ruskin's consolation

His grey diaries
instanced with Rose

Liver here tonight
Tomorrow we dine out

tho not like him
at Club Metaphysical

.

1965—1967

Autumn

Ice
on the minnow bucket

and a school of leaves
moving downstream

.

Last night the trash barrel
smoked from lighted paper
This morning
from sun burning
the frost

.

The boy tossed the news
and missed
They found it
on the bush

.

Popcorn-can cover
screwed to the wall
over a hole
    so the cold
can't mouse in

．

Truth
gives heat

He blushed
when I said

before he came
I never wore beads

．

Lights, lifts
parts nicely opposed
this white
        lice lithe
pink bird

．

O late fall
marsh—
    I
raped by the dry
weed stalk

   ■

CHURCHILL'S DEATH

> *I was painting the*
> *Whooping Crane, the*
> *fingers-flying-pinnae*
> *when the news came*

Air Minister
Sir Bird-White

man-high
yard-long stride

over
and out

  . . .

The funeral

Out of the great courtyard
past the Tower that can be seen
      on a winter day

the Tramp of Time
via Telstar
so that we may go
      with him

.

The Badlands

              Adlai Steven-
              son's death

We'd have danced
to sandstone spooks
in a beige land

but for stratified
      vacancy

.

A student
my head always down
of the grass as I mow

I missed the cranes.
"These crayons fly
in a circle ahead"
said a tall fellow.

．

Bird singing
ringing yellow
   green

My friend made green
       ring
—his painting—

   grass
the sweet bird
flew in

．

Easter Greeting

I suppose there is nothing
so good as human
immediacy

I do not speak loosely
of handshake
      which is

           of the mind
or lilies—stand closer—
smell

.

CITY TALK

I
The flower beds
        on the superhighways—
Well they have all
        the facilities
the information
        from the colleges
they force it
        and all that garbage

II
I'm good for people?—
penetrating?—if you mean

I'm rotting here—
I'm an alewife

the fish the seagull
has no taste for

I die along the shore
and send a bad smell in

.

As praiseworthy

The power of breathing (Epictetus)
while we sleep. Add:
to move the parts of the body
without sound

and to float
on a smooth green stream
in a silent boat

    ▪

They've lost their leaves
the maples along the river
but the weeping willow still
        hangs green

and the old cracked boat-hulk
    mud-sunk
grows weeds

year after year

    ▪

My mother saw the green tree toad
on the window sill
her first one
since she was young.
We saw it breathe

and swell up round.
My youth is no sure sign
I'll find this kind of thing
tho it does sing.
Let's take it in

I said so grandmother can see
but she could not
it changed to brown
and town
changed us, too.

.

TRADITION

I
The chemist creates
    the brazen
    approximation:
Life
    Thy will be done
    Sun

II
Time to garden
    before I
    die—

to meet
    my compost maker
    the caretaker
of the cemetery

  .

Autumn Night

Lisp and wisp
of dry leaves
"Put me wise
to what a tree toad is"
Boy

whose little son
now walks
"Starless night"
brings to mind the stars
those glimmering talks

  .

Sky
in my favor

to fly
to downtown crowds
home

and Bashō
on my mind

．

Nothing to speak of
on the bus ride
—a cleaned-up route—

till the courthouse—
on that grey structure the noise
of a thousand raspy wires—

sparrows!
By what law do the chirp-screech
"sparrow folk" go screwy
the late daylight hours
of fall?

．

Swedenborg

Well he saw man created according
to the motion of the elements. He located
the soul: in the blood. Retired
at last—to a house where he paid
window-tax (for increasing the light!).
Lived simply. Gardened. Saw visions.

Nothing for supper but tea.
Now he saw the soul from his "Pray,
what is matter" leave for the touchy
—heavens!—blue rose kind of thing.
Strange—he did grow a blue rose,
you know.

.

I lost you to water, summer
when the young girls swim,
to the hot shore
to little peet-tweet-
            pert girls.

Now it's cold your bright knock
—Orion's with his dog after him—
at my door, boy
on a winter
            wave ride.

.

I married

in the world's black night
for warmth
           if not repose.
           At the close—
someone.

I hid with him
from the long range guns.
           We lay leg
           in the cupboard, head
in closet.

A slit of light
at no bird dawn—
           Untaught
           I thought
he drank

too much.
I say
           I married
           and lived unburied.
I thought—

.

You see here
the influence
of inference

Moon on rippled
stream

"Except as
and unless"

.

Your erudition
the elegant flower
of which

my blue chicory
at scrub end
of campus ditch

illuminates

.

Alone

a still state hard
as sard

then again whisper-talk
preserved in chalk

At last no (TV) gun
no more coats than one

no hair lightener
Sweetheart of the whiter

walls

.

Why can't I be happy
in my sorrow

my drinking man
today

my quiet
tomorrow

.

And what you liked
or did—
no matter

once the moon
dipped down
and fish rose
from under

.

Cleaned all surfaces
and behind all solids
and righted leaning things

Considered then, becurtained
the metaphysics
of flight from housecleanings

.

Young in Fall I said: the birds
are at their highest thoughts
of leaving

Middle life said nothing—
grounded
to a livelihood

Old age—a high gabbling gathering
before goodbye
of all we know

.

North Central

In every part of every living thing
is stuff that once was rock

In blood the minerals
of the rock

.

Iron the common element of earth
in rocks and freighters

Sault Sainte Marie—big boats
coal-black and iron-ore-red
topped with what white castlework

The waters working together
      internationally
Gulls playing both sides

.

Radisson:
"a laborinth of pleasure"
this world of the Lake

Long hair, long gun

Fingernails pulled out
by Mohawks

.

*(The long
canoes)*

"Birch Bark
   and white Seder
      for the ribs"

.

Through all this granite land
the sign of the cross

Beauty: impurities in the rock

.

And at the blue ice superior spot
priest-robed Marquette grazed
azoic rock, hornblende granite
basalt the common dark
in all the Earth

And his bones of such is coral
raised up out of his grave
were sunned and birch bark-floated
to the straits

.

Joliet

Entered the Mississippi
Found there the paddlebill catfish
come down from The Age of Fishes

At Hudson Bay he conversed in latin
with an Englishman

To Labrador and back to vanish
His funeral gratis—he'd played
Quebec's Cathedral organ
so many winters

∎

Ruby of corundum
lapis lazuli
from changing limestone
glow-apricot red-brown
carnelian sard

Greek named
Exodus-antique
kicked up in America's
Northwest
you have been in my mind
between my toes
agate

∎

Wild Pigeon

Did not man
    maimed by no
        stone-fall

mash the cobalt
    and carnelian
        of that bird

.

Schoolcraft left the Soo—canoes
US pennants, masts, sails
chanting canoemen, barge
soldiers—for Minnesota

Their South Shore journey
        as if Life's—
The Chocolate River
        The Laughing Fish
and The River of the Dead

Passed peaks of volcanic thrust
Hornblende in massed granite
Wave-cut Cambrian rock
painted by soluble mineral oxides
wave-washed and the rains
did their work and a green
running as from copper

Sea-roaring caverns—
Chippewas threw deermeat
to the savage maws
"*Voyageurs* crossed themselves
tossed a twist of tobacco in"

.

Inland then
beside the great granite
gneiss and the schists

to the redolent pondy lakes'
lilies, flag and Indian reed
"through which we successfully
                    passed"

.

The smooth black stone
I picked up in true source park
       the leaf beside it
once was stone

Why should we hurry
       Home

.

I'm sorry to have missed
    Sand Lake
My dear one tells me
    we did not
We watched a gopher there

    .

My Life by Water

My life
   by water—
      Hear

spring's
   first frog
      or board

out on the cold
   ground
      giving

Muskrats
   gnawing
      doors

to wild green
   arts and letters
      Rabbits

raided
   my lettuce
      One boat

two—
    pointed toward
      my shore

thru birdstart
    wingdrip
      weed-drift

of the soft
    and serious—
      Water

．

TRACES OF LIVING THINGS

"strange feeling of sequence"—S.M.

Museum

Having met the protozoic
    Vorticellae
      here is man
Leafing towards you
    in this dark
      deciduous hall

．

Far reach
 of sand
  A man

bends to inspect
 a shell
  Himself

part coral
 and mud
  clam

 .

TV

See it explained—
compound interest
and the compound eye
 of the insect

the wave-line
on shell, sand, wall
and forehead of the one
 who speaks

 .

We are what the seas
have made us

longingly immense

the very veery
on the fence

.

What cause have you
to run my wreathed
rose words
off

you weed
you pea-blossom weed
in a folk
field

.

Stone
and that hard
contact—
the human

On the mossed
massed quartz
on which spruce
grew dense

I met him
We were thick
We said good-bye
on The Passing Years
River

.

The eye
of the leaf
into leaf
and all parts
    spine
into spine
neverending
    head
to see

.

For best work
you ought to put forth
     some effort
      to stand
in north woods
among birch

.

Smile
    to see the lake
      lay
    the still sky
And
    out for an easy
      make
    the dragonfly

.

Fall

We must pull
the curtains—
we haven't any
leaves

.

Years
   hearing and sight
      passing

walk
   to the Point—
      (between the waters)

—how live
   (with daughters?)
      at the end

.

Unsurpassed in beauty
this autumn day

The secretary of defence
knew precisely what

the undersecretary of state
was talking about

.

Human bean
and love-over-the-fence

just up
from swamp trouble

.

High class human
got no illumine

how a ten cent plant
winds aslant

around a post
Man, history's host

to trembles
in the tendrils

I'm a fool
can't take it cool

．

Ah your face
but it's whether
you can keep me warm

．

Sewing a dress

The need
these closed-in days

to move before you
smooth-draped
and color-elated

in a favorable wind

.

I walked
on New Year's Day

beside the trees
my father now gone planted

evenly following
the road

Each
      spoke

.

J. F. Kennedy after
the Bay of Pigs

To stand up

black-marked tulip
not snapped by the storm
"I've been duped by the experts"

—and walk
the South Lawn

∎

Mergansers
  fans
    on their heads

Thoughts on things
   fold unfold
     above the river beds

∎

"Shelter"

Holed damp
cellar-black beyond
the main atrocities
my sense of property's
adrift

Not burned we sweat—
we sink to water Death
(your hand!—
this was land)
disowns

■

WINTERGREEN RIDGE

Where the arrows
    of the road signs
        lead us:

Life is natural
    in the evolution
        of matter

Nothing supra-rock
    about it
        simply

butterflies
    are quicker
        than rock

Man
    lives hard
        on this stone perch

by sea
    imagines
        durable works

in creation here
    as in the center
        of the world

let's say
    of art
        We climb

the limestone cliffs
    my skirt dragging
        an inch below

the knee
    the style before
        the last

the last the least
    to see
        Norway

or "half of Sussex
    and almost all
        of Surrey"

Crete perhaps
    and further:
        "Every creature

better alive
    than dead,
        men and moose

and pine trees"
    We are gawks
        lusting

after wild orchids
    Wait! What's this?—
        sign:

Flowers
    loveliest
        where they grow

Love them enjoy them
    and leave them so
        Let's go!

Evolution's wild ones
    saved
        continuous life

through change
    from Time Began
        Northland's

unpainted barns
    fish and boats
        now this—

flowering ridge
    the second one back
        from the lighthouse

Who saved it?—
    Women
        of good wild stock

stood stolid
    before machines
        They stopped bulldozers

cold
　　We want it for all time
　　　　they said

and here it is—
　　horsetails
　　　　club mosses

stayed alive
　　after dinosaurs
　　　　died

Found:
　　laurel in muskeg
　　　　Linnaeus' twinflower

Andromeda
　　Cisandra of the bog
　　　　pearl-flowered

Lady's tresses
　　insect-eating
　　　　pitcher plant

Bedeviled little Drosera
　　of the sundews
　　　　deadly

in sphagnum moss
　　sticks out its sticky
　　　　(Darwin tested)

tentacled leaf
　　towards a fly
　　　　half an inch away

engulfs it
          Just the touch
                    of a gnat on a filament

stimulates leaf-plasma
          secretes a sticky
                    clear liquid

the better to eat you
          my dear
                    digests cartilage

and tooth enamel
          (DHL spoke of blood
                    in a green growing thing

in Italy was it?)
          They do it with glue
                    these plants

Lady's slipper's glue
          and electric threads
                    smack the sweets-seeker

on the head
          with pollinia
                    The bee

befuddled
          the door behind him
                    closed he must

go out at the rear
          the load on him
                    for the next

flower
 Women saved
  a pretty thing: Truth:

"a good to the heart"
 It all comes down
  to the family

"We have a lovely
 finite parentage
  mineral

vegetable
 animal"
  Nearby dark wood—

I suddenly heard
 the cry
  my mother's

where the light
 pissed past
  the pistillate cone

how she loved
 closed gentians
  she herself

so closed
 and in this to us peace
  the stabbing

pen
 friend did it
  close to the heart

pierced the woods
>red
>>(autumn?)

Sometimes it's a pleasure
>to grieve
>>or dump

the leaves most brilliant
>as do trees
>>when they've no need

of an overload
>of cellulose
>>for a cool while

Nobody, nothing
>ever gave me
>>greater thing

than time
>unless light
>>and silence

which if intense
>makes sound
>>Unaffected

by man
>thin to nothing lichens
>>grind with their acid

granite to sand
>These may survive
>>the grand blow-up

the bomb
  When visited
    by the poet

From Newcastle on Tyne
  I neglected to ask
    what wild plants

have you there
  how dark
    how inconsiderate

of me
  Well I see at this point
    no pelting of police

with flowers
  no uprooted gaywings
    bishop's cup

white bunchberry
  under aspens
    pipsissewa

(wintergreen)
  grass of parnassus
    See beyond—

ferns
  algae
    water lilies

Scent
  the simple
    the perfect

order
    of that flower
        water lily

I see no space-rocket
    launched here
        no mind-changing

acids eaten
    one sort manufactured
        as easily as gin

in a bathtub
    Do feel however
        in liver and head

as we drive
    towards cities
        the change

in church architecture—
    now it's either a hood
        for a roof

pulled down to the ground
    and below
        or a factory-long body

crawled out from a rise
    of black dinosaur-necked
        blower-beaked

smokestack-
    steeple
        Murder in the Cathedral's

proportions
> Do we go to church
>> No use

discussing heaven
> HJ's father long ago
>> pronounced human affairs

gone to hell
> Great God—
>> what men desire!—

the scientist: a full set
> of fishes
>> the desire to know

Another: to talk beat
> act cool
>> release   la'go

So far out of flowers
> human parts found
>> wrapped in newspaper

left at the church
> near College Avenue
>> More news: the war

which "cannot be stopped"
> ragweed pollen
>> sneezeweed

whose other name
> Ambrosia
>> goes for a community

Ahead—home town
    second shift steamfitter
        ran arms out

as tho to fly
    dived to concrete
        from loading dock

lost his head
    Pigeons
        (I miss the gulls)

mourn the loss
    of people
        no wild bird does

It rained
    mud squash
        willow leaves

in the eaves
    Old sunflower
        you bowed

to no one
    but Great Storm
        of Equinox

.

1968 — 1970

And the place
was water

Fish
    fowl
        flood
    Water lily mud
My life

in the leaves and on water
My mother and I
            born
in swale and swamp and sworn
to water

My father
thru marsh fog
    sculled down
        from high ground
saw her face

at the organ
bore the weight of lake water
    and the cold—
he seined for carp to be sold
that their daughter

might go high
on land
    to learn
Saw his wife turn
deaf

and away
She
    who knew boats
        and ropes
no longer played

She helped him string out nets
for tarring
    And she could shoot
        He was cool
to the man

who stole his minnows
by night and next day offered
    to sell them back
        He brought in a sack
of dandelion greens

if no flood
No oranges—none at hand
    No marsh marigolds
        where the water rose
He kept us afloat

I mourn her not hearing canvasbacks
their blast-off rise
    from the water
        Not hearing sora
rails's sweet

spoon-tapped waterglass-
descending scale-
    tear-drop-tittle
        Did she giggle
as a girl?

His skiff skimmed
the coiled celery now gone
    from these streams
        due to carp
He knew duckweed

fall-migrates
toward Mud Lake bottom
    Knew what lay
        under leaf decay
and on pickerel weeds

before summer hum
To be counted on:
    new leaves
        new dead
leaves

He could not
—like water bugs—
    stride surface tension
        He netted
loneliness

As to his bright new car
my mother—her house
    next his—averred:
        A hummingbird
can't haul

Anchored here
in the rise and sink
    of life—
        middle years' nights
he sat

beside his shoes
rocking his chair
    Roped not "looped
        in the loop
of her hair"

I grew in green
slide and slant
    of shore and shade
        Child-time—wade
thru weeds

Maples to swing from
Pewee-glissando
    sublime
        slime-

song

Grew riding the river
Books
    at home-pier
        Shelley could steer
as he read

I was the solitary plover
a pencil
    for a wing-bone
From the secret notes
I must tilt

upon the pressure
execute and adjust
    In us sea-air rhythm
"We live by the urgent wave
of the verse"

Seven year molt
for the solitary bird
    and so young
Seven years the one
dress

for town once a week
One for home
    faded blue-striped
as she piped
her cry

Dancing grounds
my people had none
    woodcocks had—
    backland-
air around

Solemnities
such as what flower
    to take
    to grandfather's grave
unless

water lilies—
he who'd bowed his head
    to grass as he mowed
    Iris now grows
on fill

for the two
and for him
    where they lie
    How much less am I
in the dark than they?

Effort lay in us
before religions
    at pond bottom
        All things move toward
the light

except those
that freely work down
    to oceans' black depths
        In us an impulse tests
the unknown

River rising—flood
Now melt and leave home
    Return—broom wet
        naturally wet
Under

soak-heavy rug
water bugs hatched—
    no snake in the house
        Where were they?—
she

who knew how to clean up
after floods
    he who bailed boats, houses
        Water endows us
with buckled floors

You with sea water running
in your veins sit down in water
    Expect the long-stemmed blue
        speedwell to renew
itself

O my floating life
Do not save love
    for things
        Throw *things*
to the flood

ruined
by the flood
    Leave the new unbought—
        all one in the end—
water

I possessed
the high word:
    The boy my friend
        played his violin
in the great hall

On this stream
my moonnight memory
    washed of hardships
        maneuvers barges
thru the mouth

of the river
They fished in beauty
    It was not always so
        In Fishes
red Mars

rising
rides the sloughs and sluices
    of my mind
        with the persons
on the edge

.

Alliance

Hunger
    with wonder

Mites wintering
    in rabbits' ears

Pronuba
    with yucca

Bashō's
    backwater

moon-pull
    He was full

at the port
    of Tsuruga

.

Bashō

beholds the moon
    in the water

He is full

at the port
    of Tsuruga

.

The man of law
    on the uses
        of grief

The poet
    on the law
        of the oak leaf

    .

Not all harsh sounds displease—
Yellowhead blackbirds cough
        through reeds and fronds
as through pronged bronze

    .

JEFFERSON AND ADAMS

    I

Jefferson: I was confident
the French Revolution would end well
Adams differed: What is freedom
to their thousands upon thousands
who cannot read or write—
impracticable as for the Elephants Lions
Tigers Panthers Wolves and Bears
in the Royal Menagerie of Versailles

Our minister at Paris: Lafayette
gave dinner at my house ten days before
the fall of the Bastille
The argument at table *disfigured*
by no tinsel—cool
as Xenophon Plato Cicero

2

Adams to the unexploding projectile
from the forest of Virginia: *Where was you—*
Jefferson said Dear friend, I was Stoic-trained
but longed for Tranquility—
Monticello, Horace, Epicurus
I value the passions
(the senses stimulate the mind)
though yours drew you away from me
Friend Acrid to his friend Jefferson:
—no doubt you was fast asleep
in philosophical Tranquility
when ten thousand People paraded
the streets of Philadelphia

.

Katharine Anne

A poor poet
divining Gail

The baby looked toward me
and I was born—
to sound, light
lift, life
beyond my life

She wiggles her toe
I grow
I go to school to her
and she to me
and to Bonnie

.

War

The trees full of snipers, the new kind
       of bird
Men on the hunt for Russian furs
     for Ukrainian sausage
          and Chinese girls

They floated past a crescent moon
       to Sicily—
strings of diminished pearls
    In each pearl-parachute
       a tommy gun

The Russian—only a man from Georgia
      USSR
could dance like that
    My baby son?—in some
        secret zone

.

Harpsichord & Salt Fish

THOMAS JEFFERSON

I

My wife is ill!
And I sit
            waiting
for a quorum

II

Fast ride
his horse collapsed
Now *he* saddled walked

Borrowed a farmer's
unbroken colt
To Richmond

Richmond How stop—
Arnold's redcoats
there

III

Elk Hill destroyed—
Cornwallis
carried off 30 slaves

Jefferson:
Were it to give them freedom
he'd have done right

IV

Latin and Greek
my tools
to understand
humanity

I rode horse
away from a monarch
to an enchanting
philosophy

V

The South of France

Roman temple
"simple and sublime"

Maria Cosway
      harpist
on his mind

white column
and arch

VI

To daughter Patsy: Read—
read Livy

No person full of work
was ever hysterical

Know music, history
dancing

(I calculate 14 to 1
in marriage
she will draw
a blockhead)

Science also
Patsy

VII
Agreed with Adams:
send spermaceti oil to Portugal
for their church candles

(light enough to banish mysteries?:
three are one and one is three
and yet the one not three
and the three not one)

and send salt fish
U.S. salt fish preferred
above all other

VIII
Jefferson of Patrick Henry
backwoods fiddler statesman:

"He spoke as Homer wrote"
Henry eyed our minister at Paris—

the Bill of Rights hassle—
"he remembers . . .

in splendor and dissipation
he thinks yet of bills of rights"

IX

True, French frills and lace
for Jefferson, sword and belt

but follow the Court to Fontainebleau
he could not—

house rent would have left him
nothing to eat

. . .

He bowed to everyone he met
and talked with arms folded

He could be trimmed
by a two-month migraine

and yet
       stand up

X

Dear Polly:
I said No—no frost

in Virginia—the strawberries
were safe

I'd have heard—I'm in that kind
of correspondence

with a young daughter—
if they were not

Now I must retract
I shrink from it

XI
Political honors
      "splendid torments"
"If one could establish
      an absolute power
of silence over oneself"

When I set out for Monticello
    (my grandchildren
        will they know me?)
How are my young
        chestnut trees—

XII
Hamilton and the bankers
would make my country Carthage

I am abandoning the rich—
their dinner parties—

I shall eat my simlins
with the class of science

or not at all
Next year the last of labors

among conflicting parties
Then my family

we shall sow our cabbages
together

XIII

Delicious flower
of the acacia

or rather

Mimosa Nilotica
from Mr. Lomax

XIV

Polly Jefferson, 8, had crossed
to father and sister in Paris

by way of London—Abigail
embraced her—Adams said

"in all my life I never saw
more charming child"

Death of Polly, 25,
Monticello

XV

My harpsichord
my alabaster vase
and bridle bit
bound for Alexandria
Virginia

The good sea weather
of retirement
The drift and suck
and die-down of life
but there is land

XVI

These were my passions:
Monticello and the villa-temples
I passed on to carpenters
bricklayers what I knew

and to an Italian sculptor
how to turn a volute
on a pillar

You may approach the campus rotunda
from lower to upper terrace
Cicero had levels

XVII

John Adams' eyes
        dimming
Tom Jefferson's rheumatism
           cantering

XVIII

Ah soon must Monticello be lost
      to debts
  and Jefferson himself
          to death

XIX

Mind leaving, let body leave
Let dome live, spherical dome
and colonnade

Martha (Patsy) stay
"The Committee of Safety
must be warned"

Stay youth—Anne and Ellen
all my books, the bantams
and the seeds of the senega root

.

The Ballad of Basil

They sank the sea
    All land
        enemy

He saw his boats stand
    and he
        off the floor

of that cold jail
    (would not fight
        their war)

sailed anyway
    Villon went along
        Chomei

Dante
    and the Persian
        Firdusi—

rigging
    for his own
        singing

.

Wilderness

You are the man
You are my other country
and I find it hard going

You are the prickly pear
You are the sudden violent storm

the torrent to raise the river
to float the wounded doe

.

Consider

the alliance—
ships and plants

The take-for-granted bloom
of our roadsides
       Queen Anne's Lace
       Black Eyed Susans
          rode the sea

"Specimens graciously passed
between warring fleets"

And when an old boat rots ashore
itself once living plant
               it sprouts.

.

Otherwise

Gerard Manley Hopkins

Dear friend: If the poem
is printed few
will read and fewer scan it
much less understand it
To be sure

the scanning's plain
but who will veer
from the usual stamp and pound
Other work?—I've not yet found
the oak leaves' law . . .

.

Nursery Rhyme

As I nurse my pump

The greatest plumber
    in all the town
from Montgomery Ward
rode a Cadillac carriage
    by marriage
and visited my pump

A sensitive pump
    said he
that has at times a proper
    balance
    of water, air
and poetry

■

Three Americans

John Adams is our man
but delicate beauty
touched the other one—

an architect
and a woman artist
walked beside Jefferson

Abigail
(Long face horse-name)
cheesemaker

chicken raiser
wrote letters that John
and TJ could savour

.

POEMS AT THE PORTHOLE

Blue and white
china cups
glacier-adjacent

lost
in the foothills

.

The soil is poor
water scarce
    the people clothed
        in wind and cold—
Bolivia

.

Michelangelo

If matches had been my work
instead of marble poems
    —sulphur—
  I'd suffer
less

  .

Wallace Stevens

What you say about the early
yellow springtime is also something
worth sticking to

  .

SUBLIMINAL

    Sleep's dream
the nerve-flash in the blood

    The sense
of what's seen

     "I took cold
on my nerves"—my mother

    tall, tormented
darkinfested

  .

Waded, watched, warbled
learned to write on slate
with chalk from an ancient sea

If I could float my tentacles
through the deep . . .
pulsate an invisible glow

.

Illustrated night clock's
          constellations
and the booming
                    star-ticks

Soon I rise
          to give the universe
                    my flicks

.

Honest
          Solid
                    The lip
     of tipped
lily

A quiet flock
    of words
        not the hound-
  howl
holed

  .

Night
    the sag
       of day

My mother
   all the years
      no day

  .

LZ

He walked—loped—the bridge
Saluted Peck Slip
—his friend shipped fish—
    My dish
Test

and the short verse
Now he stops for lilacs
—in the *sun's* fame
    he'd say—
Stops?

Even for death
         Z
after all that "A"
would dip his wool beret
to carp-fed roots

.

                    Peace

Dark road home
         from town—
young neighbor as he walked
      wound up tiny Swiss works—
         a firefly music

Mickey Mouse leaned on a bubble
            removed a tear
from the elephant's eye
   to a brush so he
         could scrubble

Our small boat's motor raced
         Great Blue
the heron sailing as in China
   not caring
         to win

.

Thomas Jefferson Inside

Winter when no flower

The Congress away from home

Love is the great good use
one person makes of another
(Daughter Polly of the strawberry
letter)

Frogs sing—then of a sudden
all their lights go out

The country moves toward violets
and aconites

■

Foreclosure

Tell em to take my bare walls down
my cement abutments
their parties thereof
and clause of claws

Leave me the land
Scratch out: the land

May prose and property both die out
and leave me peace

■

HIS CARPETS FLOWERED

William Morris

I

—how we're carpet-making
by the river
a long dream to unroll
and somehow time to pole
a boat

I designed a carpet today—
dogtooth violets
and spoke to a full hall
now that the gall
of our society's

corruption stains throughout
Dear Janey I am tossed
by many things
If the change would bring
better art

but if it would not?
O to be home to sail the flood
I'm possessed
and do possess
Employer

of labor, true—
to get done
the work of the hand . . .
I'd be a rich man
had I yielded

on a few points of principle
Item sabots
blouse—
I work in the dye-house
myself

Good sport dyeing
tapestry wool
I like the indigo vats
I'm drawing patterns so fast
Last night

in sleep I drew a sausage—
somehow I had to eat it first
Colorful shores—mouse ear . . .
horse-mint . . . The Strawberry Thief
our new chintz

II
Yeats saw the betterment of the workers
by religion—slow in any case
as the drying of the moon
He was not understood—
I rang the bell

for him to sit down
Yeats left the lecture circuit
yet he could say: no one
so well loved
as Morris

III
Entered new waters
Studied Icelandic
At home last minute signs
to post:
Vetch

grows here—Please do not mow
We saw it—Iceland—the end
of the world rising out of the sea—
cliffs, caves like 13th century
illuminations

of hell-mouths
Rain squalls through moonlight
Cold wet
is so damned wet
Iceland's

black sand
Stone buntings'
fly-up-dispersion
Sea-pink and campion a Persian
carpet

.

DARWIN

    I

His holy

      slowly

            mulled over

  matter

not all "delirium

        of delight"

            as were the forests

    of Brazil

"Species are not

        (it is like confessing

            a murder)

    immutable"

He was often becalmed

        in this Port Desire by illness

            or rested from species

    at billiard table

As to Man

      "I believe Man . . .

          in the same predicament

    with other animals"

    II

Cordilleras to climb—Andean

      peaks "tossed about

        like the crust

    of a broken pie"

Icy wind
    Higher, harder
        Chileans advised eat onions
  for shortness of breath

Heavy on him:
    Andes miners carried up
        great loads—not allowed
  to stop for breath

Fossil bones near Santa Fé
    Spider-bite-scauld
      Fever
  Tended by an old woman

"Dear Susan . . .
    I am ravenous
      for the sound
  of the pianoforte"

III

FitzRoy blinked—
    sea-shells on mountain tops!
      The laws of change
  rode the seas

without the good captain
    who could not concede
      land could rise from the sea
  until—before his eyes

earthquake—
    Talcahuana Bay drained out—
      all-water wall
  up from the ocean

—six seconds—
    demolished the town
      The will of God?
  Let us pray

And now the Galápagos Islands—
    hideous black lava
      The shore so hot
  it burned their feet

through their boots
    Reptile life
      Melville here later
  said the chief sound was a hiss

A thousand turtle monsters
    drive together to the water
      Blood-bright crabs hunt ticks
  on lizards' backs

Flightless cormorants
    Cold-sea creatures—
      penguins, seals
  here in tropical waters

Hell for FitzRoy
    but for Darwin Paradise Puzzle
      with the jig-saw gists
  beginning to fit

IV

Years . . . balancing
      probabilities
           I am ill, he said
   and books are slow work

Studied pigeons
      barnacles, earthworms
          Extracted seeds
   from bird dung

Brought home Drosera—
      saw insects trapped
          by its tentacles—the fact
   that a plant should secrete

an acid acutely akin
      to the digestive fluid
          of an animal! Years
   till he published

He wrote Lyell: Don't forget
      to send me the carcass
          of your half-bred African cat
   should it die

V

I remember, he said
      those tropical nights at sea—
          we sat and talked
   on the booms

Tierra del Fuego's
     shining glaciers translucent
          blue clear down
   (almost) to the indigo sea

(By the way Carlyle
     thought it most ridiculous
         that anyone should care
   whether a glacier

moved a little quicker
     or a little slower
         or moved at all)
   Darwin

sailed out
     of Good Success Bay
         to carcass-
conclusions—

the universe
     not built by brute force
         but designed by laws
   The details left

to the working of chance
     "Let each man hope
         and believe
   what he can"

Prose and Radio Plays

1937

There were three crows sat on a tree,

They were as black as crows could be;

One said to the other see

The farmer sowing his seed—

Isn't he wonderful kind to the poor

  I'm sure.

(from hearsay)

He loved the quiet and peace of his old country home. He was a quiet man. But such a career he must have, my Uncle, as to keep him making a name for himself. Changes took place in the country while he, John Julius Benjamin Beefelbein, went on making the same name. Not aggressive—a liberal who gave and accepted all. In the fight to win the good things of life, comfort and retirement from grinding work, and in order to keep his home in the country, Uncle Babe—Matty, fifteen years older than her brother, called him Babe without thinking even when he was big—entered public service at the height of which the initials J.J. did not mean an overpowering gain.

The family, the two old folks, sturdy proprietors of the resort hotel home, and their daughter and John, entered the fierce struggle to get ahead. But then when I speak of the family in those days I speak of Friedericka, the parent with the flying petticoats sometimes rustling as of sateen, asperity in her whole manner, and she wished she had taffeta. I knew her when I was playing around the place as the child of her niece—we stayed there, my mother and I, while my father was away in a sanitarium. Whereas Great-Uncle Gotlieb, tall, happy, head thrown back . . . I thought I was to call him *Great* Uncle because he had such great smiling wrinkles around his eyes . . . braided my hair and told me nursery jingles. . . . There *were* three *crows* sat *on a tree.* . . . And if he saw me at a distance outdoors he'd hold out his arms wide. He was too easy-going for Aunt Riecky. At this time Uncle John as a boy—I suppose I called him Uncle because he was next in line to Great Uncle, open, good natured—was away at school in Milwaukee, home only in summer. The folks were trying their best to give him the advantages. They knew he applied himself at books and was always busy learning to be somebody in an office. Matty was learning to be a dressmaker in town and already sewing for others, helping with John's expenses. Matty was a tall, lean strong figure of a woman, sharp eyes and nose but not bad looking. She often suffered from neuralgia and colds, all from having walked a mile crosslots in woods and marsh to country school—Gotlieb took the children on the road only when the road was passable—and she sat through her lessons with cold feet, perhaps wet. She was Asperity's daughter, though, and went through everything. She could be seen at times, a large handkerchief folded over her head and ears and tied under her chin, working on washboard and sewing machine. Once, I remember, after she'd scrubbed the floor, she stood clapping her hands hard to the words: now my strength is all gone! She inherited the virtue of work from her mother, as in a way did John. Inherited?—but in those days things were stolidly saved and passed along in the family and couldn't be changed. Riecky was the family, but I always thought my Great Uncle Gotlieb was somebody too: he was a naturally happy man. She scolded him for this or that—he stayed out fishing too long and didn't catch anything or slept after the noonday meal and beer or he dressed and cleaned the wild fowl he'd shot so late that she had to milk the cow and feed the horse and her blood was aroused, and this with her habit of work put her through the chores in a hurry. She always did what was needed, cleaning, cooking and directing. Was clean and saving and made it go. She said Gotlieb had a poor way of making it, no action, would never have money, but with her it was different. She could buy their food in winter and when spring came could have $3 left.

Many times my Uncle Gotlieb of happy actions could be seen walking outdoors, food and drink in his belly, his gun in his hand. Like a landlord, Riecky said, walking around on the lawn. He was considered a good hotel man, people liked him, he enjoyed being a proprietor. A certain class of people came out from Milwaukee—cheese makers and store owners who had money. But usually he was waiting for just anyone to blow in. He may have wanted to be a policeman but outside of town there was no chance, or game-warden, but in those days there were no laws restricting the catch of plentiful game. He must have thought of some princely office or just some good job whereby he might sleep two hours after dinner and the woodbox wouldn't even have to be filled. He sold fish and canvasback ducks to a hotel keeper in the city and John helped with this when he could.

They were not church people—this was a resort nine miles from the church the farmers were afraid of. They had a feeling about wrong-doing though, knew that you always got paid for wrong-doing, and Riecky especially knew all the orthodox sins. Was a time in Uncle Babe's life when he believed he should become a church man but he resented being preached to or thought he should be the one talking, and it seemed two hours every week wasted when he should be attending to his business and helping people. Matty, tolerant—when another German family never let a Good Friday go by without noodles, prunes and fish—says, That's alright but I wasn't brought up to be a Christian like that.

Riecky believed in working for people who paid. If they did or especially if they didn't, she cleaned until she was aroused to a frazzle, it was her morality. She left a smell of dirty, oily rags where she'd cleaned, very rank till you got used to it. You had to go through hard things in order to get somewhere in the world, she said. She did her best to rid the place of rats, would often say they should be caught alive, taken up by their tails and dipped in tar. Matty was strong like that, rising up in her frail health.

Uncle Gotlieb worshipped as he saw fit. He said, as he stood looking up, Trees are the best things a man can have that little while he lives. He would make chests of drawers in wintertime and neat little models for boats or small launches to be built later outside if he could get the materials. You loved to pass your hand over the models, so smooth, dark-rubbed walnut; one now hangs above Matty's sewing machine.

I always thought the people were really good. What held them back was something they were laboring under—

The place . . . trees thick, great branches. Robins' nests allowed on the window sills on the store-room side of the house. Evenings the red-wings, the wind died down, the little river still. The birds gathered close in a song of settling down . . . over two hundred acres . . . owned by the family—

The moss green Morris Chair. The shadows plush green in the water. Pictures of afternoons of those days: women in their chairs, the mild, wild lowland, excessively beautiful, willows, ease-ness, drooping health, the ladies with long, flowing skirts, their handkerchiefs in their laps. The Beefelbeins on such occasions dressed not unlike the guests.

—The breaths of the women wafting over the children, perfume catarrhal or from rich eating. Sweets were honored, oranges not easy to get.

—Often nothing to do. A great deal depended on the people who came to the hotel. The Beefelbeins catered mostly to two families of cheese makers, their brothers, and friends who were store men. The two cheese makers were big people—each weighed close to 300 lbs. Withal, they were democratic, and often, Riecky thought, quite common. Their wives wore silk dresses, were refined; the entire crowd demanded good food and waiting on and no matter how sick they got from boat or beer, they always, said she, ate good. After all, they shouldn't think they were Rockefellers—there were people in the world had more money than they. She would imitate them, set two teaspoons at table even when only one was needed—for coffee, the dessert being cake. Everyone knew her, though, for a woman of few dishes. She considered herself socially superior to moneyed people— the virtue of hard work was on her side—*they* could get into trouble and lazy ways, she thought, spending for rich dishes and drink. The fact that her work served trouble and that it earned her not one-half dozen fresh pineapples or one new jacket in five years . . . she had little time to think about it.

—Sometimes on spring election days, her money spent for taxes, she would serve Uncle Gotlieb with the blitz kuchen and soup and water-cress and handcheese he loved—always the handcheese in a jar back of the stove—and she would ride with him to town over the muddy road after the long winter—he had to attend to voting, didn't he?—an important day for men and they were treated to cigars by those who were running. John had a poem in his schoolbook about voters by a man named Whittier. . . . She would make it known to Gotlieb that she wanted him to buy her a blouse and a hat, thus making herself dear to him.

—He admired her caprice; it was part of her energy and he knew which side of his life the kitchen was on. I suppose she never failed to say, several times a week, after he'd gone off with his gun and come back ready to enter: Now Pa, I've just cleaned.

—The large range she cooked over was always hot, and always she made her own butter and sausages and bread and cheese. Some of the vegetables from the garden she canned. In summer a grocery wagon would come through and she liked to patronize the man who ran it as much as she could. We must patronize him, she told Gotlieb. Sometimes she traded wild fowl or fish for coffee or sugar. The stove would go out only between dinner and supper on hot summer days. Matty now has a beautiful electric range, and beside it on her little wood-and-coal heater is an oven to save electricity. Both the old folks often said, I don't know what it's coming to.

So the big cheese makers would write to Great Uncle Gotlieb to meet them in town at the depot with the two-seater: Will be 4 of us, will make it worth while for you. And when he'd get there he'd find four beside the two big men and two kegs of beer and a barrel of cheese and other food and suitcases of luggage. Uncle would have to go twice back and forth with them and then again to leave his rented buggy and one horse and bring his own horse and small buggy home, a long day, and sitting alone on this last trip, darkness closing in, mosquitoes, he thought how long he would have to wait—two months, six months, for his money—he could have got it after a month or so, Riecky at him why he didn't, but he had his pride and wouldn't ask a dollar from anyone and he knew they would pay in full and more too whenever they got around to it.

And it wasn't long before they had him making merry with them, blowing the foam off their beer mugs *splotch* on the walls. And they pressed cheese upon him. Perhaps they liked people to whom they could be in debt and surely they liked to have people in debt to them. They took enjoyment in those who owed them something. We love you to stay this way, poor, working for us, they said, we want to be your Patrons. Postponement of the pay might even extend over into the next year but then a silk dress would accompany the big check and a silver dollar for Matty and John each. It was just their leisurely, aristocratic social-democracy, perhaps even a kind of aesthetic. They were cultured and didn't have to think of money. And my Great Uncle was cultured too and couldn't demand. Really everyone accepted it as policy. The cheese people still held the mortgage on Uncle's place and although it put Gotlieb in embarrassment to have to be a little late with the interest, that's the way it was in the country. It was this confusion that kept Uncle Gotlieb doing things for them without knowing just where he was. Undoubtedly much the same thing contributed to John's later political and business decorum of letters and dinners and third persons and, as Matty said, handkerchief wavings. So as the days went on the more the Beefelbeins had to do for their boarders so as to be sure the bill would mount up to where they might sooner be paid. Meanwhile their beer would run out and Uncle could make a little profit selling them his own.

The one man paid Uncle Gotlieb or Johnny immediately upon rowing him out in the boat, and more, so as to keep them working to make it up. The other cheese man would never pay. He wanted to be rowed out onto the lake, the little river emptying into it a quarter mile down, and then rowed around in the bay, fish a little here, and a little there, the oars under the hands cracking, blistering in the hot sun. He would forget to pay, he didn't mean anything by it, he just didn't settle. Both men left the feeling with the Beefelbeins that money was the power but that it made people fat and lazy, money corrupted those who had it. Such people had it too good, Riecky said, high livers. The men sometimes sick from wine or beer had to have Gotlieb support them up the stairs to their bedrooms. I can remember seeing him half carry one of them up and Riecky's summer wurst hanging from the ceiling of the upstairs hallway.

The feeling that money was bad. Same with machines, city industries that used newer and newer machinery and threw men out of work. Money, principally, was bad.

It was a hard pull. If things had gone better, John might have continued his education in Milwaukee, this way it was broken off when he was nineteen. He came home, wondered what to do with himself. Roamed with the dog, quietly amused himself, greeted some of the old hotel guests, kept shy of new ones. He was usually a happy person like Uncle Gotlieb, looked like him, same pleasant good face, his nose more of a button, stature about the same—in fifteen years more he was to take on a plumpness making him appear bigger than his father. Plump—Matty shook her head and said he must be taking after some ancestor they'd all missed.

Often John as a boy was not to be disturbed. It seemed to him the less he did the more his mind worked. Gotlieb understood this in a way, considered the boy more refined than he was himself, educated, his world therefore a little different from that of the old stogies in the wilderness. Let him drift a bit. Johnny would take a boat, paddle out and lie in it. He would look at a tree in a certain light; his sensations the moment he looked formed the tree, he thought, and no one else would find that tree to be just what he found it, and he wondered if the song sparrow would have perched there just then if he hadn't been looking. But Riecky was watching. As John landed back on shore she said, Time for those trees to be cut, been hanging there crowded too long.

He became interested in the fyke net fishing, got together a small outfit with Gotlieb's help. When John had saved $250 he put it into a cheese factory. The man who came around had been a good talker. Wisconsin was a great dairy state, cheese factories were doing a big business. John's education cut off in his freshman year of Normal School he realized he must depend now on working with his hands and then invest his savings, depend on what money could bring as to further education and leisure. He must be able to stand up against any man. A decent supply of money was good. A decent business, a fair profit—as he looked about him he couldn't quite help coming to that conclusion so early . . . he came to it helplessly. But it may be said to his credit that he was never against most of the things money can buy. He was a man who wanted to spend money and have nice things. When a chair was without a pillow or an upholstered seat he would reach over to the sofa and get hold of one of Matty's dark red plush cushions. She would indicate he should take the little old pad that the cat used but he would wink and say, This plush is just as good. Or at table he'd butter a piece of kuchen in place of his mother's or Matty's bread maybe getting dry and hard, and with Uncle Gotlieb's smiling wrinkles acclaim buttered kuchen just as good. Riecky and Matty always held the hard view.

The way the cheese industry developed—a factory sprang up here or there in this country by itself for itself but somehow supposedly for the common good, entering the free competition against others that sprang into individual profits if lucky. Some got themselves joined to a big chain controlled possibly in New York. "Filled cheese" was produced by mixing foreign fats, animal or vegetable, with skim milk. The original butterfat extracted, a cheaper substitute used. In some cheese was found the best cottonseed oil. Much of the full cream cheese was excellent for people who could afford it. John's factory springing up north of Milwaukee was going to produce good cheese. He hit upon putting his money into this concern and letting it work for him. It failed. A big monopoly forced out, sprung, the little one. Uncle Babe went to Milwaukee to the old cheesemaker friends to try through them to bring pressure to bear—he was always to say: find the right people and through them bring pressure to bear—but they were in the business themselves. He didn't think the men in charge of the factory were really dishonest—they had to suffer with the rest—they were making a cheese that was not "filled." New York Cream Cheese it was called. Showed they believed in honest food products.

The Beefelbeins were great cheese people, always had it in some form or other. In the years Riecky was making it at home the state was producing many thousands of pounds and always doubling the amount annually. Hers was good, they knew what went into it, they were used to it. They might have bought some that was better. And again, her sausage meat—to this day Uncle John can find no sausage meat like the old people made it in their homes—he can't think what it's made of now. And shoes—paper!

Matty, dully, when she heard of John's failure: Cheese kriste. And then went about her housework with force. The way she looked at it, it was just whether you were lucky or not. Baking, weather, business, all depended on luck.

John, well, he felt—poorer. His mind went back to the Indians, he could only believe their life was best, they had no financial troubles and they had been happy with what they had. At times during his life his mind went back like this. Isolated country living: each family attending at home to its own needs, what a man could do alone was best. Still, he couldn't worry too much now, he was young and everything was possible. You had to go through hard experiences, he guessed, before the good things of life would come. Life is a struggle. The fittest survive. . . . etc. . . . He went at it harder, fishing, always the desire to make something of himself, become a director himself. Gradually he went in deeper and hired a crew of five men. Hard work but making money.

One morning he went out to raise his nets. The game warden who had to supervise for the state, see that only carp and buffalo were taken to be sold, told Uncle John he couldn't raise nets, orders from Madison. At the same time John happened to know the permission to raise nets was given as usual to a man engaged in fishing farther down the river. Immediately he got himself a letter of introduction to the governor of the state, Uncle John, went and explained his cause: he'd paid license and was law abiding, now for no apparent reason the state would do this to him. He hinted that the other man down the river had paid more to gain favors? In ten minutes the governor cleaned out the conservation department, fired everyone who had anything to do with it and thanked Uncle John for coming—just like that.

To this governor Uncle John always felt he owed a great deal. But then if anyone at all ever did anything for him he thought about it and could never do enough for that person. He would do things all his life for the person who was kind to him. Perhaps out of this experience he saw a chance for coupling gratitude, service, and self-help. If only he could enter a political career. He fished now by seine, shipped rough fish in refrigerator cars to New York. He stood in rubber waders in ice cold water to his waist, subjected himself to rheumatism, smelled of fish slime and invested his money in carefully considered places. But politics, politics, it hemmed him in. A career . . . it would not let him rest.

Fight was in the air. The governor was a fighter, all good political men were. You had to fight the big business monopolies and the poorer you were the more fight it took. You really had to find at least one financially independent friend who could furnish money for your campaigns. It was a great game. You had to know psychology . . . he wished he knew more, had had a full college education. His idol, in that young man's last year as a student, had been chosen, after preliminary tests, to represent his school in the state collegiate oratorical contest, and had then won the prize at Beloit with an oration on the character of Shakespeare's "Iago" and then won in the interstate meeting and all this was in the newspapers, so it was said that later when he went among the farmers he found they could place him right away. John wished he knew Shakespeare like that, culture. Throw in his lot with culture and property. He did not even know law. But if his heart was in the right place. . . . You had to know how to handle people who favored the "interests." For example, you advocated railroad taxation bills, showing the "interests" and the general public at the same time hotly that railroads could increase their rates and take back the amount lost through such taxation, so that the railroads would let the tax bills go through and the people would become aroused under higher rates and there was your regulation of rates to furnish the next campaign. Because you had to keep yourself in office. A constant fight.

Yet Uncle Babe was the quietest of men, easy-going, Matty said, and I always knew him to be gentle. I was about eleven when the cat was lying helpless under the front porch, a leg broken—my mother and I lived here almost entirely now, my father had died, the doctor said at the last he should have been in a hospital, but it was an unfortunate case, we hadn't enough money—and Uncle Babe, interested in the kitty almost as much as I was, jumped into his Cross-Country Rambler, went to town and brought back a doctor friend and the cat grew well, our Josephine who played for us in the railing of the stairway. John could never see any animal, anybody, suffer. Sometimes he would forget to do the actual work of caring for them—thinking about other things. He always preferred Matty to cut the heads off the poultry. But he took advancement in the world as hard and serious, as probably most young men who have any talent and intelligence, but mainly because of the strain of their schooling however short, the constant strain of competition, always one first above all, a few up and the neighbors down, the ratings, the contests, the shame if you stopped to think and be considerate and received no high mark, the prizes that drove to the quick; the desire to get ahead was paramount, nervous, forceful. He sincerely desired to become a leading force in political reform if he could get to champion the right group.

He would start close to home, would take up the cudgels for the farmers. The farmers' taxes were too high. They had no market close by for their livestock—did, yes, but it held the prices up—most cattle and hogs were shipped way to Chicago and then the meat was shipped way back again. There seemed to be no great farmer issue before the public, though. This governor wasn't doing so much for the farmers, in a way, yes, but he had his railroads to fight. Perhaps there was no field. But they always said they couldn't sell their produce for more than it cost them to produce it and this was wrong. What was the trouble? They weren't organized. There was a field. They should be made to see what was good for them, join together under a competent head, form a small monopoly, a farmers co-operative, demand good prices. People did not always know what they could do to better themselves till someone came along and pointed it out.

The oleomargarine fight had benefited the farmers and the fight was still on. Grover Cleveland had said, "I venture to say that hardly a pound (oleomargarine) ever entered a poor man's home under its real name and in its real character." The packers and the Presidents, Uncle John, extended their sentiments to the poor. One must be strong. As he saw it: butterfat and beef fat both, but yes, butterfat.

The people here had a former governor to thank for what the dairy industry had become. He was a poor man but he rose to be Wisconsin's principal spokesman for the dairy interests in state and congressional hearings. He started in this very section on a farm in beet raising or was it hops and that year the market was glutted and of course he'd borrowed heavily and now his character had to stand or fall by whether he could or could not pay back, and he had failed through no fault of his own except that he was a party to a blind system. If he couldn't pay back he had no honorable character. The story is told that The Honorable Mr. Y. went into a grocery store one day, lifted a sack of flour on his back, walked out. They'd have to knock him down if they wanted it, he said, he had no money and his family had to eat. In time, however, he entered the disastrous, free competition again by way of a different business and as luck would have it bettered himself—at the cost of his neighbors though he wouldn't have meant it that way—and paid back every dollar he owed. In fact no man was a man unless he struggled under a great load against odds. Life was a struggle. This man was energetic and experimentative but he could not get ahead as he liked. What could he do not always having land and cattle and other materials to carry out his ideas? Everything connected with farming was slow. An accurate test for determining the amount of butterfat in milk had to be invented so that the creamery man would not cheat himself nor the farmer. The test finally accepted came out of the Wisconsin College of Agriculture, was received into the creamery industry with very little opposition and into the entire United States and even foreign countries. The Babcock Test can beat the Bible in making a man honest, said a cream man.

Legislators fought each other in campaigns for leadership and in offices too. One said to himself: I must fight this thing through, I know it will be worthwhile and so-and-so will be true to me. Among these individuals were militant liberals on all sides. Great speechmaking and handclapping . . . perhaps the people would forget their troubles. Sometimes the men were lawyers, got very much interested in making intricate cases. Was it constitutional, they asked, when people organized into strikes. Uncle John, but that was later, had to pay the processing tax on a pig before such tax was declared illegal. It was important to get the labor vote, but many times a well meaning senator or governor would be told, Oh, nevermind about the labor vote, Brown will take care of that, or Payne.

The current of thought started above and came down! Spirit, mind, existed before trees and rock?

The military spirit handed down to J.J. Beefelbein—was it for him? Could he stand it? He told himself yes. He would show em he could hand back just what they gave him.

He, Beefelbein, would organize the farmers.

So he started out, sometimes with horse and buggy, sometimes with the Rambler, depending on the road, and usually carried a sack or two of Red Lime Fertilizer, the agency he'd taken as an opportunity to combine salesmanship with—salesmanship! He felt if he could get them to try what he had to offer they'd never be without it.

He followed the farmers from the barn to the house and around. Not easy to gain their attention, busy plowing, milking, making hay, feeding stock, planting, cultivating—how many hours a day did a farmer work? Only time really was the noon hour and then they wanted to rest; even J.J. liked his noontime undisturbed like his father before him. They would nod to him after their heavy meals of hot soup and heaped up plates of potatoes, almost as though the radio had come already, their heads would fall from side to side on their chests as they rested in their chairs. Same way the evenings and to bed early to get up early. He managed to tell them he was organizing a farmers' co-operative. The strength of other industries lay in the power of combining and what they could do the farmers could do. When he said, We will pay the capitalists in their own coin, this did fire them. Only trouble was: they couldn't pay to enter it. And they had joined such an organization sometime before and nothing happened. He pointed out this would be bigger, more powerful, like the labor unions only better because "we" could handle "our own" products. They didn't like the mention of labor unions but John pointed out that whereas labor unions were perhaps socialistic, the farmers' union would be the good American thing. Of course, he said, no one group should be allowed to gain ascendancy over others, this was democracy. He must have thought it funny that one side could never be right but he was a man who always tried to see both sides. They all probably implied: capitalism has to exist in order to have labor unions; price determines need; strikes cause confusion in industry. Price determines need! John saw through that—funny!—and he told them how they could turn it the other way around. When he had their attention—time is slower out here than in the cities, so much space, people acres apart, illusion of freedom is greater—he would put the question: would they give their support? And they would smile: there'd be big ones in it would get sumpn, not they. They seemed better informed, usually, than Uncle Babe. Asked didn't they trust anyone in the country, they said they felt the government should be the one—what's the government for. J.J.: Well, the people must see that the government. . . . The People: Well, they were busy getting in the hay. J.J.: If farmers can't get legislation who can, they're the mainstay. The Farmers: Our children learn that in school, lots of things, they learn wrong. Use the ballot? Yes, on election days they went to the polls and voted, yes, mainly against. In this country you have to be on your guard against the officers chosen. In the first place who chooses em? Oh yes, direct primary now. A certain governor had done sumpn for em, the prosperous ones first. Uncle John said this was a prosperous farming section, milk machines coming in for those who could afford them so join the co-op and sell your produce to us for more than you get elsewhere because we can ship it in large amounts at lower rates. He signed up some of them. Others he could believe could not pay to enter. He said to these latter that if he got enough signers he would pay their dues for them and he did that later. He could never bear misfortune and he wanted this venture to be a success. The other man who was to be associated with him was around in different nearby townships getting signers.

Uncle Babe returned home these nights, his sack of Red Lime Fertilizer gone. Matty understood he was paying his expenses each day by selling these. John hated to tell her otherwise. I had ridden along sometimes and it seemed to me he had left most of it here and there among the poorer farmers as a trial gift. Altogether, he was absorbed in his new work but he brooded over his pipe ways and means of moving on. Maybe what he really wanted was company, a close friendship, someone in prosperous circumstances perhaps—he worried over these other people. Many persons loved the poor and hard-working because it was to the interests of the former . . .

he had to in the speeches he was going to make on Memorial Day and later on the subject of organization . . . he really wished they were different. To better these people, and through that make himself a place in the country, the state, the nation . . . if only he still had the old dog to talk to. Was seeing a great deal of Phoebe Hake, she, fifteen miles away.

Sometimes he would deliberately go out over the marsh that skirted the lake and woods, the shitepoke still as grass until John's voice rose up in behalf of the people. Determined now to prepare himself for the dynamics of platform work. No light matter for a man shy and starting to take on fat. He must have been haunted by dreams of speaking so well that cannons would greet him at the various towns and villages.

He called himself a Progressive, sure to mean militant liberal. Soon he was speaking in town halls and old opera houses. He memorized his speeches but if he forgot could always put in something else. His practice of throwing the voice at times like a hand grenade into the back seats made him a recognized orator of the day and out from the woods or gardens of the vaudeville curtains he stood against would come: The question is who shall rule, labor or the big producers who control through slavery the laborers? I tell you it is our duty to curb corporation power. We have inherited, as it were, the great idea that this country is the place for free competition and we mean to have it. I am coming, Ladies and Gentlemen, to the farmers' co-operative. (Quieter:) Such a farm movement was started a few years ago that for two years agriculture defeated the corporations. This can be done again. All we want is a fair profit. When we have established a farmers' co-operative we will rest content. . . . After all, however much the economic conditions of the country stare us in the face we must look to the higher things of life . . . (Grenade:) You do want to possess this freedom from materialism. That boy of yours must have an education. . . . Uncle Babe maybe wished often that he could sink back into the sky of the curtain and be a pure idealist. And all the while the military bands. He may have remembered a former militant liberal in the state who had stuck to his post, had written way back in 1858 (in a letter to his wife but now the book is out). Uncle Babe would come away very hoarse from this kind of thing and very retiring. Sometimes on days of parades, unless he had to throw grenades into the ranks, he would join and march, the badges of his party and lodge upon him—never killed a man in his life, one old friend said. The liberal military air, a system of rank. Major F. and Commander St. B. were speakers even in peace.

John was still in the fish business in fall and spring. One of the working men was put in charge of the crew when John was away, and Matty was there. She let him go—his lime fertilizer must be going good, she thought. My mother helped with the cooking and Matty had a strong hand for business. When Matty called the men to dinner: Come now! she wasn't to be trifled with. Sometimes she'd jump into the gasoline launch, speed off down to the mouth of the river, circle around, watch the fishermen. She could handle a gun too, a good marksman. In many ways she was a better executive than her brother. As the men worked nearby she'd raise the window and call out how the rope should be passed or what kind of bolt or which parts should be put together next. John could always return to the executive mansion and find everything going at high pitch.

The old folks passed on. Great Uncle Gotlieb first. A stroke while in the woods, sat by a tree all night. His insurance company, Modern Woodman, failed. John had paid the assessments toward the last as they mounted, only to lose all. Made him dammad but of course, what could he do. The men in charge of the company were out of his reach. As time went on, thinking it over, he concluded perhaps the head men were business men used to taking profits and big salaries naturally; they couldn't understand that their salaries should be held down to the decent level of men giving service. An economist in England was way later to make that same excuse for the failure of a utility company in this country.

Riecky had stayed with my mother's mother in the north of the state as she grew older and not so well, and Grandma by way of Matty bought her gold belt buckle twice to help give the poor thing a feeling of security—she was always afraid she'd have to go to the Poor House. Wasn't long and she was gone too.

John was taking on more weight, becoming known, always advancing the cause of his leader and his party, and while he waited for things to take shape—give the people time, he said, they can't be hurried—he was opening up the land along the river into lots; could sell off a lot now and then, always a little income. The people out here did not catch an idea maybe as fast as city people. But when he thought of the masses in the city he was glad he was out here. Country people had more freedom. There in the city ground down by the industrial system—their minds were faster but could they show anything more for it?—came wandering out here sometimes either very much dressed up and no money to pay for drinks and a night's lodging, or looked very poor and spent their last nickel for drink and owed you besides—that element. He always spoke of the masses and the people as two different classes. Better to be out here, respectable owners of property, he said, better anyhow, do your own work, be your own boss. Beyond that, another class of big people who were everybody's—bosses?—he owned to the quaint separatist belief that some of these could have money control without oppressing others. In his day it was considered a good thing to liberate the mind but not to change it. Never too fast. Never appear eager for a livelihood. One had to have it but it wasn't nice to seem too eager, showed you were a gentleman of good taste not to seem hungry. J.J. had a way always of covering up money transactions, they were seldom direct. If he wanted to buy or sell something it worked through a third person who absorbed the taint, the profits. Usually lawyers, but also insurance and real estate men and even garage owners accustomed to out and out deals—they "had to take" houses, plows, furniture, in payment of debts. These masses of thirds—masses, Uncle John implied, had to work so hard and shamelessly—made business go round. Every decent family had its own or hired these ministers of buying and selling, hated and revered. They would line up prospective buyers for John's lots and hunting grounds, some of them John's own friends, and then he would choose the ones he thought would be interested and give a dinner for them, rather, Matty. But it turned out that those who really bought were the thirds on the staff of life seeing John was pinched at certain times and they could get a lot for a song. Matty had a greater respect for them than for the sportsmen who wouldn't spend so someone else could play too. She saw that the former got the best of everyone, were shrewd, saving, lived below their means and that's how they had something. It often brought her a spell of neuralgia and force as she saw how her brother must have a wild duck placed on each plate at his dinners and lose out. Later, by having eaten in the company of bankers he was to be able to borrow money. He said she must realize he was ahead there because not everyone during the depression could borrow money.

Cottages went up on the lots, they began to have neighbors. Somebody was always wanting to use the ladder when Matty wanted it. The woods were not sold. Uncle John could come back from stumping the country for himself or this senator or that to the solitude of his woods, the trees overtopping him. Always in his simple honesty he gave the neighbors the run of his garage and when he'd be ready to start work around the place—his clothes all changed, overalls on—he'd go out and find his tools not there, jacks gone, ropes gone, hammers, axe. . . . But he considered he was helping someone so all well and good. He sighed. Never got ruffled. After all, he owed them something for buying the land. He went back into the house to be comfortable again. He didn't doubt the borrowers would return the things, he was honest. Matty thought if they didn't he'd still count em his friends because he'd have forgotten who borrowed what. And of course he had in mind they'd vote for him some day. He's too trusting, no wonder he can't do business, said Matty. I think myself he must have seemed to people to be so honest that he wasn't just nor keen. While they used him, knew they could depend on him, they looked with suspicion on a man who almost liquidated his property for the sake of his neighbors.

At last the day when the farmers came around, the co-op established, Uncle Babe in charge. He was winding up his fishing for good. Filling out his income tax blank the night the man brought the news that a meeting of those interested in the co-op would be held the next night to settle it. He had made out a tan blank, the wrong color, and was now on a green one. We were all sitting around, electric lights just installed. I was there, taking a few days off from business college (my father's insurance). Matty must have made her usual remark about income tax and the like: Cheez, if they'd offer a job instead of taking money away . . . well, it won't be long before they'll want yuh to keep track of the number of jobs yuh do and pay tax on em. As the man came in with the news, Josephine's daughter gave up her chair with a loud meow and doubtless caught her toes in the black and tan crocheted rugs as she jumped down and stretched. Beer and cigars were passed.

The next day Uncle Babe gave his tax blank to a lawyer acquaintance to fill out and drove off.

For three years he was to give the hammers and ladders of his honesty to the co-op and sit in comparative comfort in the office. Things started well. A merger was soon made with a national organization and for a period of five years J.J. served on county and state committees as well, white shirt every day and fine-dot tie, and so he was led up to the World War but he was just past draft age. Unable to speak now as much as he liked since he sincerely did not believe in the war, he nevertheless kept in touch through others with the general in Congress, the governor who had befriended him.

They won and rested. He saw though that he was still up against the same things: the always stronger "interests," the monopoly of power on the one side, and on the other the people of the agricultural community in a monopoly of sleep. He won an inch for the farmers, now the boom coming on—the only boom the farmers ever had was during the war—they relaxed. Things were going well even without the co-op. Their fight collectively slackened, as good as ended. Each farmer again competed with each. Wasn't it a free capitalist country? J.J. said they should continue the good work so as to prepare for times of shortage. Shortage? This was a prosperous farming section. Yes, but they must think what they would have for the next campaign. And they were doing better now, yet many of them, John noticed, refused tractors, telephones, vacation journeys. They mustn't slip into blind, unplanned production, he warned them. Price determines need!—all a matter of the people making it otherwise. He wrote in reply to my letters to him and Matty that the co-op leaders were holding picnics, giving out pop and ice cream cones free to induce people to come to their meetings. Some came, mainly children. It was like if you made an appointment they'd say: I'll see you yesterday. Never be different, J.J. told himself, so long as times stayed good. Of course he wished these times would stay. . . . Factory workers were faster, speedup, couldn't overeat. Out here the Middle Western Ages, farmers plodding behind their horses. Many drudged and denied themselves, put every penny in their farms, then sold or rented to retire to house and lot in town, their living going out of them—on the porch railing Will Farmer sat when he came to town, the basic principle of our government, the Will of the People. What could the people do against the money power now and always controlling the government? They must put men in power who could. J.J.'s chief, almost the only person who had dared militate against the war constantly called to the forces in his state to rally—freedom of the press, freedom of speech, tax the rich, curb the trusts—these things he was fighting for alone. J.J. would do the same. He would get himself endorsed by the leaders in the state. He would give a dinner, an influential standpat Republican would be invited along with the Progressives. To show they could be liberal minded. And La Follette had said, "Get and keep a dozen or more of the leading men in a community interested in, and well informed upon any public question and you have laid firmly the foundations of democratic government." They must plan so that good times would stay, or at least come oftener.

Uncle Babe retained his determination for public service through the years he was shunted from committee to committee, and then finally he was placed on the ticket. Quite well known by this time, men began coming to take even suppers with him. Matty had spells oftener.

To escape there were his acres and his radio. He liked to turn on the negro spirituals, the melting deep . . . Christ, how they could sing . . . the blackbirds settling down . . . he could forget about government. If he were asked about negroes he said they should be treated well but implied they shouldn't be given the upper hand. Matty had no time for radio. Was getting so all people wanted to do was sit and listen in. She didn't understand radio really—just foolish this guesswork pulled out of the air. She went on baking with luck, washing with an electric machine, sewing with the old tread—still made her summer dresses. Her broom in the kitchen would sweep on ceiling and sidewalls as well as floor in loud complaint of existing conditions, or she'd balance it against her, both arms going free.

One night a man and woman came out from the city, stayed over, in the morning bought the old place—the hotel and five acres surrounding. John liked this sudden, almost accidental business deal, made him happy and Matty was glad he needn't entertain the state about it. They had, for a few years past, given up using the hotel as a hotel, and now the cottage they'd planned immediately took shape on the other side of the grove, facing the river still, same view of woods and river from the windows, besides a new vegetable garden, flower garden, new arbors, chicken coop, pier. And next to their own cottage John built one to rent out—soon it would be his and Phoebe's. Very little woodland was sold with the old place, couldn't take the risk, might disappear overnight—John took only the dead wood for his fuel, and the mass of the woods standing there was protection on the north and something to look at. Would have to be pinched hard to sell any more trees.

Soon settled down again. Some of the old furniture was brought over. Their five rooms were large enough, many windows, and John's room—he allowed no curtains there, only shades. He had a little walnut cupboard for tobacco, a cot, a desk, small heater, radio. Most winter evenings they sat together in the kitchen, played euchre, dropped their apple peelings into the coal scuttle, Matty's short, quick-cut, John's round and round, unbroken.

Though less to do here, Matty was still in her neuralgic and head troubles, a woman demanding help, so used to men working on the place that during housecleaning days when she wanted stove or ice box moved she'd say, They can do this anytime now, I'm ready. Thereby she took in the neighbors. Private property before life. And as time went on she knew the courts upheld her. When the strikes came on in Detroit she read: "The right of an owner to his property is upheld by the circuit court." But the problem of neighbors staying to sit or to use the now fewer and fewer Beefelbein tools she could not always control as she liked. She was always ahead though. Her little business with her hens was fair. In one way or another she had managed to save $1000. Even during the depression she continued to gamble on her stock market, to pocket little revenues and clip coupons on coffee and soap.

The monopoly of sleep expanding. But Uncle John was running for the Assembly. He may have dreamed of serving the nation in the coming Presidential campaigns, of being called to conventions here or there: We need your help to nominate Hyle. Or Payne. Or Beefelbein. But the crash came, and then the depression, without him.

And April elections followed, sun and rain, Prairie Chickens, Phoebe . . . was still working in a drug store, giving a little each week to her mother, had asked John to invest her savings—turned out bad—made a feeling between them that should never have arisen, but he was now confident of getting into office and providing for them all.

Party feeling was intense while men huddled under a bridge and streets of people slowly died of hunger.

J. J. had been endorsed by party leaders and they were cheered when they spoke. At last a real start. Several important issues, but they had to limit themselves to what one address could adequately hold. For J.J. that meant principally the question of putting people back to work and a system of relief. On this he could give his whole heart, sound radical even, socialistic, though of course he was really becoming a Progressive Democrat soon voting for the Franklin D. Roosevelt deal.

Three days before spring election when the voters would declare themselves—for him—J.J. went out to the haystack to practice his speech of thanks to the people for supporting him. Trying out a new tone-placement to be ready for outdoor engagements. Matty, stepping out the back door heard: two million five hundred thousand. And again something like: three billion seven hundred twenty-six million. . . . The former likely the number of unemployed or the number of times he'd thought of them. Matty seeing the garden unplowed, a boat unrepaired, probably a fence down: no ground work, only figgers, figgers.

Election time, she thought, just mouth to mouth. People were living that way now instead of better. The newly married couple renting the cottage— They've got nothing, she said, go without hats or caps in winter, they live from mouth to mouth.

But to go back to Uncle Babe in the haystack, sheltered from the ill wind of depression . . . when it did strike him, poor man, he was not influential enough to keep out of the newspapers. In fact that very noon a man drove into the yard telling him the utility company which had both their savings was down so low that he feared it would never come back, and the next day it got around. Now the people still had, many of them, the feeling that a man to lose $8000, 8000 eggs in one basket, must be a poor business man . . . the system that permitted investment and crash was bad, of course, but every man must take care of himself. And doubtless, regarding John, the amount of his failure grew as it spread . . . $18,000 . . . $28,000 . . . someone said, I heard $38,000. So it passed from mouth to mouth and burned them up. Enemy papers, the day before election made the most of it. The organs of the opposition attacked me most bitterly, but I am in fighting trim and I feel confident of victory ahead . . . so an older, richer, nationally known mosquito-in-the-brush had long ago said favorably to the millions, a lawyer he became for the property holders of Milwaukee— Since lawyers, he'd said, in times of depression like the present are the only class that prospers. Uncle John couldn't fight now. Whether he just hadn't built up a successful campaign for himself, or the people were suspicious and resentful of a man in their midst who'd had enough money to retire before he was old . . . at any rate, he lost out.

He saw himself now suffering with the rest. His life past the middle, soon gone . . . what was it for? No use trying to sell any land now, nobody could buy. Mortgage the house, the woods, no, keep away from pain . . . go back to the Indians, they were happy . . . until their lands were taken away.

Night. Went to his room, the window. The big dipper, couldn't see it, different now . . . why did it move around, different positions? What were the stars? Maybe we weren't meant to know. If he'd broken into education a little further? They probably taught some damthing to fool the people. We learn wrong.

Next morning Matty baked without luck. Well, they still had cheese and their home.

He went over the land, heard bullfrogs—he'd had them imported a few years before, saw the yellow-heads in the rushes, the little river and the lake, all in a land of slavery, blue heron stands, finish, form, if city folks could see, advanced into summer, took his new stand against the bankers.

Government control of . . . same radio cushion . . . money, credit. Set-back, had a cold since April . . . government now controlled by it, wrong, but give it time. Change money. The government wouldn't have to be changed, would it?—not overthrown by . . . coughing. He felt as unsteady as a Whittier voter, or he began to feel what was best but couldn't bring himself to it. What was this talk of classes, anyway. But yes, if only the middle class and lower class would join together. Feed a cold, starve a fever. As a liberal, Uncle John did both, and the interests of both classes lost their point simultaneously. He was afraid that something must be done, anything though to keep a nation from passing away.

Think of it, I told Uncle Babe, goes down in the ocean, this country, bubbles, is gone! Not a plant to grow a whisker on. J.J. jumping in after it with a book on Money: What It Is. There it is!—the masses of workers with a government which is themselves and by them the mines, factories, forests, farms, railroads, banks, owned, and the right to work guaranteed, vacation too! A reasonable profit? No, all profit went down in the ocean, so did graft. Down with a fierce love of independence, Hamilton! Look, "our" woods. In your old age a pension and your same old pride a new one. A living science working for just such good Russ . . . Germans as you. Organized methods. Powerful tractors. Price-decline. Production costs in the barn fell and the haystack moved to the consumer!

The food which Matty always allowed John to provide was not very nourishing now, she said, only common, coarse food. He brought home less meat, almost no candy. Apples, lemons, were high. If only somebody would give a dinner, show they remembered what he'd done for them and give him a job. To help others. He'd worked hard in his younger days and since, to keep what he had. Now he'd have been ready to give his time and money for other concerns.

Farmers, organize for the benefit of society. But collective farming? Not own their land? Could a man be depended on to work land he didn't own? What people want is better living, walnut furniture, pottery, violets, theatres. . . .

Maybe some man put in control. Hard to know which one to trust. In 1912 the American people had elected President Wilson on the belief that he would lower the cost of living! Sometimes it was Wilson, sometimes the Pope, then again Coughlin, or the local police officer.

He met a man one day. We were riding home in John's Ford V8. I was on vacation—had taken a cut, working now for $2 a week more than room and board. The elderberry bushes beside the road were holding out their white blossom-plates where the pies would come. This man walking, dusty, a small sackload on his back, held out his hand.

J. J.: Going far?

Man: West, I guess, wherever I can find work. Know of any?

He had worked 35 years, it turned out, and now had nothing. John gave him some of our rolls and bananas and 50¢.

Uncle John worried over him. Pressure to bear. Yes, but as a whole, he said, the common people didn't know what was good for them, couldn't govern themselves. My uncommon Uncle! I suppose he couldn't forget they had repudiated him at the polls, but he said the more prosperous farmers were against relief for those in the towns who had nothing and if they didn't watch out they wouldn't have a friend in the legislature. They really didn't appreciate what was done, could be done, for them—he was led to this belief once long ago when he had given a ditch, a right-of-way straightout to a group of men who wanted to buy it. They never even thanked him. I saw his sadness, couldn't tell him just then that people don't want things done for them. He went on that he at least had a place to be in these hard times. Still, that man, and there must be many more, would see the ocean . . . if he had good luck, whereas he, John Beefelbein, had no means of seeing it, had to stay on in his old place.

He would gladly give the man more sackloads if he could.

1951—1952

I divined this comedy, Dante, before I went in. But I had to have a job. "Like one who has imperfect vision, we see the things which are remote from us." O brother, we saw tho the eyes were shot. We had light if not love. We had business.

Nystagmus ("The poet's eye, in a fine frenzy rolling"), the searching movement, combined with 80% vision. You'll have to use a magnifying glass, we can't give you glasses to reach print. Good-bye to proof reading. Good-bye to a living. No! That low, rangy, glass-walled office and plant in the Frank Lloyd Wright setting, clean-mowed acres, tulips, petunias, evergreens—I would apply there. Not literature but light fixtures and pressure cookers. Out of daylight into Wade Light.

I was the September dandelion—forty, female—seeking a place among the young fluorescent petunias. I keep cropping up in the world's backyards while here in America, on all sides they shear civilization back to the seventeen-year-old girl, not yet young shall we say.

I entered the window-walled office of personnel. Or was it a corner of a little theatre? What would the director be like? A properly placed man may expand his influence over the whole of your sight. We met ideally, as strangers do, without prejudice, without violence . . . courteous before the guessed-at depth. All art between us. Will he help me? He is not usual. He moves as in a dance to be considerate. As if to speak, against the room's outdoor backdrop, of Renoir? Of Einstein? Is he the master economist with a sense of the relative value of things? The artist with a sense of needing fewer things? The political observer with a knowledge of electronics? What does he know really, sweetly, by touch?

He said, "You read."

Beethoven: "It is impossible to say to people, 'I am deaf'." But I said it: I have an eye handicap.

"I wonder if you should . . . we have a switchboard opening. You might try it."

I went in. Lights, polished glass, blond satin finished desks, glossy haired and bald-headed efficiency. Shine. Lamps to be produced. Lamps to be sold. The antique sweatshop base with a new shine. You'll never have to polish this brass, a lacquering process, won't tarnish. This is the lust that will never rust.

The shade by the door, the grey parchment face, cracked in a half smile. Shall I appear alive or let myself be carried along? I suppose man is, the most sensitive physical part of him, an electrical apparatus, switches, wires, etc. . . . How much do I give to Wade lamps? It takes 1028 human bodies to build a star. Purely business.

The girl at the switchboard shouted, "Come in—if you can—it's my birthday, you know. Once a year and at Christmas this happens—nylons, table lamps, candy, help yourself. The bosses, the old honeypots, must like me a little bit, anyhow. Sit down. Let me tell you what goes. They're all good enough guys, family men, church, golf, they're after the business, they'll lay on you, of course."

You see in a place of this kind, she said, the switchboard girl is one of their outlets. They do a great deal of their sweating thru you. You'll make the contact and in haste, also they relax thru you. You're a part of it when their bags are full and you jazz em when they're down.

"Get me the Howard Hotel, a single."

"Good, I like to sleep close."

That was Mendau, the burnt-out fuse in the beautiful suit who still thinks he's got something to sell.

"Give me Philadelphia." Give me Europe. I'm waiting, operator, for the Paris pick-up. I'm on wartime Montparnasse, gas mask, phosphorescent heels, illuminated brooch. "What's that?" What does it look like? There they call it what it is.

The Japs: We had neither hens nor eggs. We went requisitioning. A miserable village. On the way back we began to look for Chinese girls.

They don't make em as sensitive as geiger counters.

"Goddamit what the hell happened to that call to Lethal Steel? Sleeping at the switchboard?"

"I reported to you, sir, that Dan Blaine will talk."

"Christ if you can't get anybody but Dead-End Daniel—"

"What was the name they wanted?" Somebody by the name of Christ. Please pass the blood. Human matériel is obsolescing.

As for the work itself, she plays an intricate chess. You gamble with the red and the white and the green, without benefit of spa.

I lost. "No natural aptitude."

Dante? Yes, go ahead.

The evening's automobiles, men from work, shot silently through green lights. Encased motors give man the swift, shining precision that his mind as he drives can't give him. Well, he makes his get-away in beauty. He passes gleaming. And somewhere along the speedway for men with motors is home, woman.

I must have been aglow myself as I stood there—I was a banner headline in running lights: YOUNG MAN GOES HOME—after twenty years as newspaper printer. Although mid-twentieth century of the middle ages continued had brought me the printing press, I'd found that Wm. James was right: "The sensational press is the organ of a state of mind which means a new 'dark' ages that may last more centuries than the first one. Then illiteracy was brutal and dumb and power was rapacious without disguise. Now illiteracy has an enormous literary organization and power is sophistical," and this organization, as good an avenue for plunder as any business is, protects and is protected by that other and still more expensive organization, war. I'd found that a job does not necessarily sustain life. Grime, guts, gloom, the crash and roar of the big presses, speed, overtime speed, reason jarred. Throw the forms away for the last time, I was away to my childhood home in the country.

Benj glided up to the curb in his own silent, white tired speed-gleam. I recalled my sister's remark on a certain small red beauty in the neighborhood, "They've bought a hummingbird—you can't haul anything with it."

"But why do you do it," shrieked Benj, "It's lunacy!—alone, isolated, when everybody else is gearing himself for the fight for survival."

"Are men afraid of their own selves? Give us peace and we'll survive."

"But nobody to talk with!"

"Talk, these days, is dangerous. My friend the poet says 'Talk is a form of love'. Maybe I'll find that form in the millennium after the next."

"And what about Norma? Aren't you marrying her in June?"

"Why is it that women about to be married need a mineralogical fulfillment—silver, diamond?"

"You'll find a flood. In that lowland in the spring it won't take a forked stick to find water. What *do* you expect to find?"

"The ancient present. In me the years are flowing together."

I awoke the next morning to twitterings out of leaves on every side, mixed with a marsh hush that I must have known soon after I'd known life in this world. The river had risen in the back land to within six feet of the house. Here in the lush wash, you go back to the exuberant source and start over. My mother, not too happily married, lived on her nerves on this stream, hunted and fished, grew flowers as big as plates in the Nile-like silt and said—how often she said it—"I've got a new pain."

The goddam dragon flies mating all over hell, said Jackie from my office, once long ago, and Jackie was a lady, unintellectual but enlightened, one to whom diamonds held no lure.

No lady is the other office woman by her own insistence, weak-voiced and slight of build though she is. She is the proof reader, Francie Canoye who sits in her monastic, windowless cell, abhorrent of anything approaching profanity, but who manages to domineer over some sixteen men—printers, editors, bosses—with a desperate, old maid, bitter, obscene purity.

Francie's impeccably penciled initials in the corner of her galleys soon stood among us men for Finance Capitalism. This small piece of steel flesh with a bad heart and spleen, a military bearing which was her only patrimony, maintains a deadly hatred of labor unions despite a ready acceptance of holiday pay. Two weeks paid vacation she never gets because she refuses it on the grounds that there is no one to whom she can trust her job.

This is the woman who carries her portable possessions to and from work with her every day in a big bag resembling an enormous, pendulous, inverted bladder, never trusting their safety with her landlady. Sometimes the bag contains empty milk bottles—her own serious admission—to protect herself against landlady and landlord should the situation arise. Actually, she has nothing. A brother who died of leukemia had thereby depleted his and her own savings. Poor old thing, she marches along the street under the heavy weight of nothing. If she'd had money, she'd have quit—no, more likely as the self-appointed carrier of civilization she'd have gone on suffocating at her post. It's generally agreed that Francie knows her gothics and her futuras, but day after day of stepped-up tensions, dead lines, the whole deadly, competitive madness, have left their mark. And natural that sheer noise should affect her as she grows older. Not that she would complain to the owners. She looked belligerent, one particularly distressing day, when even her young copyholder shouted in near delirium, "Can't hear the stars, too close to the big press."

Through an age of violence and sudden death such as ours, a culture that hardly distinguishes between credulity and superstition, a culture that forever oscillates between a search for a movie with a Holy Grail theme and a search for the next meal, proof reader Francie Canoye guides her once sharp mind by sheer force of will.

"Triskaidekaphobia thought they'd stump me on that one they didn't get me on Capuchin and bailiwick either Christ was a Jew they say—impossible! take it back to the editors I'm afraid of Frank Dane's bull neck the linotype boys are late today and sloppy we need a Hitler over here to make things move the moon changes tomorrow so we'll get different weather do you pray?" And when Francie runs on thus the ads in the night's paper loom up with tender *lions* for tender *loins*, or *grease-free* ginghams for *crease-free* ginghams or unconditional *surrender* (on tires) instead of unconditional *guarantee*. So she loses her night's sleep and starts the morning of the next day by laying into the men who had failed to make the corrections which if marked hadn't been changed because the proofs had come back too late from the proof reader's desk. At such a time her grey figure stood before you like the sandpiper's out at my yard's "shore line," a clam shell on long, thin legs with nervous-nodding head. Once a child came along, asked what kind of a bird that was and "What does it kill?" The truth was that often in her "brute goodness," her only laxative from tight-bound days and too many candy bars, was to let an error fly where it would among the stench along her own close-confined portion of beach.

But now I—at least I—was home. I looked toward the water's edge where lay milk bottle, electric light bulb, whiskey flask. China's great blue heron, Poor Joe, look at him go. A knock at the door-who in hell? I hung from a cold cigarette. A woman, her hair burning in the morning sun.

"Parachute?"

"No, I'm one of the last of my line—legs." She stood there with more than one range of intensity and a basket of chicken and salad. It was Marion Dollman from the hill.

"Come in." We sat at table. Five feet from us on the other side of the window a yellow warbler was busy at her compact nest, three eggs of her own and a cowbird's. The birds building in the bush under my nose!

The girl passed the salt. "You look at me as though you expected to find something of a world . . ." The world, we said, will come from scientists on the tail of their terror-literature, if it comes. Still, we'd make our own.

"Tell me," she said, "What do you know to be true? Not merely that roughly radiation dies away according to the formula r equals one over time."

"Not roughly. Knowing goes best with the quietest touch. Otherwise it's somebody else's stuff. Even so I can only indicate."

Her tender-spoken "No terror here." And "With all deference to what we could be together, no two persons can ever become one, each must be free to desire what the other has indicated. At least we'd make it a point, wouldn't we, never to be familiar no matter how close we got?"

"And together, isolated from a great portion of humanity, as all with feeling are, these days . . . while the flood recedes and the grass starts fast to mow me in my prime."

"Isn't it glorious? Let's trim green thought in one place and let it grow wild in another."

The lovely greenery—I hadn't too much of it in my pocket or in any bank. But we don't need a third of the things, the sheer, literal litter that people do in our savage cities.

Let's sit here in the long afternoon and last.

radio adaptation
of William Faulkner's
novel

DOC PEABODY *as narrator*

Anse Bundren's wife Addie was dying. When Anse finally sent for me of
his own accord I said: He has wore her out at last. And when it got far
enough into the day for me to read weather signs I knew it couldn't have
been anybody but Anse that sent. I knew that nobody but a luckless man
could ever need a doctor in the face of a cyclone. And I knew that if it had
finally occurred to Anse himself that he needed a doctor, it was already
too late. Their cotton and corn farm lay on top a steep hill. My team
couldn't make the last several yards up the steep but Anse got me up
there—my 250 pounds—with the help of a rope. "What the hell does
your wife mean," I say, "taking sick on top of a durn mountain?"

ANSE (*thick, gentle voice*)

I'm right sorry, Doc.

PEABODY

Well, let's go in.

Sound of footsteps, door closing.

PEABODY *as narrator*

The girl Dewey Dell was standing by the bed fanning her. Addie turns
her head. She's been dead these ten days. I suppose it's having been a part
of Anse for so long that she cannot even make that change, if change it
be. I can remember how when I was young I believed death to be a
phenomenon of the body; now I know it to be merely a function of the
mind—and that of the minds of the ones who suffer the bereavement.
The nihilists say it is the end, the fundamentalists, the beginning; when in
reality it is no more than a single tenant or family moving out of a
tenement or a town. Beneath the quilt she is no more than a bundle of

sticks. I turned to Anse standing there with his arms dangling, the hair pushed and matted upon his head like a dipped rooster.

PEABODY

Why didn't you send for me sooner?

ANSE

Hit was jest one thing and then another. That ere corn me and the boys was aimin to get up with, and Dewey Dell a-takin such good keer of her, till I jest thought . . .

PEABODY

Damn the money. Did you ever hear of me worrying a fellow before he was ready to pay?

ANSE (*low-voiced, concerned*)

She's goin, is she?

Silence

ANSE

I knowed it. Her mind was sot on it. She laid down on her bed. She says: I'm tired.

PEABODY

And a damn good thing.

PEABODY *as narrator*

Suddenly Addie looks at me. Her eyes like lamps blazing up just before the oil is gone. She probably wants me to get out and everybody else. I've seen it before in women. Seen them drive from the room them coming with sympathy and pity, with actual help, and clinging to some trifling animal to whom they never were more than pack-horses. That's what they mean by the love that passeth understanding: that pride, that furious desire to hide that abject nakedness which we bring here with us, carry with us into operating rooms, carry stubbornly and furiously with us into the earth again.

ADDIE (*rather loud*)

Cash. You, Cash! I want the boy. (*weaker*): Anse, Jewel, Darl?

ANSE (*kindly and close in*)

The boys went for another load, Ma. Them three dollars, you know. They thought you'd wait.

ADDIE (*weakly but clearly*)

I smell wet leaves and earth (*fade to background during next two speeches*) geese flying north . . .

PEABODY

She seems to be talking to herself.

ANSE

I'll go out and see if them boys are coming. (*door closing*)

ADDIE (*stronger, closer in*)

I was young then. I was teaching school. One day in early spring a man appeared, turning his hat round and round in his hands and I said, "If you've got any womenfolks, why in the world don't they make you get your hair cut?" He said, "I ain't got none." And that was Anse and I took him. And when I knew I had my child, Cash, I knew that living was terrible and that words are no good; words don't ever fit even what they are trying to say at. We had to use each other by words but most of all by blood, blood coursing, boiling, whipping—only by something like the whip could my blood and their blood unite in one stream. I loved Anse but my aloneness was violated. When I found I had Darl I saw only one thing—Anse had tricked me. But no, I had been tricked by words older than Anse or love and the same words had tricked Anse too. And when Darl was born I asked Anse to promise to take me back to Jefferson when I died. Father had said that the reason for living was to get ready to stay dead for a long time. I knew that father had been right, even when he couldn't have known he was right any more than I could have known I was wrong. Anse was dead and didn't know it. Anse was dead. (*Falters, weaker, then suddenly tries to raise up and call*): Is Anse dead?

PEABODY

Calm yourself, Addie.

ADDIE

As I lay in the nights I heard the words that are the deeds, and the other words that are not deeds, and that are just the gaps in people's lacks, coming down like the cries of the geese out of the wild darkness. But I found it—the reason for life was the duty to the alive, to the terrible blood, the red bitter blood boiling through the land. My children were of the wild blood of me and of all that lived, of none and of all. Then I found that I had Jewel—when Jewel was two months gone. Then Dewey Dell, then Vardaman. And then I could get ready to die.

PEABODY *as narrator*

So she died. The child Vardaman, was somewhere about. Dewey Dell sat motionless awhile, then Anse reminded her to get supper.

ANSE

We got to keep our strength up. And Cash'll need to eat quick and get back to work so he can finish the coffin in time.

PEABODY *as narrator*

I stepped out into the twilight, Dewey Dell behind me. I could feel the 17-year-old girl's big dark eyes boring a hole through my back.

DEWEY DELL (*low, rich voice*)

I'll have to look for Vardaman. (*Lower, fuller, more intimate—she always speaks from the depths but now as though to herself alone*): You, Doc Peabody, could do so much for me if you just would and if you just would then I could tell you and then nobody'd have to know it except you and me and Darl and Lafe. You could help me if you would.

Sound of door

ANSE

God's will be done. (*sighs*) Now I can get them teeth I been needin for so long.

DEWEY DELL (*off some distance, voice raised*)

Vardaman. (*Louder*): You, Vardaman. Bring that fish for supper. Come now, right away.

VARDAMAN

(*little child's voice, always tiny, distinctive, thin, "talking to himself like a cricket in the grass," Faulkner says, "a little one"*): Here I am right here by the porch. Yuh, I've got a fish, my fish, hey, where's my fish? I cut his guts out but Dewey Dell wants to cut him up for supper. (*Starts crying*): And that man—he came and kilt my Maw. He came and kilt my Maw.

DEWEY DELL (*normal voice*)

Stop that.

VARDAMAN (*no longer crying*)

My mother is a fish.

PEABODY *as narrator*

Yes, Addie Bundren was dead but to get her into her grave how many miles away in Jefferson where she asked to be buried with her kinfolk—that was another matter. As one of the neighbours said, "It's just like Anse to marry a woman born a day's hard ride away and have her die on him." *A day's* hard ride! With the rain falling and rivers rising up over the bridges who knows how many days.

ANSE (*as if looking out over the land, rubbing his knees*)

No man mislikes it more than me. And me without a tooth in my head, hoping to get ahead enough to get my mouth fixed where I could eat God's own victuals as a man should. And her hale and well as ere a woman in the land until that day, ten days ago.

PEABODY *as narrator*

Jewel, Darl and Cash came home. We ate. Cash started making the box.

Sound of sawing and, occasionally, nailing.

ANSE (*to Cash*)

I aint much help carpentering, Cash.

CASH

Darl is here.

DARL

Next thing it'll do, Cash, is rain. Think you'll get the coffin made tonight? Here's a lantern. (*To himself*): It takes two people to make you, and one people to die. That's how the world is going to end. Dewey Dell wanted her to die because then she'd get to town.

DEWEY DELL (*as if to herself*)

God gave woman a sign when something has happened bad.

DARL (*to himself*)

Yes. Cash is nailing her up. Jewel sitting there looking disconsolate. (*To Jewel*): It's not your horse that's dead, Jewel.

JEWEL

Goddam you. You always were a queer one.

DARL (*as narrator but as though to himself*)

The air smells like sulphur. Cash works on, arm bared. Below the sky sheet-lightning slumbers lightly; against it the trees, motionless, are ruffled out to the last twig, swollen, increased as tho quick with young. It begins to rain. The first harsh, sparse, swift drops rush through the leaves and across the ground in a long sigh, as though of relief from intolerable suspense. They are as big as buckshot, warm as though fired from a gun; they sweep across the lantern in a vicious hissing. From behind Pa's slack-faced astonishment he muses as though from beyond time, upon the ultimate outrage. (*To Cash*): The lantern's getting wet. (*Sound of saw ceases.*) Here, you'd better put on Mrs. Tull's raincoat. (*Again as narrator*): Cash hunts the saw. After awhile we find it in Pa's hand. (*To Cash*): Going to bevel all those boards? It'll take more time.

CASH

Yuh. The animal magnetism of a dead body makes the stress come slanting, so the seams and joints of a coffin are made on the bevel. It makes a neater job.

Sound of sawing and nailing and rain and then fade out.

PEABODY *as narrator*

It's almost day when Cash finishes. Four of us carry the coffin to the house. Addie could not want a better box, Cash is a good carpenter. And why not? Didn't she pick out these boards herself? Before she died, Cash brought each board to her for her approval. Darl lies down for a couple of hours.

DARL

I know. I know. In a strange room you must empty yourself for sleep. And before you are emptied for sleep, what are you. And when you are emptied for sleep you are not. And when you are filled with sleep, you never were. I don't know if I am or not. How often have I lain beneath rain on a strange roof, thinking of home.

Silence

PEABODY *as narrator*

On the day of the funeral Brother Whitfield came in wet and muddy to the waist. He had swum the river on his horse. The rain washed the bridge out.

WHITFIELD (*chants*)

The Lord comfort this house. The Lord giveth . . . The Lord put his grace on this house. May she rest in peace. I went down to the old ford and swam my horse over, the Lord protecting me.

SEVERAL MEN (*chanting*)

The Lord giveth. The Lord giveth. The Lord giveth . . .

NEIGHBOR (*rough drawl*)

That ere bridge was built, let's see, in 1888. I mind it because the first man to cross it was Doc Peabody coming to my house when Jody was born.

PEABODY

If I'd crossed it every time your wife littered since it'd a been wore out long before this.

Sudden laughter at this remark as release, then sudden quiet as they realize indiscretion and take sidelong glances at each other.

NEIGHBOR

Only the Lord can get Addie Bundren across the river after this rain. A misdoubtful night last night with the storm making. I knowed it was an evil day when I seen that team of Peabody's come up lathered, with the broke harness dragging and the neck-yoke betwixt the off critter's legs. Not too bad a wind but the rain. It'll take Anse a week to go to Jefferson and back. It's the cotton and corn I mind. Washed clean outen the ground it will be. A fellow wouldn't mind seeing it washed up if he could just turn on the rain himself. Who is that man can do that? Where is the colour of his eyes? Ay, the Lord made it to grow, the Lord giveth. . . .

MEN CHANTING (*not quite in unison*)

The Lord giveth. The Lord giveth. The Lord giveth . . .

PEABODY *as narrator*

And the next day they should have started off. I said, "Anse, how about the wheel for the wagon, will Jewel get it fixed?"

ANSE

Jewel will git back with it, I reckon, Doc.

NEIGHBOR

Take my wagon, Anse.

ANSE

Thank yuh, but I'll wait for ourn. She'll want it so. She was ever a particular woman.

NEIGHBOR

You'll have to go way around by Samson's bridge. It'll take you a day to get there. Then you'll be 40 miles from Jefferson. Take my team and get started right away, Anse.

ANSE

We'll wait for ourn. I'm goin fishin in the slough.

NEIGHBOR

That slough aint had a fish in it never that I knowed. Aint no good day to fish anyhow.

ANSE

It's one in here. Dewey Dell seen it.

NEIGHBOR

Tell you what—let's all get started to where you're goin and when we get to the river me and you'll take our poles and catch some fish.

ANSE

One in here. Dewey Dell seen it.

VARDAMAN

Pa shaves every day now because my mother is a fish.

Sound of wagon creaking fading in and occasionally mules snorting. Then sudden stop.

PEABODY *as narrator*

At long last the wagon was ready, the mules hitched to it. Everybody gathered in the yard ready to go. Dewey Dell climbs onto the wagon, her leg coming along from beneath her tightening dress: that lever which moves the world; one of that caliper which measures the length and breadth of life. She sits on the seat beside Vardaman, drops a basket of lunch in the bottom of the wagon and holds a square package on her lap.

ANSE

You, Jewel, leave that horse behind and come sit with us in the wagon. It aint respectful to your Ma to ride that horse like you wuz goin to a circus. A durn spotted critter of a horse, wilder than a catty-mount, a deliberate flouting of her and me. Her wanting us all to be in the wagon with her that sprang from her flesh and blood.

JEWEL (*evenly but staunchly*)

I'm taking my horse.

Sound of Darl laughing.

JEWEL

I didn't laugh, that was Darl.

ANSE

How many times I got to tell you, Darl, it's laughing like that that makes folks talk about yuh. Right on the plank where she's laying.

DARL (*toning down his laughter*)

All right, let's go. Good-bye Doc, see you some day.

PEABODY

Good-bye, good-bye. (*Lowering voice*): And time, I'd say. (*Wagon creaking fades in and then fades out*). (*As narrator*): I heard the rest of the story from Darl later.

Sound of wagon creaking and mules.

DARL *as narrator*

Kind of nice, the mud whispering on the wheels. And Jewel's horse moving with a light, high-kneed driving gait just back of us.

CASH

It'll be smelling in a couple of days now.

ANSE

It's a hard country on a man; it's hard. Eight miles of the sweat of the body washed up outen the Lord's earth, where the Lord himself told him to put it. Nowhere in this sinful world can a honest hard-working man profit. And the towns live off them that sweats. It's only in heaven every man will be equal and it will be taken from them that have and given to them that have not by the Lord.

CHANT OF MEN'S VOICES WHISPERING

Nowhere in this sinful world can a honest hard-working man profit. Nowhere in this sinful world . . .

VARDAMAN

There's the river, Pa, there's the river. See?

ANSE

We're getting to Samson's at dusk-dark. How's the bridge?

DARL

Washout out, just like Tull's. No, just under in the middle, out at both ends but swaying back and forth like a grass carpet.

ANSE

We'll stay at Samson's for the night and if it don't rain cross over in the morning.

SAMSON

Howdy, folks. Unhitch your mules, Anse, and come in to supper.

ANSE

We'll stay in the barn, thank yuh, we've got something in the basket.

SAMSON'S WIFE

Look here, come on in to supper and then go to sleep in a bed. You've got to get your rest. I believe in respect for the dead but you need your sleep.

ANSE

No thank yuh, ma'm, I wouldn't be beholden.

SAMSON

The best respect you can pay her now is to get her in the ground the quickest you can. You better give up going to Jefferson, Anse, and go over here to New Hope, only three miles, bury her there.

DEWEY DELL (*with great urgency*)

Pa, you promised, you gotta take her to Jefferson—if you don't do it, it will be a curse on you. You promised, you've got to.

ANSE

Did I say no?

SAMSON (*lowers his voice as if to himself*)

Stubborn, the lot of em. Those bone-gaunted mules of theirn . . . and that girl watching me. If her eyes had a been pistols I wouldn't be talking now. (*Raises his voice to speak directly to them*): Well, come in later on to sleep just as my wife said.

ANSE

I thank yuh but I'll stay up with her. I don't begrudge her it.

DEWEY DELL (*to herself*)

I took the knife from the steaming fish and killed Darl. Darl's eyes. Because he knows.

ANSE (*to himself*)

Now I can get them teeth. That will be a comfort, it will.

DARL

Look up in the sky.

VARDAMAN

Buzzard.

Silence.

Sound of rooster crowing. Noises of dawn. Sound of wagon creaking along.

DARL

Yes, the bridge submerged in the middle. Sagging and swaying.

Sound of wagon creaking gives over to water swirling.

CASH

Well—a fellow could walk across yonder on the planks and logs that have caught up on the ford past the jam—showing nothing under em though—might be quicksand built up there. What you think, Darl?

DARL

Let Pa, Dewey Dell and Vardaman walk across on the bridge, the water won't be too high for that. And then we'll go in the wagon over the ford best we can.

PEABODY *as narrator*

Sure, there they were, ready to go through the water. That girl, too, with the lunch basket on one arm and that package under the other. Just going to town. Bent on it. They would risk the fire and the earth and the water and all just to eat a sack of bananas.

DARL

Jewel—

JEWEL

I'll go ahead on the horse. You can follow me in the wagon.

DARL

Right. And Jewel, take the end of the rope upstream and brace it. Will you do that, Jewel?

JEWEL

I don't give a damn. (*Voice in high tension above increasing sound of water swirling and logs jamming*): Just so we do something. Sitting here, not lifting a goddam hand . . .

DARL (*above the noise*)

The motion of the wasted world accelerates just before the final precipice. Doc Peabody, would you have gone over?

PEABODY *as narrator*

An irrevocable quality. I can see it—the mules stand, their forequarters already sloped a little, their rumps high.

Sound of mules breathing with a deep groaning sound.

DARL

Jewel's horse is sinking. No, there he is again. Cash, steady the coffin. Wait—here comes a log! Cash! We're gone!

PEABODY *as narrator*

I know just how it was—a log surged up out of the water and stood for an instant upright upon that surging and heaving desolation like Christ.

CASH (*yelling*)

Darl, get out. (*Frantically*): Look out! Jump!

Sound of crash and destruction and animal cries. Then dead silence.

PEABODY *as narrator*

The wagon, the box with the dead, Darl, Jewel, Cash's carpenter tools, Cash himself, did you think they wouldn't get out of it? Cash had a broken leg but he claimed it bothered him none. They hitched up somebody's team, laid Cash on top of Addie and here they go again.

Sound of wagon creaking along and perhaps sounds of life along the road—car passes sounding its horn, etc. . . .

DEWEY DELL

Pa, I gotta stop.

ANSE

Can't you wait till we get to town—we aint got time if we want to get there by dark and get the hole dug.

DEWEY DELL

No, I gotta go in the bushes. I won't be long.

Sound of wagon ceases.

JEWEL

Taint nothing to dig a hole. Who the hell can't dig a hole.

DARL

I'll bet Dewey Dell changes clothes. Sure, there she is already. Sunday dress, beads and shoes and stockings.

ANSE (*long suffering*)

I thought I told her to leave them clothes to home.

DARL (*to himself*)

I wonder what she'll accomplish in town.

Sound of creaking of wagon fades out and city street noises fade in. Sound of footsteps and a screen door opening and closing. A small bell sound as of door or ringing of cash register.

MALE VOICE, *drug store clerk*

Yes ma'm?

Silence.

DRUG CLERK

Yes, ma'm?

DEWEY DELL

I want something, suh . . . can we talk private . . .

DRUG CLERK

What is your trouble?

DEWEY DELL

Well—female trouble, suh. I've got ten dollars. Lafe said I could get it at a drug store.

DRUG CLERK

But ma'm, you've come to the wrong place—

DEWEY DELL

This is a drug store, aint it? We'll never tell you sold it to us, never, suh.

DRUG CLERK

Listen, you go on home, buy yourself a marriage license with that ten dollars.

DEWEY DELL (*pleading*)

If you've got something, let me have it.

DRUG CLERK (*to himself*)

It's a hard life they have, sometimes a man . . . (*Raises his voice and speaks directly to her*): Look here, the Lord gave you what you have even if He did use the devil to do it. (*Lowered voice again as if to himself*): Funny looking set, that's her family out there on the street I guess, in the wagon. I heard somebody say they were running around getting cement—*cement*—for the boy's broken leg. And the wagon smells as though there was something dead in it. They'll all hole up in jail the lot of em. This girl's not bad looking, though—I might as well play along with her. (*Normal voice again but with a reckless, philandering quality*): Well, here's something then—

DEWEY DELL

It smells like turpentine. You sho this will work? Is this all there's to it?

DRUG CLERK

I tell you what you do. You come back at ten o'clock tonight, I'll give you the rest of it.

Silence. Then montage of voices, each as if talking to himself.

VARDAMAN

Hurry up, Dewey Dell. Hit smells.

DARL

How does your leg feel, Cash?

CASH

Fine. The stuff is cool on it.

VARDAMAN

Jewel hasn't got a horse anymore.

ANSE

I wouldn't be beholden.

CASH

It don't bother me none.

DEWEY DELL

I just know it won't work. I just know it won't.

VARDAMAN

We can sleep on the straw tonight with our legs in the moon. Jefferson is no longer a far place.

CASH

Ah—go easy. For the sake of Christ.

Now they speak directly to each other.

PEABODY

Go easy! (*Snorts*) Raw cement! Don't you lie there, Cash and try to tell me you rode six days on a wagon without springs with a broken leg and it never bothered you.

CASH

It never bothered me much.

PEABODY

Raw cement! You mean it never bothered Anse much. Don't tell me. And don't tell me it aint going to bother you to have to limp around on one short leg for the balance of your life—if you walk at all again. God Amighty, why didn't Anse carry you to the nearest sawmill and stick your leg in the saw? That would have cured it. Then you all could have stuck his head into the saw and cured a whole family . . . Well, now you've got her in the ground, where is Anse, anyhow, what's he up to now?

CASH

He's taking back them spades he borrowed.

PEABODY

Of course he'd have to borrow a spade to bury his wife with. Unless he could borrow a hole in the ground. Too bad you all didn't put him in it too . . .

DARL

Here comes Pa now.

VARDAMAN

Who's she coming with him? Who's she?

CASH

Looks like the woman he borrowed the spades of.

Sounds of footsteps fading in.

ANSE

Young uns, meet Mrs. Bundren.

PEABODY *as narrator*

And damned if he didn't have teeth too.

ACT I, SCENE 3

William's room. He is now 30, Alice is 24.

WILLIAM (*writing in his journal at table*)

She's gone. A part of myself was lowered into the grave with her today.
Minny—Minny Temple is dead. (*Rises with gesture of futility*) Death or
life—it's all one meaning. What about that part of me left here to fight
through this nothingness—the nothingness of this egotistical fury!
William James, what about it? All the years of study—introspection—
give it all up! Restrict myself to anatomy. What then?—count vertebrae
for the rest of my life? I read Biblical texts to console myself these days.
I *expect philosophy* to pull me out. Do I have the strength—the sheer
physical and mental strength—to develop a complete conception of
things? Because in the end if I want a philosophy with no humbug in it
I'll have to write it myself! (*Consults his watch*) Harry! I wish you'd get
here—the boat must have been late. I wonder if he'll know. It's so hard
to forget her *life*. Minny—Harry. His stories—his characters touch us
as she did—their orbits come out of space and lay themselves for a
short time alongside ours, then off they whirl again into the unknown.
After his year in England he'll come home healthier and happier—the
only one of father's children moving into something like mental
equilibrium. (*Alice is at the door, enters in a silent, reflective mood, stands*)
Eh . . . Alice!

ALICE

I've decided to stay.

WILLIAM

Little sister—

ALICE

It wasn't—*wrong*—of me to have considered—?

WILLIAM

Who can be considered educated who hasn't thought of—of ending one's life. But you'll stay here?

ALICE

Here with good mother and poor dear old good-for-nothing papa. (*Brightening*) While William is at hand being William and Harry is taking possession of London as Henry James, the novelist. Yes, I'll fight the Irish cause from here!

WILLIAM

That's my old Bottled Lightning speaking—(*The door is softly pushed open by Harry, overcoat on arm, hat on head and holding package and valise. Alice and William throw their arms about him and relieve him of his things.*)

WILLIAM

You know?

HARRY

Minny . . . (*now disengaged from his brother and sister*) It's the living who die and the writers who go on living.

ALICE

Minny's death marks the end of our youth.

Darkness

Notes and Contents Lists

Abbreviations

CC	Cid Corman
LN	Lorine Niedecker
LZ	Louis Zukofsky

BOOKS BY NIEDECKER

BC   *Blue Chicory*. A posthumous collection prepared by Cid Corman. New Rochelle, N.Y.: The Elizabeth Press, 1976.

MFT   *My Friend Tree*. Edinburgh: Wild Hawthorn Press, 1961.

MLBW   *My Life by Water: Collected Poems, 1936–1968*. London: Fulcrum Press, 1970.

NC   *North Central*. London: Fulcrum Press, 1968.

NG   *New Goose*. Prairie City, Ill.: Press of James A. Decker, 1946.

T&G   *T&G: The Collected Poems (1936–1966)*. Penland, N.C.: The Jargon Society, 1969.

COLLECTIONS OF NIEDECKER LETTERS

BYHM   *"Between Your House and Mine": The Letters of Lorine Niedecker to Cid Corman, 1960 to 1970*. Edited by Lisa Pater Faranda. Durham, N.C.: Duke University Press, 1986.

LN: W&P   *Lorine Niedecker: Woman & Poet*. Edited by Jenny Penberthy. Orono, Maine: National Poetry Foundation, 1996.

NCZ   *Niedecker and the Correspondence with Zukofsky, 1931–1970*. Edited by Jenny Penberthy. New York: Cambridge University Press, 1993.

NIEDECKER MANUSCRIPTS

MS   I use this abbreviation to refer to both her typed and holograph manuscripts.

EA   "THE EARTH AND ITS ATMOSPHERE." The 106-page typescript prepared by LN
          in June 1969 when Cid Corman offered to publish a book. She notes on the
          title page: "chosen by LN from main body of poems—to be called The
          Selected—"

FPOP   "FOR PAUL AND OTHER POEMS." Typescript dated December 1956.

H&SF   "HARPSICHORD & SALT FISH." Typescript prepared for publication by LN in
          1970. Published posthumously by Pig Press in Durham, U.K., 1991.

"NG"MS   "NEW GOOSE" typescript. Collection of short poems dated 1945.

VV   "THE VERY VEERY." The 24-page typescript prepared at the same time as
          "THE EARTH AND ITS ATMOSPHERE" in June 1969. LN notes on the title page:
          "Selected from The Selected."

The "HARPSICHORD & SALT FISH," "THE EARTH AND ITS ATMOSPHERE," and "THE VERY
VEERY" (H&SF, EA, VV) typescripts make up the Lorine Niedecker Collection at the
Boston University Library. Cid Corman's copy of "HOMEMADE POEMS" is in the Berg
Collection at the New York Public Library; Jonathan Williams's copy of "HANDMADE
POEMS" is part of his private collection. LN's own library plus assorted manuscripts and
papers constitute the Lorine Niedecker Collection in the Dwight Foster Public
Library in Fort Atkinson, Wisconsin. The privately held Roub Collection contains
manuscripts, papers, and an extensive collection of photographs. The remainder of
Niedecker's manuscripts and papers, including her posthumous bequest, is subsumed
within the Louis Zukofsky Collection in the Harry Ransom Humanities Research
Center (HRHRC) at the University of Texas at Austin. A typescript of Niedecker
poems is included in the Edward Dahlberg Collection, also at the HRHRC at the Uni-
versity of Texas at Austin.

Poems

1921–1922

LN graduated from Fort Atkinson High School in June 1922 at the age of nineteen. The following two poems appeared in the school yearbook, *The Tchogeerrah*. She told CC that "When I was 18, I bought a Wordsworth and took the book with me down here toward evening. I didn't quite know, yet I think I was vaguely aware that the poetry current (1921) was beginning to change" (*BYHM* 49). In Sept. 1922, she enrolled at Beloit College and stayed until 1923 when she was summoned home to care for her ailing mother.

Reminiscence [1921]

The light of day is growing dim,
And fires, the western skies illume,
From bays and creeks, the blackbirds call,
Oh, Canadian honker, we know 'tis fall.
On the edge of the river the muskrats build,
They're silently working while all else seems killed.
'Tis a sign that the winter'll be long and severe—
So runs the Indian prophecy drear.

The winds blow wild; all day 't has blown,
And grey and sere has Nature grown.
E'en now the light is fading fast
And my longing heart turns to the days that are past.
Oh, the cozy warm room that is waiting for me
With the books all mine and the comforts so free.
Turn backward, years that are flying along,
To-night all to youth does surely belong.

Oh, why is our life not always young?
In youth, our gayest songs are sung,
We wish for life and love and fame,
We care not for serving; ourselves our thoughts claim.
I did not realize the true way to go—
Just thought the ultimate good I'd know,
Only let me feel young and willing to work
I'd not grudge the failure, nor would I shirk.

I open a book, with light turned low,
Recall the friends of long ago—

Ah, here are Ruth and Joe and Bill!
And how care-free were Mary and Phil!
Then the class page with writings, "Good luck to you!"
But our dreams have reality known too soon;
Oh, Tchogeerrah,'tis now that my mind you have changed,
I will work out those plans so long arranged.

Wasted Energy [1922]

Refinement of speech is a thing that we preach
All in vain it would sometimes seem,
For this is the age when slang is the rage,
And vocabularies, a dream.

I used to make rhymes; now I hand people lines
(And they're boresome and foolish, no doubt),
But however folks feel—one thing is so real—
A great many "expire and pass out."

When Tom, Dick, and Phil are conversing,
The effect is entirely unique,
We can't quite make out what they're talking about
But we gather it's Sheba or Sheik.

I tell Tom of the quake that made Mexico shake,
"Well, ain't that the berries?" quotes he.
When describing a quail or a sunset or whale—
They're "wonderful!"—each of the three.

It's amazingly queer, but from all sides we hear
Of the "crooks" and "tough birds" in our town,
Of "wild women," of "guys," many "I wonder why's,"
"Juicy" tales and requests to "pipe down."

Any brains do you say? You may put them away
By this modernized method of talk.
An argument clinch? Say, "Oh, yes, that's a cinch,"
"Absolutely" is still better—less thought.

The American tongue is found lacking by some,
So they take a few words from afar.
But "Pas auf" and "trez bean" are as common,'twould seem,
As Uncle Joe Cannon's cigar.

1928–1936

LN married Frank Hartwig in Nov. 1928 and moved with him to Fort Atkinson where she worked as a library assistant at the Dwight Foster Public Library. She published a regular book review column, "Library Notes," in the *Jefferson County Union*. In 1930, after the Depression struck, she lost her job and her marriage, and returned to Black Hawk Island to live with her parents. Reading the Objectivist issue of *Poetry* in Feb. 1931 led to her lifelong correspondence with LZ. He introduced her to avant-garde magazines such as Eugene Jolas's *transition*, which encouraged her to pursue the surrealist tendencies already visible in her writing. LN visited LZ in New York during this period, meeting Jerry Reisman, George and Mary Oppen, Charles Reznikoff, and others. LZ and Jerry Reisman visited her on Black Hawk Island in Sept. 1936.

LN excluded from her published books all writing from this period. However, the following works have survived in MS and in magazines. During this period, her experimentation in other genres was part of her larger poetic project. See "UNCLE" (in the final section of prose and radio plays).

Transition   **Unpublished in book form.**

The Will-o-the-Wisp; a Magazine of Verse 3 (1928): 12.

Mourning Dove   **Unpublished in book form.**

Parnassus: A Wee Magazine of Verse 2.2 (15 Nov. 1928): 4.

SPIRALS   **Unpublished in book form.**

Promise of Brilliant Funeral   Submitted on Jan. 31, 1933, and published in *Poetry* 42.6 (Sept. 1933): 308, as the first of a pair of poems. The second in the pair is the earlier submission, *"When Ecstasy is Inconvenient."* LN rejected "SOMNAMBULISTIC JOURNEY" as an alternative title for the two poems. A letter to Harriet Monroe dated Aug. 5, 1933, revises the final line of the second stanza from "had" to "seen."

When Ecstasy is Inconvenient   Submitted on Nov. 5, 1931, and published in *Poetry* 42.6 (Sept. 1933): 309, paired with *"Promise of Brilliant Funeral,"* both under the title "SPIRALS."

Also in *Poetry Out of Wisconsin*, eds. August Derleth and Raymond E. F. Larsson (New York: Henry Harrison, 1937) 198.

PROGRESSION   **Unpublished.**

An earlier shorter version, now lost, went to *Poetry* on Jan. 31, 1933. The accompanying letter to Harriet Monroe notes that the poem "was written six months before Mr. Zukofsky referred me to the surrealists for correlation." She explains that "poetry to have greatest reason for existing must be illogical. An idea, a rumination such as more or less constantly roams the mind, meets external object or situation with quite illogical association. Memory, if made up of objects at all, retains those objects which were at the time of first perception and still are the most strikingly unrecognizable. In my own experience sentences have appeared full-blown in the first moments of waking from sleep. It is a system of thought replacements, the most remote the most significant or irrational; a thousand variations of the basic tension; an attempt at not hard clear images but absorption of these. Intelligibility or readers' recognition of sincerity and force lies in a sense of basic color, sound, rhythm" (*LN:W&P* 177–78).

The present text is a later version of the poem sent to Ezra Pound on Jan. 6, 1934, and unknown until 1995 when it was found by Burton Hatlen in the Ezra Pound Papers at the Beinecke Library, Yale University.

Canvass; For exhibition; Tea   Unpublished in book form.

Submitted unsuccessfully to *Poetry* on Feb. 12, 1934. See next note.

Beyond what; I heard; Memorial Day   Unpublished in book form.

Submitted unsuccessfully to *Poetry* on May 31, 1934.

All six poems, which LN described as "experiment[s] in planes of consciousness," were published in *Bozart-Westminster* (Spring/Summer 1935): 26–27. Her intention was for each group of three poems to be printed side by side on a double-page spread. In a Feb. 12, 1934, letter to Harriet Monroe, she refers to the *"Canvass"* trilogy as "[a]n experiment in three planes: left row is deep subconscious, middle row beginning of monologue, and right row surface consciousness, social banal; experiment in vertical simultaneity (symphonic rather than traditional long line melodic form), and the whole written with the idea of readers finding sequence for themselves, finding their own meaning whatever that may be, as spectators before abstract painting. Left vertical row honest recording of constrictions appearing before falling off to sleep at night. I should like a poem to be seen as well as read. Colors and textures of certain words appearing simultaneously with the sound of words and printed directly above or below each other. All this means break-up of sentence which I deplore though I try to retain the great conceit of capitals and periods, of something to say. It means that for me at least, certain words of a sentence—prepositions, connectives, pronouns—belong up toward full consciousness, while strange and unused words appear only in subconscious. (It also means that for me at least this procedure is directly opposite to that of the consistent and prolonged dream—in dream the simple and familiar words like prepositions, connectives, etc . . . are not absent, in fact, noticeably present to show illogical absurdity, discontinuity, parody of sanity)" (*LN:W&P* 181–82).

Stage Directions   Unpublished in book form.

MS dated Aug. 1934.
Bozart-Westminster (Spring/Summer 1935): 27.

Synamism   Unpublished.

Undated MS on which LN notes: "Finish of Sub-entries at least for the present. Stage Directions is the 'theatre'?" *"Stage Directions"* and *"Synamism"* may well have been parts of a larger work called "SUB-ENTRIES."

Will You Write Me a Christmas Poem?   **Unpublished.**
The otherwise undated MS bears the following note: "Reworking of poem by Lorine Niedecker, L.Z.—Xmas 1934." LZ's revisions to the MS:

> stanza 3, line 2: in the damp development of winter
>
> stanza 9, line 4: And where are we?
>
> stanza 11, line 5 is deleted.
>
> stanza 12, line 1: The Christian cacophony
>
> The present text does not reflect LZ's "re-working."

NEXT YEAR OR I FLY MY ROUNDS TEMPESTUOUS   **Unpublished.**
Dated by LZ "Xmas 1934" (found by the editor in the LZ Collection, HRHRC, Austin, Texas in 1996). Handwritten on small pieces of paper pasted over the printed text of a bi-weekly calendar, 27 sheets long; each sheet is 5 $^1/_2$ × 4 $^3/_8$ inches. The calendar's original text is only just legible bearing platitudes such as "True bravery is / shown by performing / without witness what / one might be capable / of doing before all the / world"(Jan. 13–26).

DOMESTIC AND UNAVOIDABLE   **Unpublished in book form.**
Undated MS.
Published—with minor revisions to the stage or camera directions—in *Bozart-Westminster* (Spring/Summer 1935): 27–28. These revisions may have been made by Jerry Reisman. Early in 1935, LZ had sent Pound a copy of Reisman's short scenario of LN's "DOMESTIC AND UNAVOIDABLE." Many years later, Reisman recalled, "Actually I did nothing to LN's play. I simply added instructions for a cameraman. Lorine's plays struck me as being conceived for the screen rather than the stage" (letter to editor, April 5, 1989).
The present text is drawn from *Bozart-Westminster*.

THE PRESIDENT OF THE HOLDING COMPANY and FANCY ANOTHER DAY GONE
Unpublished in book form.
Published together and titled "TWO POEMS" in *New Democracy* (May 1936): 60–62, in a section called "New Directions" edited by James Laughlin.
Published together in *New Directions* 1 (1936): n.p.
No MSS or printer's typescripts survive. In both appearances of "FANCY . . ." the first two speakers are "HE". I take this to be a printing error and change the first speaker to "SHE".

News   **Unpublished.**
Undated MS. Speculatively dated early 1936: lines 64–65 "over and down Payroll Hill / fashions mornings after" are adapted in "My coat threadbare" (see p. 95) published in 1936.
MS annotations are addressed to Zukofsky: "I first had as first line *Your* wit, the lover said. Maybe *To Wit:* shd be title and leave out the lover said since I'm no longer

in depression [] (Zu)" And referring to the last line or lines, she says, "might leave out but (. . .) feeling of wings, wingjabs."

1936–1945

This is the period of LN's folk project. Of the total 88 folk poems, 70 were grouped in two collections—41 in the published volume *New Goose* (Prairie City, Ill.: The Press of James A. Decker, 1946) and 29 in the unpublished manuscript also titled "NEW GOOSE." The two collections are preceded here by 16 uncollected poems which appeared in two earlier overlapping sequences: a 13-poem undated "MOTHER GOOSE" MS, very likely one that LN submitted unsuccessfully to *Poetry* on Feb. 25, 1936, and a 17-poem "MOTHER GEESE" selection published in *New Directions* 1 (1936): n.p.

These 16 poems do not yet register the local speech habits or the local history that enter her work once she starts research for the WPA's Wisconsin state guide in 1938.

O let's glee glow as we go   Unpublished in book form.
In the 13-poem "MOTHER GOOSE" MS probably sent to *Poetry* on Feb. 25, 1936.
In the 17-poem group, "MOTHER GEESE," *New Directions* 1 (1936): n.p.

Troubles to win   Unpublished in book form.
In the 13-poem "MOTHER GOOSE" MS probably sent to *Poetry* on Feb. 25, 1936.

A country's economics sick   Unpublished in book form.
In the 13-poem "MOTHER GOOSE" MS probably sent to *Poetry* on Feb. 25, 1936.

***Lady in the Leopard Coat*   Unpublished in book form.**
In the 13-poem "MOTHER GOOSE" MS probably sent to *Poetry* on Feb. 25, 1936.
In the 17-poem group, "MOTHER GEESE," *New Directions* 1 (1936): n.p.

Jim Poor's his name   Unpublished in book form.
In the 13-poem "MOTHER GOOSE" MS probably sent to *Poetry* on Feb. 25, 1936.

Scuttle up the workshop,   Unpublished in book form.
In the 13-poem "MOTHER GOOSE" MS probably sent to *Poetry* on Feb. 25, 1936.
In the 17-poem group, "MOTHER GEESE," *New Directions* 1 (1936): n.p.

There was a bridge once that said I'm going   Unpublished in book form.
In the 13-poem "MOTHER GOOSE" MS probably sent to *Poetry* on Feb. 25, 1936.

When do we live again Ann,   Unpublished in book form.
In the 13-poem "MOTHER GOOSE" MS probably sent to *Poetry* on Feb. 25, 1936.

Missus Dorra   Unpublished in book form.
In the 13-poem "MOTHER GOOSE" MS probably sent to *Poetry* on Feb. 25, 1936.
In the 17-poem group, "MOTHER GEESE," *New Directions* 1 (1936): n.p.

No retiring summer stroke   Unpublished in book form.
In the 13-poem "MOTHER GOOSE" MS probably sent to *Poetry* on Feb. 25, 1936.

To war they kept   Unpublished in book form.
In the 17-poem group, "MOTHER GEESE," *New Directions* 1 (1936): n.p.

Petrou his name was sorrow   Unpublished in book form.
In the 17-poem group, "MOTHER GEESE," *New Directions* 1 (1936): n.p.

The eleventh of progressional   Unpublished in book form.
In the 17-poem group, "MOTHER GEESE," *New Directions* 1 (1936): n.p.

Young girl to marry,   Unpublished in book form.
In the 17-poem group, "MOTHER GEESE," *New Directions* 1 (1936): n.p.

I spent my money   Unpublished in book form.
In the 17-poem group, "MOTHER GEESE," *New Directions* 1 (1936): n.p.

Trees over the roof   Unpublished in book form.
In the 17-poem group, "MOTHER GEESE," *New Directions* 1 (1936): n.p.

NEW GOOSE

The completed typescript of *New Goose* went to the Press of James A. Decker in Sept. 1944, and was published in March 1946, a small book $4^{1/2} \times 6$ inches.

Don't shoot the rail!   *NG, MFT, T&G, MLBW* [EA].
MFT variant line 4: he is falling asleep.

Bombings   NG, T&G, MLBW.

Hop press   NG.

Ash woods, willow, close to shore,   *NG, T&G, MLBW* [EA].
NG variant line 7: the wornout roof hanging there
LN regretted that this poem was excluded from *MFT*.
EA variant line 1: Ash woods, willows close to shore
An undated letter (probably late 1930s) from LZ to LN letter finds signs of Thomas Hardy in the poem, especially in the inversions of speech for rhyme. He praises the movement of the poem, particularly "now twitter."

The music, lady,   *NG*.
Titled *"Fascist Festival"* in the 13-poem "MOTHER GOOSE" MS (probably sent to *Poetry* on Feb. 25, 1936) and in the 17-poem group, "MOTHER GEESE," *New Directions* 1 (1936): n.p.

For sun and moon and radio   *NG*.
In the 17-poem group, "MOTHER GEESE," *New Directions* 1 (1936): n.p., as a two-stanza poem, beginning with the following stanza:

> In speaking spokes the mighty
> come down from welding wires
> to light up the farmers
> with electricity.

She had tumult of the brain   *NG, T&G, MLBW* [EA, VV].
In the 13-poem "MOTHER GOOSE" MS probably sent to *Poetry* on Feb. 25, 1936. In the 17-poem group, "MOTHER GEESE," *New Directions* 1 (1936): n.p.

My coat threadbare   *NG, T&G, MLBW.*
In the 17-poem group, "MOTHER GEESE," *New Directions* 1 (1936): n.p. Possibly derived from the longer, unpublished, undated poem *"News,"* speculatively dated 1936 (see p. 79). The spelling "Capital" occurs in all appearances of the poem.

Mr. Van Ess bought 14 washcloths?   *NG, T&G, MLBW.*
In *NG* the "14" of line 1 is "fourteen" and "church" of line 4 is "Methodist Church".
Revised to the present text for *T&G* and *Origin* ser. 3, 2 (July 1966): 5.

Not feeling well, my wood uncut.   *NG, MFT, T&G, MLBW* [EA].

Remember my little granite pail?   *NG, MFT, T&G, MLBW* [EA].
In *NG* and *MFT* line 3 ends with an exclamation point.

A lawnmower's one of the babies I'd have   *NG.*

My man says the wind blows from the south,   *NG, MFT, T&G, MLBW* [EA, VV].
An undated letter from LZ to LN has high praise for this poem, seeing it as quintessential Niedecker.

Du Bay   *NG.*

I'm a sharecropper   *NG, MFT, T&G, MLBW.*

Here it gives the laws for fishing thru the ice—   *NG.*

On Columbus Day he set out for the north   *NG.*

Black Hawk held: In reason   *NG, MFT, T&G, MLBW* [EA].
LN's notes on *Life of Black Hawk* edited by J. B. Patterson are dated May 28, 1941 (HRHRC).

We know him—Law and Order League—   *NG, T&G, MLBW.*
In *Furioso: A Magazine of Verse* 1.1 (Summer 1939): 5, with "A working man appeared in the street," under the title of "TWO POEMS FROM 'NEW GOOSE.'"
An undated letter from LZ to LN reports that his friends are crazy about this poem.

The clothesline post is set   *NG, MFT, T&G, MLBW* [EA].

I said to my head, Write something.   *NG.*

Grampa's got his old age pension,   *NG, T&G, MLBW.*
NG omits dollar sign in line 2.
LN ignores LZ's suggested revision of the final line: you can have everything I got.

There's a better shine   *NG, MFT, T&G, MLBW* [EA].
In the 13-poem "MOTHER GOOSE" MS (probably sent to *Poetry* on Feb. 25, 1936)

and in the 17-poem group, "MOTHER GEESE," *New Directions* 1 (1936) n.p., the poem has a variant line 4: and many's the time.

Revised to the present text for LZ's *A Test of Poetry* (New York: Objectivist Press, 1948).

MLBW uses only three bullets between lines 4 and 5; the present text adopts the four used in all other appearances.

The museum man!   *NG, T&G, MLBW* [EA].

Line 2 in *MLBW*: I wish he'd take Pa's spitbox!

The present text adopts the line 2 used in all other appearances including *Origin* ser. 3, 2 (July 1966): 5.

An undated letter from LZ to LN notes that she's right to spend half her time copying and editing her mother's statements. He says that the spitbox lines make a perfect poem and he envies the gold mine of poetry that LN has available to her.

LN to Ron Ellis in 1966 refers to this poem: "My mother who was a kind of Mother Goose, straight out of the people etc. told me this just as it is. You see at this time—1930s—there was this rage to get poetry into direct, simple speech . . ." (*LN:W&P* 94).

That woman!—eyeing houses.   *NG, T&G, MLBW* [EA].

Hand Crocheted Rug   *NG.*

They came at a pace   *NG.*

I doubt I'll get silk stockings out   *NG.*

To see the man who took care of our stock   *NG, T&G, MLBW* [EA].

NG line 2: As we slept in the dark, blackbirds flying

Revised to the present text for *T&G* and *Origin* ser. 3, 2 (July 1966): 6.

Letter to Ron Ellis in 1966 refers to this poem: "This one not understood by most—it was a depression poem and those years were not over yet when I made my 1st visit to NY whose streets frightened me as much as not having money" (*LN:W&P* 95).

A monster owl   *NG.*

An early version can be reconstructed from LZ's letter to LN, March 9, 1938:

> A monster owl
> out on the fence
> flew away. Now
> what's it the sign
> of. The sign of
> an owl I guess.

LN adopts LZ's revisions for *NG*.

Gen. Rodimstev's story / (Stalingrad)   *NG, T&G, MLBW.*

Birds' mating-fight   *NG, MLBW.*

From my bed I see   *NG.*

Asa Gray wrote Increase Lapham: *NG, T&G, MLBW.*

According to LN's letter to LZ, July 11, 1961, she planned to use the following revision for *MFT:*

> Great grass! The shoots Michaux
> brought back to Philadelphia
> by way of Bartram and known to Linné
> bear Jefferson's name.

> Asa Gray wrote Increase Lapham:
> pay particular attention
> to my pets, the grasses—
> on these lie fame.

In fact, the poem was not included in *MFT,* and the above version was never published. *Origin* ser. 3, 2 (July 1966): 6.

Pioneers   *NG, T&G, MLBW* **[EA].**

In *NG* and *T&G,* the two halves of the poem are divided by three bullets.
Excerpted in EA: Between fighting . . . swayed back and forth from food-lack. ("Food-lack" is an EA revision of "lack of food.")

Well, spring overflows the land,   *NG, MFT, T&G, MLBW* **[EA].**

Audubon   *NG, T&G, MLBW.*

The present text uses the line 5 of *NG, T&G,* and *Origin* ser. 3, 2 (July 1966): 4.
MLBW variant line 5: with fear

van Gogh   *NG, T&G, MLBW* **[EA].**

NG variant line 1: I have at times to sit in the dunes
Revised to the present text for *Origin* ser. 3, 2 (July 1966): 4.

What a woman!—hooks men like rugs,   *NG.*

The brown muskrat, noiseless,   *NG.*

The broad-leaved Arrow-head   *NG.*

"NEW GOOSE" MANUSCRIPT

The 29-poem typescript, dated 1945 (although the opening letter/poem is dated 1943), remained unpublished in LN's lifetime.

To a Maryland editor, 1943:   **Unpublished.**

MacCloud is Norman MacCleod, who in 1943 ran the Creative Writing Department at the University of Maryland and edited the *Maryland Quarterly* (first issue 1944).

Summer's away, I traded my chicks for trees   Unpublished.
An undated letter from LZ to LN has high praise for this poem. He cautions her not to change anything saying there's no need to embellish a poem so instinctively right.

She was a mourner too. Now she's gone   Unpublished.

Seven years a charming woman wore   Unpublished.

The land of four o'clocks is here   Unpublished in book form.
In the 17-poem group, "MOTHER GEESE," *New Directions* 1 (1936): n.p.

Just before she died   Unpublished.
An undated letter from LZ to LN comments on the originality of the poem's movement, which he finds to be close to William Blake's "Chimney Sweep."

Brought the enemy down   *T&G, MLBW.*
Origin ser. 3, 2 (July 1966): 8.

Nothing nourishing,   Unpublished.

The number of Britons killed   Unpublished.

Old Hamilton hailed the man from the grocery store: Unpublished.

Motor cars   Unpublished in book form.
The present text is a revision of an earlier version in the 17-poem group, "MOTHER GEESE," *New Directions* 1 (1936): n.p. Here is the variant second stanza of the earlier version:

> Will the sugar bowl
> of taffy color
> > speeding
> stop to eat people?

Allied Convoy / Reaches Russia   Unpublished.

Depression years   *T&G, MLBW* [FPOP].
The "NG" MS version is untitled with variant lines 2–3: I was certified, / then for weeks I raked leaves
Revised to the present text for FPOP (see p. 165) with a variant title, *"Depression ballad."*
In *Origin* ser. 3, 2 (July 1966): 8, the title changes to *"Depression years."*

Coopered at Fish Creek,   Unpublished.

A working man appeared in the street   Unpublished in book form.
In *Furioso: A Magazine of Verse* 1.1 (Summer 1939): 5, with "We know him—Law and Order League—" under the title "TWO POEMS FROM 'NEW GOOSE.'"

Woman with Umbrella   Unpublished in book form.
Accent 13.2 (Spring 1953): 96.

Automobile Accident   Unpublished.

Look, the woods, the sky, our home.   Unpublished.

Coming out of Sleep   Unpublished.

Voyageurs   Unpublished.

I walked / from Chicago to Big Bull Falls (Wausau),   Unpublished.

See the girls in shorts on their bicycles   Unpublished.
   An earlier draft version has a variant line 1: These girls ride their bicycles in shorts

When Johnny (Chapman) Appleseed   Unpublished.

Tell me a story about the war.   *NG, MLBW* [FPOP].
   The "NG" MS version is substantially different, reflecting its Mother Goose folk context:

>   The Marshal of France made a speech,
>   told the people they were hungry.
>   The psychologist said: reach a porterhouse steak—
>   place your ounce of beef on a doll's plate.
>   The Bishop beseeched the people to sleep.

   Revised to the present text for FPOP (see p. 144).

Poet Percival said: I struck a lode   Unpublished.

Terrible things coming up,   Unpublished.

1937   Unpublished [FPOP].
   Untitled in "NG" MS. Revised to the present text for FPOP (p. 164).

Their apples fall down   Unpublished.

The government men said Don't plant wheat,   Unpublished.

1945–1956

Very little poetry survives from the years 1945 to 1948. In May 1944, LN had begun work as a stenographer and proofreader for Hoard's, the Fort Atkinson printer of the prominent regional journal *Hoard's Dairyman*, and the job and her home life with aging parents claimed all her time. She did recover some independence with her 1946 move from her parents' home to her own newly built one-room cottage.

   Many of these poems predate the "FOR PAUL" project. Others were written "FOR PAUL" groups 1–8 but were not included in FPOP.

New!   Unpublished.
   MS dated Nov. 22, 1945.

(L.Z.)   Unpublished.
   MS dated 1945.

Chimney Sweep   **Unpublished in book form.**
  MS dated Jan. 1948.
  Golden Goose 1 (Summer 1948): 29.

Swept snow, Li Po,   *T&G, MLBW.*
  Two drafts on a single MS page dated Jan. 1948; draft (i) follows:

Home

  Swept snow, Li Po,
  by dawn's 40-watt moon
  to the road that flies
  to black office
  away from home.

  Tended my little oil-burning
  stove as one would a cow—
  she gave heat—till spring.
  River-marsh-frog-clatter—
  peace breaks out—

  no fact is isolate—
  grasses, heron, China,
  days of light:
  Saturday,
  Sunday.

Draft (ii) revises draft (i) as follows:
  line 1: Swept my snow, Li Po,
  line 9: Now river-marsh-frog-clatter—
  line 12: grasses, heron, China, three
  lines 14–15:

  Saturday, Sunday,
  memory.

A third version appeared in *New Mexico Quarterly* 20.2 (Summer 1950): 209:

  Swept snow, Li Po,
  by dawn's 40-watt moon
  to the road that hies to office
  away from home.

  Tended my brown little oil-burning stove
  as one would a cow—she gives heat.

> Spring—marsh frog clatter
>   peace breaks out
> No fact is isolate
> Grasses, heron, China,
> light:
> Saturday, Sunday.

In the *New Mexico Quarterly*, the above is number "II" of "TWO POEMS"—"I" is an untitled version of *"Wartime"* (see p. 172).

Regards to Mr. Glover   Unpublished.

MS dated June 10, 1948.

LN letter to LZ, May 23, 1948: "by the way I had begun something embodying the conversation with Glover, so when you write 'Regards to Glover'—jiggers, there's my title. [] and now when I see the second line of God LL.D: 'Only sometimes does one feel that intimate'—Zu could I use it and quote it?" (*NCZ* 147).

Sunday's motor-cars   Unpublished in book form.

Undated MS, breaks line 6 in two after "waking".

In "THREE POEMS," *New Directions* 11 (1949): 303, with "I rose from marsh mud" and "Don't tell me property is sacred."

Let's play a game.   Unpublished in book form.

Poem XI in "FOR PAUL: GROUP TWO" MS dated Dec. 14, 1950, adds two lines between the present lines 10 and 11:

>   Trees and stars?
>   Of course, if they console you.

variant line 14: one constellation is:

LN's annotation: "(constellation simply a child's mispronunciation of consolation—you didn't get that? Believe I'd like 'Trees and stars? Of course, if they console you' taken out. Those were the additions. You understand Diddy [Paul] is the speaker on the right side??)"

LN adopts LZ's suggested "console-ation" in line 14.

Revised to the present text on an undated MS and published in "FOR PAUL: GROUP TWO," *New Mexico Quarterly* 21.1 (Spring 1951): 207.

Lugubre for a child   Unpublished in book form.

This poem overlaps with and replaces the earlier "You have power politics, Paul" (MS dated Dec. 14, 1950):

> You have power politics, Paul,
> You have "I'll call you, I'll call—"
> which Indians did aptly

and more—in the forest an Indian girl,
her washing spread out on a rock,
let a song fall.

You now see man hide behind
his ribs' loose grates, his kind
eye closed, the other one screwing
the savage sprays
of our steel woods' life-everlasting,
a filing refined.

But wait! In still wilder states
he'll be Needle That Clicks. Rays
will cause counters to sing
counter to sense
and man, the weapon, must obsolesce
as he radiates.

LN to LZ, Dec. 30, 1950: "I figure the Lugubre for a child to take the place of the somewhat crazy You have power politics, Paul. Ah, how does it sound? [ ]" (*NCZ* 171).

The first draft of "Lugubre for a child" is poem XV in the "FOR PAUL: GROUP TWO" MS (undated, possibly Dec. 30, 1950):

variant line 6: Some flowers have pistons,
variant line 16: Dear fiddler: how'll you carry
variant lines 19–20: stinging rays/on little whirring things?

LN offers an alternative to line 19 ("rays," deleting "stinging") and also alternative lines 18–20:

> counter to sense
>   in the presence
> of man's stings?

On the MS, LZ suggests a revision of line 6: "Watch! in some flowers".

Revised for poem XV of "FOR PAUL: GROUP TWO," *New Mexico Quarterly* 21.1 (Spring 1951): 209, where line 6 reflects LZ's revision and lines 19–20 become those of the present edition: rays/on small whirring things

In "Changes in FOR PAUL" (Jan. 29, 1955), LN revises line 16 ("Dear Fiddler: How'll you carry") to the present line 16 and deletes a question mark at the end of the stanza. At this date the poem was still part of the "FOR PAUL" project.

Could You Be Right **Unpublished in book form.**

Untitled on MS dated Jan. 4, 1951.

variant line 5: But think of Troy, we had the word

MS dated Jan. 16, 1951, adopts LZ's revision of line 5 ("But think of Troy, it was a word") and revises lines 7–8 as follows:

so go up in a kite.
Still, could she be right?

Accent 13.2 (Spring 1953): 97, adds the title and reverts to the earlier lines 7–8 reflected in the present text. She ignores LZ's suggestion to drop "yet" in line 7.

This poem arises out of LN's debate with LZ over her use of the word "obsolesce" in "You have power politics, Paul" (see pp. 380–81).

Look close   Unpublished.
MS dated Feb. 27, 1951.

***If I were a bird*   Unpublished.**
Undated MS. LZ notes alternative title on MS: "Tally of Contemporaries" and also his suggested deletions from stanza 5—line 12: the depths; line 13: and; line 14: cut sky

LN to LZ letter, March 15, 1951: "Yes, I'll use If I were a bird sometime in FOR PAUL" (*NCZ* 178).

High, lovely, light,   Unpublished.
A draft version dated March 30, 1951, titled in LN holograph as "Rondel" with variant lines 5–7:

> You at your mountain-height—
> your cello plied with Easter
> bow lovely, light—

and variant lines 11–12:

> sleep? In what season
> timed, tuned, tight,

LZ's suggested changes: line 4 deletes "down"; line 11 revises "In" to "To"; line 12 revises "tight" to "bright".

Revised close to the present text for poem I of "FOR PAUL: GROUP III" MS dated Sept. 27, 1951, with a variant line 6: your cello and bow for Easter—

"Changes in FOR PAUL" (Jan. 29, 1955) alters line 6 to the present "your cello and bow in Easter's".

***Letter from Paul*   Unpublished.**
MS dated Sept. 27, 1951.
Poem V of "FOR PAUL: GROUP FOUR" MS (undated, probably 1951).

Two old men—   *T&G, MLBW.*
Poem IV of "FOR PAUL: GROUP FOUR" MS (undated, probably 1951).
"Changes in FOR PAUL" (Jan. 29, 1955) omits the poem.
Origin ser. 3, 2 (July 1966): 9.
LN to LZ, July 31, 1951: "Ladwig—yes, an old friend of my father's. . . . A priceless thing Walter Ladwig said when he was here the last time: 'I had an old friend

in Milwaukee who wanted come and live with me—we'd take turns cooking and washing dishes, he said, we're both alone, it would work out—I said "But our way of living is so different, you spit, I don't spit" and that very night he killed himself—and left $100,000.' Perfect?" (*NCZ* 182).

Paul, hello   Unpublished.

Poem V of "FOR PAUL: GROUP FOUR" MS (undated, probably 1951).

"Changes in FOR PAUL" (Jan. 29, 1955) moves this poem to the "very end." At this date the poem is still part of "FOR PAUL."

So this was I   Unpublished in book form.

MS dated Nov. 1951.

Titled "Poem" in *Accent* 13.2 (Spring 1953): 96.

Am I real way out in space   Unpublished.

Poem V of "FOR PAUL: GROUP SIX" MS, dated Oct. 22, 1952.

"Changes in FOR PAUL" (Jan. 29, 1955) omits the poem.

On a row of cabins / next my home   Unpublished.

Undated MS.

Part of "FOR PAUL: GROUP SEVEN" MS (undated, probably 1952/3).

In moonlight lies   Unpublished.

Poem III of "FOR PAUL: GROUP 8" MS, dated Dec. 31, 1953.

"Changes in FOR PAUL" (Jan. 29, 1955) omits the poem.

The cabin door flew open   Unpublished.

An alternative poem IV of "FOR PAUL: GROUP 8" MS (undated). LN offers a variant "generally happy" for line 12.

The elegant office girl   Unpublished.

Poem VII of "FOR PAUL: GROUP 8" MS (undated).

The first two stanzas are inserted into the second (Aug. 30, 1955) and third (1956) versions of the five-page "Dear Paul," cited in full in the note to the condensed version printed in this edition (see pp. 395–401).

When brown folk lived a distance   Unpublished.

Sent to Dahlberg Aug. 30, 1955, for his proposed anthology.

FOR PAUL AND OTHER POEMS

In 1947, LN visited the Zukofskys in New York. Already she had been taking great delight in LZ's written accounts of his young son, Paul, born in 1943. In 1949 she began her "FOR PAUL" project and, with her resignation from Hoard's in June 1950 due to her deteriorating eyesight, she would work on the poems unimpeded.

Many of the poems are addressed directly to Paul, some quote LZ's letters to her, others refer to her life on Black Hawk Island and to her family—her mother and father died in the course of the project, her mother in July 1951 and her father in June 1954.

The "FOR PAUL" project began with the composition of numbered poems gathered into eight groups. The first group was published under the title of "FOR PAUL" in *New Directions* 12 (1950): 181–85, and the second group under the title of "FOR PAUL: GROUP TWO" in the *New Mexico Quarterly* 21.1 (Spring 1951): 206–11. She wrote the eight groups steadily between 1949 and 1953. The surviving MSS for groups 6–8 appear to be incomplete. At some point after 1953, LN abandoned the grouped structure, and between 1955 and 1956 arranged the poems in a collection named "FOR PAUL and Other Poems" (FPOP). A typescript titled "Changes in FOR PAUL" (Jan. 29, 1955) lists ongoing revisions. The FPOP MS (Dec. 1956) divides the poems into two sections: "FOR PAUL" (43 poems) and "OTHER POEMS" (29 poems). The texts of eight of the poems carry LZ's suggested deletions, many of which LN adopted. His deletions generally remove direct references to Paul. FPOP was never published despite her efforts to find a publisher. She reduced the collection to 41 poems for a book that Jonathan Williams considered publishing. By the early 1960s, having given up hope of publishing it in book form, she dismantled the collection and published most of its contents in magazines.

FOR PAUL

Paul   *T&G, MLBW* [**FPOP**].

Poem I of "FOR PAUL" MS, dated Nov. 20, 1949. In the MS, in poem I of "FOR PAUL," *New Directions* 12 (1950): 181, in FPOP, and in *T&G*, line 1 reads "Dear Paul".

What bird would light   *T&G, MLBW* [**FPOP**].

Poem II of "FOR PAUL" MS, dated Nov. 20, 1949 and poem II of "FOR PAUL," *New Directions* 12 (1950): 181.

Nearly landless and on the way to water   *T&G, MLBW* [**FPOP**].

Poem III of "FOR PAUL" MS, dated Nov. 20, 1949, poem III of "FOR PAUL," *New Directions* 12 (1950): 181–82, and FPOP, all include the following variants:

stanza 1 adds lines 6–7:

> who'd asked the carpenter, "Homer,
> did you write that book?"

stanza 2 adds 3 words to the start of line 1: Yes, Paul dear, Homer's . . .

stanza 2 also adds a line 7: People like us, child, see through it.

LN's note on the 1949 MS: "Notice alternative on other side of page. Tell me which lines to keep. I like yr. suggestion 1st stanza but the child belongs to my present view not to the one I lost and yet I like the surrealism—saw and see both. Last stanza—I didn't like *in* in each of first 3 lines so do you like the change?"

On FPOP, LZ suggests the omission of the variant words and lines noted above. LN adopts his revisions.

Understand me, dead is nothing   Unpublished in book form [FPOP].

Poem IV of "FOR PAUL" MS, dated Aug. 21, 1950, and poem IV of "FOR PAUL," *New Directions* 12 (1950): 182–83. On FPOP, LZ suggests that LN omit the poem.

How bright you'll find young people,   *T&G, MLBW* [FPOP].

Poem V of "FOR PAUL" MS, dated Aug. 21, 1950. LN's annotation refers to the final rhyming word of the poem: "I like this but do you think reader remembers Diddle [Paul] all that long?"

Poem V of "FOR PAUL," *New Directions* 12 (1950): 183.

The spelling of "Einsteind" is consistent in all appearances.

If he is of constant depth   *T&G, MLBW* [FPOP].

Poem VI of "FOR PAUL" MS, dated Aug. 21, 1950, poem VI of "FOR PAUL," *New Directions* 12 (1950): 183, and FPOP, all include variant lines 3–4:

> numbers plus the good in em—
> all the technique by the time he's twelve

The young ones go away to school   *MFT, T&G, MLBW* [FPOP].

An early MS dated March 1, 1950:

> The young ones go away to school
> come home to moon
>
> like Frederick the Great
> what was it he ate
> that had to be sown in the dark of the moon?
>
> Looking for rain?
> Wait for the moon to change
>
> But Edwin—Edwin's glorious—
> runs all over his acres without a hat
> as though he knew
> > the moon
> changes every day

LN offers a variant final word: noon

A revised MS—poem VII of the "FOR PAUL" MS, dated Aug. 21, 1950—and poem VII of "FOR PAUL," *New Directions* 12 (1950): 183–84, have one variant, for line 8: how people run their acres without a hat

Revised to the present text for FPOP.

In "EIGHT POEMS," *Monks Pond* 1 (Spring 1968): 7.

Some have chimes   *T&G, MLBW* [FPOP, EA].

Poem VIII of "FOR PAUL" MS, dated Aug. 21, 1950, poem VIII of "FOR PAUL," in *New Directions* 12 (1950): 184, and in "THREE POEMS," *Granta* 71.12456 (1964/5): 19.

O Tannenbaum   *T&G, MLBW* [FPOP].

Poem IX of "FOR PAUL" MS, dated Aug. 21, 1950, and of "FOR PAUL," *New Directions* 12 (1950): 184–85, begins with the following companion poem:

> You are far away
> sweet reason
>
> Since I saw you last, Paul,
> my sight is weaker . . .
>
> I still see—
> it's the facts are thick—
> thru glass:
> a peace scare on Wall St.

Poem IX of "FOR PAUL" MS, dated Aug. 21, 1950, continues with:

> O Tannenbaum they sing
> round and round
> one child sings out:
> atomic bomb
>
> not all suckling
> where Paul is
> and check-writing
> but as the queen, Elizabeth,
>
> . . . . . .

In *New Directions* and FPOP lines 1–2 above are revised to the following three:

> O Tannenbaum
> the children seem to sing
> round and round

FPOP omits the companion poem "You are far away."

For subsequent appearances, LN adopts LZ's suggested omissions from lines 1–3 and 6–8 noted on FPOP.

In the great snowfall before the bomb   *T&G, MLBW* [FPOP].

Poem XIV of "FOR PAUL: Group Two" MS, dated Dec. 30, 1950.
variant stanza 1, lines 3–5:

> at windows,
> the only glow of contemplation
> in our time

LN offers a variant ending to this stanza, adding a 6th line: along this road. variant stanza 3, lines 2–6:

> I took my bundles of hog feeder price lists
> by Larry the Lug,
> I'd never got anywhere
> because I'd never had suction,
> you know, pull, favor, drag,

Poem XIV of "FOR PAUL: GROUP TWO," *New Mexico Quarterly* 21.1 (Spring 1951): 208, adopts the variant stanza 1, line 6 ("along this road") offered on the MS and revises stanza 3, lines 2–6:

> I carried my bundles of hog feeder price lists
> by Larry the Lug,
> I'd never got anywhere
> because I'd never had suction,
> you know: pull, favor, drag,

Revised to the present text for FPOP.

T&G variant stanza 1, line 4: along the road

Not all that's heard is music. We leave   *T&G, MLBW* **[FPOP]**.
Poem X of "FOR PAUL: GROUP TWO" MS, dated Dec. 14, 1950, poem X of "FOR PAUL: GROUP TWO," *New Mexico Quarterly* 21.1 (Spring 1951): 206, and FPOP, all include the following variants:

line 1: Not all that's heard is music. Paul, we leave

line 5: but fascists'—you have the world. Remember the little

LN adopts LZ's suggested omissions from lines 1 and 5; the suggested omissions are noted on FPOP.

Tell me a story about the war.   *T&G, MLBW* **[FPOP]**.
A revision of the earlier "NG" MS version, "The Marshal of France made a speech" (see p. 378). The revision reflects the new context of the "FOR PAUL" poems.
In the "FOR PAUL: GROUP TWO" MS, dated Jan. 16, 1951, in poem XVI of "FOR PAUL: GROUP TWO," *New Mexico Quarterly* 21.1 (Spring 1951): 209, and in FPOP, there is a variant line 1: Tell me a story about the last war.
In MS it is paired with "Laval, Pomeret, Pétain" (MS dated Jan. 16, 1951). In FPOP, *T&G* and *MLBW,* the poems appear as adjacent but separate poems.

Laval, Pomeret, Pétain   *T&G, MLBW* **[FPOP]**.
On the "FOR PAUL: GROUP TWO" MS, dated Jan. 16, 1951, it is paired with "Tell me a story about the war" (see note above).
variant line 1: Yes, Laval, Pomeret, Pétain
variant line 8: Now let's practice your dance.

Revised to the present text for FPOP.

T&G line 8: Now let's practice your dance

Thure Kumlien   Unpublished [FPOP] and Shut up in woods   *T&G, MLBW* [FPOP, EA].

Both of these poems derive from two longer and closely related MSS.

The first is a "FOR PAUL: GROUP TWO" MS dated by LZ as "earlier" than Jan. 18, 1951:

> I'd like to tell you about a man
> of a hundred years ago.
> He was here while the wild white swans
> were still afloat. Bigwigs wrote
> from Boston: Thure, we must know
> about the sandhill crane,
> is it ever white with you and how many
> eggs can you obtain?
>
> Grandchildren played with his mounted birds.
> "Imagine playing horse
> with a pink flamingo! Imagine eight of us
> schooled and exposed to a course
> of music" one of them sums it up,
> grandchildren of her own.
> "And gathered around the first lamp—
> kerosene—how we shone."
>
> For Thure   The Solitary Tattler,
> Wilson's Phalarope.
> He exchanged dried New England plants
> for those around his home
> at Koshkonong. One day he found
> an aster down in the ditch
> by the old turnpike—to it he gave
> his name as tho he were rich.
>
> . . .
>
> The trouble with war for a botanist—
> he daren't drop out of the line
> of march to examine a flower—can only
> hope to come back sometime
> or now in power wars when half
> the world is shell-burst

> observe a sky-exotic
> attract a bomber-bird.
>
> . . .
>
> Dear little Curlew
> how are you
> on Willow St.
> your ear on all us pipers
> as we bleat.

LN's annotation: "I did better on an ode to Koshkonong in high school. ["Reminiscence"; see p. 367] Unless you insist I won't use it. Second stanza might be omitted and third begin: He saw The Solitary Tattler 'is it ever white'—they changed color as do herons and egrets in various stages of growth in various sections of country as they fly up this way from Florida."

The above draft is revised for poem XVII of "FOR PAUL: GROUP TWO," *New Mexico Quarterly* 21.1 (Spring 1951): 210, with the following changes:

lines 3–4:

> He was here when wild swans were still
> afloat. Bigwigs wrote

lines 13–end:

> of music" as one of them now sums it up
> to grandchildren of her own.
> "And gathered around the first kerosene
> lamp, how we shone."

> For Thure the solitary tattler
> opened a door
> to learned birds—with their latest books—
> who walked New England's shore.
> One day by the old turnpike that still crosses
> the marsh, down in the ditch
> he found a new aster—to it he gave
> his name as tho he were rich.

> The trouble with war for a botanist—
> he daren't drop out of the line of march
> to examine a flower. What flower?
> Shell-burst—observe a sky-exotic
> attract a bomber-bird.

> Dear little curlew
> how are you on Willow St.
> your ear on us pipers
> who bleat?

Substantial condensations occur to produce the finished *"Thure Kumlien."* These revisions are first seen when sent to LZ on the MS titled "Changes in FOR PAUL" (Jan. 19, 1955): the poem is revised to the present text plus a not yet omitted final stanza, "The trouble with war for a botanist . . . attract a bomber-bird." FPOP omits this final stanza. (At this point, in Jan. 1955, LZ appears to have returned to the MS of "I'd like to tell you about a man" dated "earlier than Jan. 18, 1951" and noted her condensations in the margin.)

The second MS, dated Jan. 18, 1951, expands on the earlier version:

> He was here before the wild white swans died out
> and old country courtesy. Boston bigwigs wrote:
> Dear Thure, tell us about the sandhill crane,
> is it ever white with you . . . please send us
> Solitary Tattlers' eggs. A latin scholar,
> "shut up in the woods", he broke land,
> made knives and forks, fumbled English gently:
> "Now is March gone and I have much undone . . ."
>
> Snow. Christine sick. There are two kinds of artists,
> those who write for the people and those who write
> for art's sake. Strong storm with colors. Marsh grass
> over my head. Sent 500 insects to Berlin.
> When the money comes from Leyden we'll buy coats
> and shoes. Chopped five lengths of ash. Both hens laid.
> Cleaned grain in the wind. Baby's coffin—I owe
> two basswood boards . . . when the money comes from Leyden.
>
> He saw Wilson's Phalarope, the beauty
> among the waders. Grandchildren played
> with his mounted birds. Imagine playing horse
> with a pink flamingo, sighs one of them who now
> has grandchildren of her own. And how they shone
> gathered around the first kerosene lamp.
> In the ditch by the old turnpike that still crosses
> the marsh he found a new aster and gave it his name.
> . . .
>
> The trouble with war for a botanist—
> he daren't drop out of the line of march

to examine a flower. Or when half the world
is shell-burst, observes a sky-exotic
attract a bomber-bird.

. . .

Dear little curlew
how are you on Willow St.
your ear on us sandpipers
as we bleat.

Soon after writing this draft, she would begin the substantial revisions that lead to
"Shut up in woods," poem XVIII of "FOR PAUL: GROUP TWO," *New Mexico Quarterly*
21.1 (Spring 1951): 210. There it is revised to the present text with lines 1, 4–5, 6–9
enclosed in quotation marks. LN's "Changes in FOR PAUL" (Jan. 29, 1955) notes that
she has removed the quotation marks.

Your father to me in your eighth summer: Unpublished in book form [FPOP].
Poem IV of "FOR PAUL: GROUP III" MS, dated Sept. 27, 1951.
"FOR PAUL: CHILD VIOLINIST," *Quarterly Review of Literature* 8.2 (1955): 117.
On FPOP, LZ suggests that LN omit the poem. However, she saves lines 10–14 as
the fifth stanza of the condensed version of another poem, "Dear Paul" (see p. 153).

To Paul now old enough to read: *T&G, MLBW* [FPOP, EA].
The present text has its origins in a much longer poem, an undated, possibly 1945,
MS:

Crèvecoeur

Letters from an
American Farmer (1782)

What a shame, said my mind, or something that inspired my mind,
that here, with no masters to bleed us
thee shouldst have employed so many years tilling the earth
and destroying so many flowers and plants
without knowing their structures and uses . . .
In a little time I became acquainted with every
            vegetable that grew in my neighborhood;
in proportion as I thought myself more learned,
            proceeded further . . .

perched within a few feet of a humming bird,
its little eyes like diamonds reflecting light on every side,

elegantly finished in all parts,
quicker than thought.

Thought: man, an animal of prey, seems
to have bloodshed implanted in his heart.
We never speak of a hero of mathematics
or a hero of the knowledge of humanity.

Men are like plants, the goodness, flavour of the fruit
comes out of the soil in which they grow;
we are nothing but what we derive from the air,
climate, government, religion, and employment.

Men of law are plants that grow in soil cultivated by the hands of others,
once rooted extinguish every other vegetable around.
In some provinces only they have knowledge,
as the clergy in past centuries in Europe.

In Nantucket, but one lawyer finds the means to live,
grazing land held in common.
I once saw sixteen barrels of oil boiled out of the tongue of the whale.
No military here, no governors, no masters but the laws
and their civil code so light.
Happy, harmless, industrious people,
after death buried without pomp, prayers and ceremonies—
not a stone or monument erected—
their memory preserved by tradition.
I saw, indeed, several copies of Hudibras.

Astonishing how quick men learn who serve themselves.
At night the fireflies can be caught and used as a reading light.

A Russian came to me, interested in plants.
Why trouble to come to this country?
Who knows, he said, what revolutions Russia and America may one day
bring about.

(coda)

Men who work for themselves learn
fast. The firefly
two pairs of wings and a third to read
by
    disappearing.

The next surviving draft is much revised. Poem V of "FOR PAUL: GROUP III" MS,
dated Sept. 27, 1951, departs from the present text in stanza one:

> To Paul reading books: Once
> there lived a farmer, Crèvecoeur,
> who tried to save his heart
> from too much hurt.

and in line 17: Learn Crèvecoeur and learn fast
FPOP omits the above first stanza and retains the line 17 above.
Revised to the present text for *Combustion* 15/*Island* 6 (n.d.): 32.

What horror to awake at night   *T&G, MLBW* [FPOP].

Poem II of "FOR PAUL: Group III" MS, dated Sept. 27, 1951. Variant line 5 in MS
and FPOP: I've spent my life doing nothing.
An undated letter from LZ to LN praises the poem, particularly its use of sound.
LZ notes with approval echoes of T. S. Eliot's "Fragment of an Agon," of Lord
Rochester's "Ode to Nothing," and Robert Burns's "This ae night."

Sorrow moves in wide waves,   *T&G, MLBW* [FPOP].

As poem I of the "FOR PAUL: GROUP FOUR" MS (undated, probably 1951), the poem
merges with "Old Mother turns blue and from us," creating a four-stanza poem.
By the time of FPOP, the four stanzas have divided into two discrete poems.
At the end of "Sorrow moves in wide waves," LN acknowledges her source:
"(after Henry James)." LN ignores LZ's suggested omission of "illimitable"
on FPOP.
In *T&G* the poem is subheaded "H.J."
MLBW mistakenly capitalizes the first letter of line 2.

Jesse James and his brother Frank   *T&G, MLBW* and May you have lumps in your mashed potatoes   *T&G, MLBW* [FPOP, EA].

As poems VI and VII of "FOR PAUL: GROUP III," these were independent poems until
their linked appearance in *T&G* and *MLBW*.
Although "Jesse James and his brother Frank" is omitted from FPOP at the time of
"Changes in FOR PAUL" (Jan. 29, 1955), I include it here for copytext reasons.
"May you have lumps in your mashed potatoes" appeared alone in *Origin* ser. 2, 2
(July 1961): 28.

Old Mother turns blue and from us,   *T&G, MLBW* [FPOP].

In its "FOR PAUL: GROUP FOUR" MS appearance (undated, probably 1951) the poem
forms the third and fourth stanzas of "Sorrow moves in wide waves." Thereafter, it is
an independent poem.
Origin ser. 2, 2 (July 1961): 28.

I hear the weather   Unpublished [FPOP].

Very likely a descendant of the "weather poem" with a "fugue of r's" referred to by
LZ in a letter to LN dated March 9, 1938.

Poem II of "FOR PAUL: GROUP FOUR" MS (undated, probably 1951), lines 3–4:
> or is it my mother
>> breathing

"Changes in FOR PAUL" (Jan. 29, 1955) offers variant lines 3–4:
> or is it my breathing
>> mother

Revised to present text for FPOP.

Dead   *T&G, MLBW* **[FPOP]**.

Poem III of "FOR PAUL: GROUP FOUR" MS (undated, probably 1951) is substantially different:

> The shining brown steel casket—
> What is its value really,
> we already have a concrete vault.
>
> "I don't know, they seem to want it.
> Look at your automobiles—"
> She who wheeled dirt for flowers
>
> lay there deaf to death
>> parked
> in her burnished brown motorless automobile.
>
> She could have grown a good rutabaga
> in the burial ground
>> edged by woods.
>
> What is life
>> in those woods one of her pallbearers
>>> after a deer
>
> "I like a damfool followed a deer
>> wanted to see her jump a fence
> never'd seen a deer jump a fence—
>
> pretty thing
>> the way she runs."

FPOP and *Black Mountain Review* 6 (Spring 1956): 191, omit the opening line of the present text. In *BMR* it is part of a numbered group of "FOUR POEMS."

Can knowledge be conveyed that isn't felt?   Unpublished [FPOP].

Poem VII of "FOR PAUL: GROUP FOUR" MS (undated, probably 1951).

On FPOP, LZ suggests she omit "Generator boy, Paul," in line 7.

Ten o'clock   Unpublished [FPOP].

Poem I of the "FOR PAUL: GROUP SIX" MS, dated Oct. 22, 1952, is followed by three bullets and two additional stanzas:

> Gun-night, said the kid next door,
> hit the feathers, flatten,
> tomorrow oil up your squeak box
> and saw it off in Manhattan.
>
> Who *is* this Shakespeer? Gimme a gander—
> beard like a sea cook's. Rounded the Horn?
> *What kind of man is he? Why, of mankind.*
> Okay, like us, he was born.

"Changes in FOR PAUL" (Jan. 29, 1955) notes her omission of these stanzas. On Aug. 30, 1955, MS sent to Dahlberg, the final line replaces "me" with "us." On FPOP, LZ suggests that she omit the entire poem.

Adirondack Summer   Unpublished [FPOP].

Poem II of "FOR PAUL: GROUP SIX" MS, dated Oct. 22, 1952, where the poem is untitled.

On FPOP, LZ suggests that she condense the title "*Adirondack Summer*" to "*Summer*." A trace of this unpublished poem appears in "PAEAN TO PLACE," stanza 20:

> Maples to swing from
> Pewee-glissando

Spelling of "peewee" in MS and FPOP changes to "pewee" in *T&G* and *MLBW.*

The slip of a girl-announcer: Unpublished [FPOP].

Poem III of "FOR PAUL: GROUP SIX" MS, dated Oct. 22, 1952.

LN to LZ, Aug. 12, 1952: "Your letter is TERRIFIC. . . . It prompts me to descend practically to doggerel. . . . Dare I use it FOR PAUL?" (*NCZ* 197).

Now go to the party,   Unpublished in book form [FPOP].

Poem IV of "FOR PAUL: GROUP SIX" MS, dated Oct. 22, 1952.

Origin ser. 2, 2 (July 1961): 30.

Dear Paul: *T&G, MLBW* [FPOP, EA].

This is a condensation of the original five-page poem, titled in MS, "FOR PAUL: PART v" and dated Dec. 12, 1951:

> Dear Paul:
> the sheets of your father's book of poetry
> are to be bound for England?
> At last, after the hardships
>
> He can say: take back to your ship
> a gift from me,

something precious, a real good thing . . .
such as a friend gives to a friend.

You ask what kind of boats in *my* country
on my little river.   10
Black as those beside Troy
but sailless tar-preserve-black fish barges
and orange and Chinese red rowboats
in which the three virtues
          knowledge, humanity, energy
infrequently ride.

Ask me rather what kind of people
          —here they kick the book of poetry open—
because you can't keep people from water
they'll cut thru to it   20
rut thru in the soft
dig under and come up in the middle,
by water they go for Helen
in water seek their own image
fish Sunday's quiet
by water uncork their beer
on days off
                    to see light behave
                    double moon on the wave
water where bobbed likely the first life on earth.   30
Right of way—
you can't keep em from it.

Ask me what kind of children.
Who are the kids of the calm-moving wet,
of Saturday-Sunday parents.
One with listening eyes like yours
little Sat Sun shall we say
sits in the thinning wild rice
watching wide sky wash
away from the laundry.   40
One.

What we have is the Sunday school crowd
laying waste the countryside
with their long sticks.

Beat the grass
whip Queen Anne's lace
bow low, my family of young poplars
oh holy day

The sons and the daughters
on their way to water,   50
your floaters, your doters,
your wigglers, your little pond scum
turtle torturers, danglers of frogs
in any mud puddle
your wuttle-gutt goop longs
            —they can't talk—
the pings and the ack acks
dealing death to the little green thing
cute kids
kee-yute tribe   60
who at six steer the motor boat
straight to the dock

No they can't talk
they combust
or they mush it

Dennie's the spitwit kid
chewer of seaweed inland
            juices, breaks up into acids
related to what was his name
            who could speak no English   70
            his tongue runneth all on buttered fish
yet asleep in his army blankets
as sweet a child as any

And there's always the army
to make a man of him.
Take his brother, 19,
no better butter-mutter
no clear song, fished out
left town
            empty in the head   80
                        swish swash
but good with three bullets on a knife

After me
     backward
          the cockpit
               fell out

Give me silk
     or nylon
          and down
               with your art   90

You saw Guppy the fleet type submarine, Paul
I give you Gulpy

To hear him
he could hold up his arm
and keep the bomb from falling
or he could drop it.

Frog jabber
grab her
she's mine to pierce
ready for love   100

Gloater, soaker, roaring river boater
emptied, poured out, done,
stick out your tongue
mammoth oar-muscle baby

The day of the giant armored fishes
               was a clear thing

Five-year-old Chief Noise
guns strewn over his lawn
his Uncle a Justice
held us up one night by the garden gate   110
throws the cat by the tail at noon
cries to get her in out of the rain
               after dark

He'll take no backwash from anybody

What does the father do?
             He steals. I mean
             he works for a steel company.
Well, why not?—
steals from himself

as they from him   120
his time, his life.
His pleasure in his work
       flows by.

He's left loved
for the spending of his wages
       on things he won't want.

All children begin with the life of the mind—
if there were no marsh or stream
imagine it

99 children go into business   130
       selling angleworms,
the hundredth develops free fingers in John Sebastian brook

Boys who play the fiddle never amount to anything
the storekeeper screamed
with the radio in his face
so he raised his son to shop work
turn screws, grind scissors
and in the end own stores
      force his rivals to the wall then buy em out
          selling and buying   140
         how are you dying
            worn out at fifty
               nevermind the mind

while poets and players
of serious song
stand the stress

All along the water
50,000 crusading children
beat their way to the pretty sea shells.
Find yourself a starfish and you'll see the sea open   150
And still there's no miracle.
Sold into slavery
sold

Brother
      sold to the factory assembly line
      for "a worthwhile goal—an automobile"
      costing more than my house.

The boy overshot his goal at dusk
hit a cow on the road
that carried no lantern   160
jumped over the moon
slid into a grave ready-blossoming
               —wild mustard and quack—
the car repaired
sold

Road boat upset
hooked as by love
the greatest thrill
since his tongue froze to the pump handle
this is the boy who'd defend you in war   170
and so doing crush you
haul over and love you

When other friendships are forgot
yours will still be hot

Put that in your Opus
5 f's for forte

One boy there was with a camera:
"I need nests 6 or 7 feet from the ground
and on which the sun shines
most of the day. Prothonotary, please.   180
I'm told if anybody knows where these nests are
it will be you."
He was a minister's son
          I never saw him—
                    driven off his course by the wind

Comes a measure marked autumn
the passing of the little summer people,
schools of leaves float downstream
past lonely piers

soft still-water twilight   190
morning ice on the minnow bucket
Riddle me this:
               book
               brook
                    Bach
                    unlock

> ships'
> gifts
>
> and I'll tell you
> how freedom grows   200

Two other MS versions of the five-page poem survive: one went to Dahlberg on Aug. 30, 1955, for inclusion in a proposed but never published anthology. It is titled "Part V of FOR PAUL, 9 year old violinist" and it includes the following variants:

line 3: are bound for England?

lines 5–8: The direct speech is enclosed in quotation marks.

line 66: "Dennie" is replaced by "Danny".

lines 175–76 ("Put that . . . forte") are omitted and replaced by the following excerpt from an early and subsequently rejected (see p. 136) "FOR PAUL" poem:

> The elegant office girl
> is power-rigged.
>
> She carries her nylon hard-pointed
> breast uplift
> like parachutes
> half-pulled.

The third long MS version of the poem is in FPOP with the following variants:

line 3: are to be bound for England?

lines 5–8: The direct speech is enclosed in quotation marks.

line 66: "Dennie" is replaced by "Reggy,"

line 126: "The elegant office girl" lines above are inserted between "on things he won't want" and "All children begin . . .".

The "FOR PAUL: CHILD VIOLINIST" selection in *Quarterly Review of Literature* 8.2 (1955): 117–19, included what LN described in an Aug. 30, 1955, letter to Dahlberg as a "section" of the long poem "Dear Paul": lines 1–16 ("dear Paul: . . . in frequently ride.") and lines 127–32 ("All children begin . . . John Sebastian Brook"). Here is her Nov. 16, 1955, statement to Dahlberg: "The reason I took a section out (for *Quart. Rev. of Lit.*) of the long FOR PAUL poem I sent you was that it wasn't going with editors as it was and the mood of those few lines seemed to fit in with the others for Weiss [ed. of QRL]. But I have always felt that that long poem, section V of the series which I called FOR PAUL, is a whole, a rangy, perhaps too long poem but nevertheless a poem."

The poem *"Autumn"* in *Poor.Old.Tired.Horse.* 9 (undated, possibly 1965): 1, is drawn from lines 188–91 of "Dear Paul" (see p. 217).

T&G and *MLBW* duplicate the *QRL* version to which they add lines 10–14 from

"Your father to me in your eighth summer" (see p. 146) followed and concluded by lines 186–91 ("Comes a measure marked autumn" . . . "morning ice on the minnow bucket").

The *T&G* and *MLBW* versions make two revisions: line 16 reads, "Sometimes ride." and line 28 (of the present text) reads, "Yes, comes a measure marked Autumn". *MLBW* differs from *T&G* in the addition of line 18: if there were no marsh or stream.

EA uses only lines 1–16, printing them in quatrains with an amended line 9: You ask what kind of boats

My father said "I remember   *T&G, MLBW* [FPOP].

In poem I of "FOR PAUL: GROUP SEVEN" MS (undated, probably 1952/3) there is a second stanza:

> Play those little records again
> no sweeter music
> than the violin.

The Aug. 30, 1955, MS sent to Dahlberg adds an additional line to the start of the second stanza, "Now I enjoy the stove" and revises "records" to "discs".

FPOP revises line 11 to "Now I need a stove".

Revised to the present text for "THREE POEMS," *Granta* 71.12456 (1964/5): 19.

Origin ser. 3, 2 (July 1966): 9.

No quotation marks used until *MLBW*.

You know, he said, they used to make   *T&G, MLBW* [FPOP].

In poem II of "FOR PAUL: GROUP SEVEN" MS (undated, probably 1952/3) and in FPOP, lines 1–2 read:

> The old man said you know they used
> to make mincemeat with meat,

He built four houses   *MFT, T&G, MLBW* [FPOP, EA, VV].

Poem III of "FOR PAUL: GROUP SEVEN" (undated, probably 1952/3).

In a numbered group of "FOUR POEMS," *Black Mountain Review* 6 (Spring 1956): 192.

In Europe they grow a new bean while here   *T&G, MLBW* [FPOP].

An undated early MS:

> In Russia they grow a new bean (being) while here
> we tie bundles of grass
> with a strand of itself as they used to American grain
> —against the cold blast
>
> around my house—my neighbor: Do yet in Russia I guess
>
> From his sister in Maine: We've found a nice warm place
> (in the hay?)

for the winter. Charlie sleeps late, I'm glad for his sake,
it shortens the day.

    Around my house in America yet.

variant final line: Around my house old bean in America yet.
A second MS, dated Dec. 1, 1951, shows the following line revisions:

    line 1: In Russia they grow a new bean while here

    line 3: With strands of itself as they used to American grain,

    line 10: Around my house the old bean in America yet.

Poem IV in "FOR PAUL: GROUP SEVEN" (undated, probably 1952/3) revises:

    line 3: with strands of itself—as my grandfolks used to grain

    line 5: From my cousin in Maine: We've found a nice warm place

The rest of the poem is revised to the present text.
    A change from "Russia" to "Europe" is marked on the above MS in LZ's hand. However, in "Changes in FOR PAUL" (Jan. 29, 1955), LN notes: "I kept: In Russia they grow a new bean but changed Russia to Europe!" The change is hers and it occurs two or three years after the above MS. My speculation is that LZ would have retrieved his copy of the undated (probably 1952/3) MS in order to examine her revision and, at the same time, would have inscribed her change.
    Revised version published in a numbered group of "FOUR POEMS," *Black Mountain Review* 6 (Spring 1956): 191–92.

Paul / when the leaves   *MFT, T&G, MLBW* [FPOP, EA, VV].
    Poem I of "FOR PAUL: GROUP 8" MS, dated Dec. 31, 1953.
    "FOR PAUL: CHILD VIOLINIST," *Quarterly Review of Literature* 8.2 (Spring 1955): 118.
    On the Aug. 30, 1955, MS sent to Dahlberg, the poem includes a dedication: "For the ten year old violinist."
    Untitled in "EIGHT POEMS," *Monks Pond* 1 (Spring 1968): 6.
    VV dedicates the poem *"To the Child."*

I've been away from poetry   *T&G, MLBW* [FPOP, EA, VV].
    On Aug. 30, 1955, MS sent to Dahlberg:
    variant line 3: and now the leaves need raking
    variant lines 5–6: between your house and mine / I must scratch green.
    FPOP variant line 6: Scratch green.
    Revised to the present text in *Elizabeth* 9 (March 1966): 30, where it is titled *"Autumn."*
    Also in *Of Poem, An Anthology*, ed. James Weil (New Rochelle, N.Y.: The Elizabeth Press, 1966): 59.

I am sick with the Time's buying sickness.   *T&G, MLBW* [FPOP].

MS dated March 10, 1954, provides two early versions:

(i)
Yes, my Time's waste.
My future ready to be filled, waits.

If this costly cold can
flanged to my house for flowing oil
to a stove not costing as much
were a piano

I'd sing, dear friend,
that thirtieth: "When to the sessions
of sweet silent thought"
"sorrows end."

(ii)
If I were buying a little piano
instead of an oil drum
—more dollars for this cold can
than bought my stove—

I'd sing, dear friend,
that thirtieth tune "When to the sessions
of sweet silent thought"
"sorrows end."

Revised for FPOP with one variant from the present text, line 3: serves a stove not costing as much.

Revised to the present text for *Origin* ser. 3, 2 (July 1966): 9.

The death of my poor father   Unpublished [FPOP].

On the Aug. 30, 1955, MS sent to Dahlberg, variant lines 14–15: to probe the trees / at the river

Revised to the present text for FPOP.

To Aeneas who closed his piano   *T&G, MLBW* [FPOP, EA].

MS dated Oct. 3, 1953, carries two drafts:

(i)
To Aeneas who closed his piano
to dig a well thru hard clay
Chopin left notes like drops of water.
Aeneas could play the Majorcan sickness,
the pig-boat whips, Aurore, all the countries'
narrow sand-strips. "O Frederic" he sighed

"think of me digging below the surface—
we are of one pitch and flow."

LN's annotation: "Was amazed and delighted to find it fell into stanzas with end rhymes (as over). Do you like this block or the other (over)? Aeneas is a Greek Catholic name. The McA's say Anis but if they're spelling it Aeneas as they do, I suppose it ought to be pronounced Eenēás? If I keep this for FOR PAUL I might use Enos instead? Aurore is George Sand's 1st name."

> (ii)
> To Aeneas who closed his piano
> to dig a well thru hard clay
> Chopin left notes like drops of water.
> Aeneas could play
>
> the Majorcan sickness,
> the pig-boat whips,
> Aurore, all the countries'
> narrow sand-strips.
>
> "O Frederic, think of me digging below
> the surface—we are of one pitch and flow."

Alternative last stanza:

> "O Frederic—can you forgive
> this well deep piano?
> —we are of one pitch
> and flow."

LN's annotation: "sandstrips—they dig here till they come to a sand-strip."
A single stanza attached to the above MS alludes to LN's friendship with her neighbor Aeneas McAllister and to a proposal of marriage (there is no indication that the stanza was to be included with the Aeneas poem):

> I don't know what wave he's on
> if he'll be slowed.
> Once was one extended his hand.
> I've lived on a bigger river—
> I present a load.

"To Aeneas who closed his piano" is poem II of "FOR PAUL: GROUP 8" MS, dated Dec. 31, 1953, revised to the present text. LN's annotation: "Chopin got sick in Majorca and had that terrible journey home. I've tried everything: the rough sea journey etc. but always come back to original."
Origin ser. 2, 2 (July 1961): 30.

My friend the black and white collie   Unpublished [FPOP].

An alternative poem V of "FOR PAUL: GROUP 8" MS (undated) inserts two lines between the present lines 3 and 4:

> A silent long tail-waving moment
> then I embraced her.

Another undated MS reduces the above line 4 to "A tail-waving".
Revised to the present text for FPOP.
LN to LZ, Feb. 2, 1953: "I guess you said or Celia: better to have a dog at my door than the wolf! Lovely huge collie, beautiful face" (*NCZ* 212).

"Oh ivy green   Unpublished in book form [FPOP].

Three drafts for "FOR PAUL: GROUP 8" precede the present text. The first is undated:

> "Oh ivy green
>   oh ivy green—"
> you spoke your poem
> as we walked a city terrace
> and said if you could hear
>   —sneeze
> sneeze on the corner—
>   Handel clean
> Christmas would be cherished
> Christmas would be cherished
>
>   To the mother
>   color
> does not matter
> with her son's cold
> no better
>   unless
> a friend should tender
>   rest and hold
> her warm till winter's old
>   warm till winter's old

The second, poem VIII of "FOR PAUL: GROUP 8" MS (undated), revises the above draft: "cherished" of lines 9 and 10 changes to "green" and "till winter's old" of lines 19 and 20 changes to "in green cover." On this MS, LZ suggests changes: he restores the "cherished" of line 10 though not of line 9, changes "color" of line 12 to "ivy," deletes "tender" from line 17 and "rest and" from line 18, and changes lines 19 and 20 to "in a green cover."

An alternate poem V of "FOR PAUL: GROUP 8" MS, dated Dec. 31, 1953, adopts LZ's changes and revises further by compressing lines 6 and 7 into the following line:—and I heard you sneeze—

Revised to the present text for "FOR PAUL: CHILD VIOLINIST," *Quarterly Review of Literature* 8.2 (1955): 118–19, and FPOP.

LN's poem refers to Paul Zukofsky's poem "O ivy green" based on Henry VIII's "As the holly groweth green." LZ quotes Paul's complete poem in "A"-20. See *"A"* (Berkeley: University of California Press, 1978): 436.

As I shook the dust   Unpublished in book form [FPOP].

In a numbered group of "FOUR POEMS," *Black Mountain Review* 6 (Spring 1956): 192–93.

They live a cool distance   Unpublished in book form [FPOP].

"FOR PAUL: CHILD VIOLINIST," *Quarterly Review of Literature* 8.2 (1955): 119. LN to LZ, Sept. 29, 1955: "Very difficult problem to state—I feel I haven't yet got it all, left out maybe their love of this thing. The stoic enters in but is only one aspect. I hope the poem doesn't get over just the one idea that it's a principle. It's a compulsion to express thru difficulties, a love of the thing. At any rate, *don't* set it up between us" (*NCZ* 224).

***Violin Debut*   Unpublished [FPOP].**

OTHER POEMS

Horse, hello   *T&G, MLBW* [FPOP].

MS dated June 28, 1949.

New Directions 12 (1950): 185. In MS and magazine, the poem is presented as a single stanza with variant lineation. Only in *MLBW* does the first line appear as a title—not adopted here.

An undated letter from LZ to LN praises the poem as one of her best. He notes its passion and its relation to the English epigrammatic tradition.

Energy glows at the lips —   *T&G, MLBW* [FPOP].

In both the MS dated Nov. 20, 1949, and in *New Directions* 12 (1950): 185–86, the present poem is a single six-line stanza to which the following second stanza is appended:

> Time on his wrist,
> soft wool zippered suit,
> he speaks:
> Got pure gold, boss,
> if we clip the gopher now.

In FPOP the six-line stanza has been broken into the present two three-line stanzas, but the "Time on his wrist" stanza remains.

Revised to the present text for *T&G*.

Hi, Hot-and-Humid   *T&G, MLBW* [FPOP].

Undated MS, *New Directions* 12 (1950): 185, and FPOP all have a variant line 3: She marsh wallows, frog bickering

Woman in middle life   Unpublished [FPOP].

We physicians watch the juices rise   Unpublished [FPOP].
    MS dated June 4, 1952.

***1937*   Unpublished [FPOP].**
    Untitled in "NG" MS.

***European Travel/(Nazi New Order)   T&G, MLBW* [FPOP].**
    MS dated "Nov '45?" and titled "European Travel/1943–44."
    Revised to the present text for FPOP.

***Depression years   T&G, MLBW* [FPOP].**
    The early "NG" MS version is untitled with variant lines 2–3: I was certified,/then
for weeks I raked leaves
    Revised to the present text for FPOP with variant title, *"Depression ballad."*
    Titled *"Depression years"* in *Origin* ser. 3, 2 (July 1966): 8.

So you're married, young man,   Unpublished [FPOP].
    There are five previous drafts. Of the two dated Oct. 22, 1953, the first begins with
LN's note: "First version which to MD states the case better than the second but the
second is less jingly. Mebbe I shdn't ever have gone to NY to meet the real writer but
shd. have stayed in my little country patch and written country ballads to be sung with
a geetar! Do I dare use the second version for FOR PAUL with a preface about a banjo or
guitar in place of a violin? Of course St. Louis Blues streams through my head and a
much better thing it is than I cd. do."

>   What's wrong with marriage?
>   Women's rich fads.
>   Women and those "buy! buy!"
>   technicolor ads.
>
>   They need spinners and dryers
>   they need nylon slips
>   they need deep-well cookers
>   they need power shift.
>
>   You'll find the same man
>   working twice to give
>   all the things to his wife
>   she demands but why live
>
>   if you can't take time
>   to be home from this grave
>   or you do and your wife's out
>   with another slave.

> She'll sue for divorce
> he'll blow his brains,
> the old work horse
> free at last of his reins.
>
> Oh that diamond-digging St. Louis
> woman was a breeze—
> now the gals got you trembling
> before a deep freeze.

The second draft (dated Oct. 22, 1953) is a four-stanza poem beginning with the first two stanzas above, adding the following as the third stanza (where it remains in the present text):

> A man works two shops—
> home at last from this grave
> he finds his wife out
> with another slave.

and closing with the final stanza above.

Next, two undated versions, the first of which is an alternative poem VI of the "FOR PAUL: GROUP 8" MS (undated), and comprises stanzas 1, 2, 3, and 5 of the present text. LN ignores LZ's suggestion that she change "this" in line 10 to "his" and "his" of line 11 to "the".

The second of the two undated versions is six stanzas long: stanzas 1 and 2 of the present text plus stanzas 3 and 4 of the first version dated Oct. 22, 1953, with the following small revision, to the opening two lines of stanza 3:

> You'll find the same man's
> Got two jobs—he must give

A fifth draft, an alternative poem IV of the "FOR PAUL: GROUP 8" MS dated Dec. 31, 1953, adds a title, "*If you were Pete/and I played guitar*" to the present text (FPOP).

"Changes in FOR PAUL" (Jan. 29, 1955) omits the poem, but it is restored by the time of FPOP (Dec. 1956).

She grew where every spring   Unpublished [FPOP].

I sit in my own house   Unpublished in book form [FPOP].

LN adopts Dahlberg's 1956 suggested revision to her Aug. 30, 1955, version. He suggests that she omit the two opening and two closing lines:

> Time moves, no,
> explodes,
> [I sit in my own house
>
> . . .

> of our day.]
> I'm a fool
> I am wise.

Revised to the present text for FPOP.
Origin ser. 2, 2 (July 1961): 30.

On hearing / the wood pewee   *T&G, MLBW* [FPOP].
Untitled in the following FPOP version:

> This is my mew
> as our days in a wild-flying world
> last—
>
> be alone.
> Throw it over—all fashion,
> feud.
>
> Go home where the greenbird
> is—the trees where you pass
> to grass.

As above in *Neon* 4 (1959): n.p.
T&G adds the title and alters the lineation slightly.
Revised to the present text for *MLBW*.

Along the river   *MFT, T&G, MLBW* [FPOP, EA, VV].
In both poem VI of "FOR PAUL: GROUP FOUR" MS (undated, probably 1951) and FPOP, the poem opens with the following line: I take it slow
T&G variant line 6: gave me this
LN to LZ, Dec. 24, 1962: "I wonder if we dare to close the gap someday—What we feel, see, inside us and outside us melted together absolutely. There's this new sense in poetry—even I with lines into each other as 'Along the river'—your contrapuntals—" (*NCZ* 327).

He moved in light   *T&G, MLBW* [FPOP, EA].
On MS dated Dec. 14, 1950, the poem is paired with "Keen and lovely man moved as in a dance."
Poem XIII of "FOR PAUL: GROUP TWO" MS, dated Dec. 30, 1950, and poem XIII of "FOR PAUL: GROUP TWO," *New Mexico Quarterly* 21.1 (Spring 1951): 208.
LN to LZ, March 15, 1951: "I feel I'm on the way to something, especially with the use of lines and words that look backward and forward as "he moved in light . . ." (*NCZ* 177–78).

Keen and lovely man moved as in a dance   *T&G, MLBW* [FPOP].
On MS dated Dec. 14, 1950, the poem is titled *"Office Blues,"* with variant lines 2–3:

to be considerate in his outdoor-lighted
glass-walled office. Industrial relations

LN's annotation: "(Industrial relations and business weren't all he knew, that's my meaning. But if the above doesn't do it, put Business in place of Industrial relations. How involved can you make this?—are *you* the lawyer-poet?) I've put back say and said—you can't condense this kind of thing—it's either this or nothing. These on this page I hadn't intended for FOR PAUL but now I don't know—Blues song and both springing out of looking for a job—what do you think?"

On the MS, LZ suggests a revision of line 2: lighted almost outdoor.

The "FOR PAUL: GROUP TWO" MS, dated Dec. 30, 1950, numbers the poem XII and revises lines 2–4:

to be considerate in his lighted, glass-walled
almost outdoor office. Business

wasn't all he knew. He knew music, art. The guy

Poem XII in "FOR PAUL: GROUP TWO," *New Mexico Quarterly* 21.1 (Spring 1951): 207, revises line 4: wasn't all he knew. He knew music, art.

Revised to the present text for FPOP.

He lived—childhood summers   *T&G, MLBW* [FPOP].

Six versions of this poem survive.

(i) undated, possibly part of the MS dated Aug. 21, 1950:

He lived. He had it—childhood summer
        thru bare feet
then years of handling money,
        silver cold and heat.

Forever the flood—out of it came
        his wood, dog,
woman, lost her, daughter—
        dog paws are warm.

He planted trees, buried carp
        beneath the rose,
Saw motion in the stillest
        as the marsh rail goes.

To bankers on the high land
        he opened his wine tank
and sent his only daughter
        to work in the bank.

(ii) MS dated Nov. 23, 1951:

He lived. He had it—childhood summers
        thru bare feet
then years of handling money,
        silver cold and heat.

Forever the flood—out of it came
        his wood, dog,
woman, lost her, daughter,
        finish, prologue.

He planted trees, buried carp
        beneath the rose,
saw how grass-still
        the marsh rail goes.

To bankers on the high land
        he opened his wine tank
who sent his only daughter
        to work in the bank.

But to her he gave a source
        to sustain her,
a weedy speech when she spoke,
        a marshy retainer.

LN offers alternative lines 5–6:

beside the river. Out of the flood
came wood, dog

(iii) MS dated Dec. 1, 1951:

He lived. He had it—childhood summers
        thru bare feet
then years of handling money,
        silver and heat

beside the river—out of the flood
        came his wood, dog,
woman, lost her, daughter
        and she'll be gone.

He planted trees, buried carp
        beneath the rose,
saw how grass-still
        the marsh rail goes.

To bankers on the high land
  he opened his wine tank
and sent his only daughter
  to work in the bank.

But for her he was a source
  to sustain her,
a weedy substance in her speech,
  a marshy retainer.

LZ suggests LN remove "he had it" from line 1 and "then" from line 3, that she restore her earlier "finish, prologue" to line 8, and that she replace "who" with "He" in line 15.

(iv) A reconstruction in LZ's holograph dated Dec. 12, 1951:

Out of flood, came
  his wood, dog
woman, lost her, daughter,
  finish, prologue

He lived the water, buried carp
  beneath the rose,
Where like still grass
  the marsh rail goes

To bankers on high land
  opened his wine tank
that had his only daughter
  work in the bank.

But gave her a source
  to sustain her
a weedy speech—she spoke,
  a marshy retainer

His childhood summer
  thru bare feet
years of handling money,
  cold and heat

(v) The version in *Golden Goose* 4.5 (Oct. 1952): 6, and also in FPOP is a revision of the Dec. 1, 1951, draft; lines 1–8:

He lived—childhood summers
  thru bare feet
then years of handling money's
  cold and heat

> beside the river—out of flood
> > came his wood, dog,
> woman, lost her, daughter,
> > finish, prologue.

line 11: where grass-still
line 17: But he gave her a source
line 19: a weedy speech
The sixth and final revision (which is the present text) appears in *T&G* and *MLBW*.

I rose from marsh mud,   *T&G, MLBW* [**FPOP, EA, VV**].
Conceived in June 1945—see *NCZ* 151.
LN's Dec. 20, 1948, letter to Eugene Magner at the Lockwood Memorial Library, State University of New York, Buffalo, responds to his request for drafts that reveal compositional method:

> I find that the main steps in a recent poem are at hand and enclose them. The papers are numbered in order of composition, beginning with mere note-taking to preserve images and idea. No. 2, a mere sketch, while at office work, intended free verse form. No. 3 after saying the lines to myself before sleep at night and on waking. No. 4 as sent to James Laughlin IV for New Directions. Final version, no. 5 . . . will ask Mr. Laughlin to make two slight changes.

Enclosure no. 1, typescript with holograph annotations below:

> the primordial slime—bits of things like algae. hair-like plants, equisetum—fern-like foliage with hollow stem. Planted willows in it. make my own beginning of creation. Arose from the primordial mud to go to a wedding, expensive affair in church. candles, satin, diamonds. One of those little girls who is a slave to International Sterling Silver. A long step from algae to the girl-slave, free to be a slave, a mind to support the silver kings. A long step from cell-division to the sweating of the male while the other takes her time acquiring silver and diamonds, donning and taking off satins. And he goes on sweating to pay for em. The church, with no other good for us than its rich silence, its candles and its organ tones. With some people there can be no procreation with The Church . . . and International Sterling.

Holograph notes:

> > mental cell division
> > earliest organism hardest thing in world—diamond—can't melt it
> > All history passed thru me in that half hr in church
> > white
> > gleam
> > rich silence with organ tones
> > silver
> > diamonds

sensuous green free vs hard silver convention
All flesh is grass
all blood and bones = grass

Enclosure no. 2, holograph MS:

Up from marsh mud
birds noisy
green frogs

to see her in the rich shade
of the church
little white slave girl

Satin, gleaming silver
These two united to serve
Solid Silver

Possession

Enclosure no. 3, typescript:

Up from marsh mud
algae, equisetum, willows,
sweet green, noisy
birds and frogs

to see her wed in the rich
rich silence of the church,
the little white slave-girl
in her diamond fronds.

Now in aisle and arch
the satin secret collects.
These two united to serve
Solid Silver. Possessed.

Enclosure no. 4, typescript with the following variants:

line 1: I arose from marsh mud,
lines 11–12: United for life to serve / silver. Possessed.

Enclosure no. 5, typescript with the following variants:

line 1: I rose from marsh mud,
line 9: In aisle and arch

In "THREE POEMS," *New Directions* 11 (1949): 302, with "Don't tell me property is sacred" and "Sunday's motor cars." Appears here with line 6: Now in aisle and arch
LN regretted that this poem was excluded from *MFT*.

In *Poor.Old.Tired.Horse*. 1 (undated, probably March 1962): n.p., with *"Linnaeus in Lapland."*

Dear Mona, Mary and all   Unpublished [FPOP].

The Aug. 30, 1955, MS sent to Dahlberg inserts a line between present lines 9 and 10: Instead of by the government

Don't tell me property is sacred!   *T&G, MLBW* [FPOP].

Undated MS.

With "I rose from marsh mud" and "Sunday's motor cars" in "THREE POEMS," *New Directions* 11 (1949): 302, with a variant final line: with poor eyes and a house.

In FPOP line 3, "rolling" is replaced with "riding."

***Wartime   T&G, MLBW* [FPOP].**

Untitled in MS dated 1945, in the *New Mexico Quarterly* 20 (Summer 1950): 208, and in FPOP.

In *NMQ* it is number "I" of "TWO POEMS"—"II" is "Swept snow, Li Po."

In MS and FPOP, variant line 4: whose stillness is alive.

In MS, *NMQ*, FPOP, and *T&G*, variant line 7: with noise and flame, by learning change

Revised to the present text for *MLBW*.

The poem *"News,"* lines 5–6, offers an early occurrence of line 12 (see p. 79).

February almost March bites the cold.   *T&G, MLBW* [FPOP, EA].

MS dated March 5, 1951:

line 1: In February almost March I bite the cold.

LN's alternative line 1: In February almost March we bite the cold.

line 8: There are no objects here, only velocities.

LZ notes his suggested omissions from lines 1 and 8 on the MS.

MS dated March 19, 1951, accepts his suggestions and revises to the present text.

LN to LZ, dated March 15, 1951: "I have lots to say about Feb. almost March but we're both fed up talking about it. Her a goddess? Because I mention Eden (God?)? You see, this thing of changing a poem means a different thing, different rhythm and pretty soon the whole original idea and movement in the mind of the writer is gone and the whole thing would have to be done over. However, I'll keep your suggestions. Copy of it enclosed" (*NCZ* 178).

Montevallo Review 1.4 (Summer 1953): 12, with a variant line 8: no object here

People, people—   *T&G, MLBW* [FPOP, EA].

First appearance FPOP.

In a five-poem group titled "IN EXCHANGE FOR HAIKU," *Neon* 4 (1959): n.p.

July, waxwings   *T&G, MLBW* [FPOP, EA].

FPOP has two variants:

line 1: July, the waxwings.
line 4: a dead

In the five-poem group titled "IN EXCHANGE FOR HAIKU," *Neon* 4 (1959): n.p., line 1 reads as above and line 2 reads: on my berries

In EA, line 1 reads: July—waxwings

Old man who seined   *MFT, T&G, MLBW* [FPOP, EA, VV].
First appearance FPOP.

In a five-poem group titled "IN EXCHANGE FOR HAIKU," *Neon* 4 (1959): n.p., in "EIGHT POEMS," *Monks Pond* 1 (Spring 1968): 5, and in *The Voice That is Great Within Us: American Poetry of the 20th Century*, ed. Hayden Carruth (New York: Bantam, 1970).

***Mother is dead*   *T&G, MLBW* [FPOP].**
Until *T&G* and *MLBW*, this was the first poem in a numbered three-poem sequence titled "THE ELEMENT MOTHER." FPOP titles the poem *"She's Dead."* The second poem in the sequence is *"The graves"* (see following note) and the third is *"Kepler"* (see below). The sequence survives in FPOP and in *Origin* ser. 2, 2 (July 1961): 29, but dissolves in *T&G* and *MLBW*.

LN to LZ, March 23, 1956: "got started on a poem about my mother—this is her birthday and the snow and Marcus Aurelius and my overloaded loneliness˙ and it's a temptation to write like Yeats, a kind of mellifluous, lush overloading (kind of folk element in it tho at that) but I must not" (*NCZ* 227).

***The graves*   *T&G, MLBW* [FPOP, EA, VV].**
Early MS dated 1945:

> The Graves and the Other Woman
>
> You were my mother, peony bush,
> you worried over life's raw push.
> But you, my father, catalpa tree,
> were as serene as now—he refused to see
> that the woman he shaded hotly cared
> for his purse petals falling—his mind in the air.

Revised to the present text for FPOP.
Origin ser. 2, 2 (July 1961): 29.
See preceding note, for *"Mother is dead."*

***Kepler*   Unpublished in book form [FPOP].**
Origin ser. 2, 2 (July 1961): 29.
See note above for *"Mother is dead."*

Bonpland   Unpublished [FPOP].

Happy New Year   *T&G, MLBW* [FPOP].

MS dated Jan. 4, 1951, has variant lines 6–10:

> My friend, two thousand years
> beyond you
> I hand you this:
> you were right.
> Happy New Year

LN's annotation: "Happy New Year—as I hear it sung there is slight pause after bitter and so winter brotherhood comes together—these phrases that look forward and back are fascinating to do but I suppose there's a limit. Trees could have apostrophe after it. What started the whole thing aside from 'better than bitter' was an inversion: 'with sorrow clean' Silly? We still get our deepest feeling of beauty from old trad. lit."

The MS carries LZ's suggested changes to the above lines 6–10.

A later MS dated Jan. 12, 1951, adopts his suggestions:

> My friend, you were right.
> Two thousand years
> beyond you
> I hand you this:

LN's annotations: "Would hyphens in 'bloom with snow' make it less trite? or snowbloom? (kind of effeminate)."

Both MSS are numbered XVI of "FOR PAUL: GROUP TWO" and both merge the present stanzas 1 and 2. The poem "Happy New Year" becomes poem XIX in "FOR PAUL: GROUP TWO," *New Mexico Quarterly* 21.2 (Spring 1951): 211, which also merges stanzas 1 and 2.

Revised to the present text for FPOP.

MLBW hyphenates "snow-/clean" (lines 10–11).

1957–1959

In Feb. 1957 LN began a menial job at the Fort Atkinson Memorial Hospital; she would retire in Nov. 1963.

Between 1957 and 1959, her five-line stanza with its rhyming third and fourth lines predominates: "did I create a new form . . . influence of haiku I suppose . . ." (*NCZ* 230). These "five-liners" first occur during the "FOR PAUL" project: the 1950 "Lugubre for a child," and the 1956 "July, waxwings," "People, people," and "Old man who seined." They are next seen in MS in 1957 and 1958.

In *T&G* and *MLBW* she grouped many of these five-liners (most of which are single-stanza poems) in a section titled "IN EXCHANGE FOR HAIKU." The title is first used in

Neon 4 (1959): n.p., where it groups five poems: "July, the waxwings," "Old man who seined" (two stanzas), "People, people," "Linnaeus in Lapland" (two stanzas), "Fog-thick morning." Another selection of five-liners appears numbered but untitled in *Origin* ser. 2, 2 (July 1961): 27—"Hear," "Springtime's wide," "How white the gulls," "My friend tree," and "New-sawed." EA names a group of 13 poems "IN EXCHANGE FOR HAIKU"; two of these are "The soil is poor" and "Michelangelo," poems which are subsequently grouped with "POEMS AT THE PORTHOLE" in H&SF (see pp. 286–87). One of the prominent five-liners of the period, "My friend tree," the title poem of the 1961 volume published by Ian Hamilton Finlay's Wild Hawthorn Press in Edinburgh, Scotland, is not grouped with "IN EXCHANGE FOR HAIKU" in *T&G* and *MLBW*, but rather with the folk poems.

Linnaeus in Lapland   *T&G, MLBW* [EA].

MS dated 1957 includes "Fog-thick morning."

In a five-poem group titled, "IN EXCHANGE FOR HAIKU," *Neon* 4 (1959): n.p.

Also in *Poor.Old.Tired.Horse.* 1 (undated, probably March 1962): n.p., with "I rose from marsh mud" and in "EIGHT POEMS," *Monks Pond* 1 (Spring 1968): 5.

Fog-thick morning—   Unpublished in book form.

MS dated 1957 includes "Linnaeus in Lapland."

In a five-poem group titled "IN EXCHANGE FOR HAIKU," *Neon* 4 (1959): n.p.

Hear   *T&G, MLBW* [EA].

In the 13-poem MS dated Jan. 1958.

Origin ser. 2, 2 (July 1961): 27; one of five numbered poems.

Cricket-song—   Unpublished.

MS dated 1957 and perhaps sent to LZ with her Sept. 2, 1957, letter: "when I suddenly came on the review of *Some Time* in *The Times Book Review* I was moved to write a pome and I diddit—two stanzys of my 5 liners" (*NCZ* 238).

The poem appears again on the MS dated Jan. 1958, one of 13 poems (all "five-liners").

***Musical Toys*   Unpublished.**

In the 13-poem MS dated Jan. 1958.

I fear this war   Unpublished.

In the 13-poem MS dated Jan. 1958.

Van Gogh could see   Unpublished.

In the 13-poem MS dated Jan. 1958.

No matter where you are   Unpublished.

In the 13-poem MS dated Jan. 1958.

How white the gulls   *T&G, MLBW* [EA].

In the 13-poem MS dated Jan. 1958.

Origin ser. 2, 2 (July 1961): 27; one of five numbered poems.

Springtime's wide   *T&G, MLBW* [EA].

In the 13-poem MS dated Jan. 1958, variant lines 1–2:

> Springtime's
> Wide water-

Origin ser. 2, 2 (July 1961): 27—one of five numbered poems.

White   Unpublished.

In the 13-poem MS dated Jan. 1958.

Dusk—   *T&G, MLBW* [EA].

In the 13-poem MS dated Jan. 1958:

> In spring when the small fish spawn
> goes a boat along shore—
> someone scything grass?
> > Slippery
> Man.

Revised for MS dated June 8, 1962, published in "5 POEMS," *Origin* ser. 2, 8 (Jan. 1963):
27, with one variant from the present text, line 1: Shore-dusk
In *T&G* lines 2 and 3 are reversed:

> How slippery is man—
> He's spearing from a boat

Revised to the present text (minus the dashes) for "EIGHT POEMS," *Monks Pond* 1 (Spring
1968): 8.

LN to LZ, Dec. 25, 1957: "she talked of her neighbors and out came this bit—was
I listening to Chaucer??—In spring when the small fish spawn—so I've used it for a
five-liner" (*NCZ* 241–42).

Beautiful girl—   *T&G, MLBW* [EA].

In the 13-poem MS dated Jan. 1958, variant lines 1–2:

> Beautiful girl
> pushes food upon her fork

New-sawed   *T&G, MLBW* [EA, VV].

In the 13-poem MS dated Jan. 1958.
Origin ser. 2, 2 (July 1961): 27; one of five numbered poems.

My friend tree   *MFT, T&G, MLBW* [EA, VV].

Sent to Paul Zukofsky with a letter and sketch dated Oct. 15, 1959: "Here is one of
the tree workers way up near the top of my big ash tree, one foot on one branch and
the other on another branch. Wonderful to watch him. They did it with ropes and a
gasoline run saw. $90 well spent. I hail the sun and the moon. . . . I still have 14 trees
on my lawn. But you do have a feeling about destroying a tree" (*LN:W&P* 62–63).
Origin ser. 2, 2 (July 1961): 27; one of five numbered single-stanza poems.

1960–1964

Many of the poems in this section were written during LN's friendship from mid-1960 to late 1962 with the Milwaukee dentist Harold Hein. Her second book—the first in 15 years—appeared in 1961 when Ian Hamilton Finlay's Wild Hawthorn Press published *My Friend Tree,* a small collection of 16 poems, 9 of them reprinted from *New Goose,* illustrated with linocuts by Walter Miller, and introduced on a loose-leaf sheet by Ed Dorn. LN offered two alternative titles: *Great Grass!* and *Don't Shoot the Rail.*

In May 1963, she married Al Millen, and in Nov. 1963, she was able to retire from her hospital job in Fort Atkinson and move with Al to an apartment in Milwaukee. The last two poems in this section reflect the new geography. LN and Al spent weekends on Black Hawk Island, first in her small cottage and then in their new home, within sight of the cottage but closer to the Rock River and built high to escape the floodwaters.

In Leonardo's light   *T&G, MLBW.*
   Origin ser. 2, 2 (July 1961): 26.
   LN to LZ, Aug. 22, 1960: "Harold [Hein] brought me his notes on Leonardo da Vinci and I was so fascinated I wrote a poem. . . . Closest to a love poem I ever writ" (*NCZ* 265).

You are my friend—   *MFT, T&G, MLBW* **[EA].**
   MS dated Sept. 15, 1960:

> Why do I press it: are you my friend?
> You bring me peaches
> and the high bush cranberry
>   you carry
> my fishpole
>
> you water my worms
> you patched my boot
> with your mending kit
>   nothing in it
> but my hand
>
> The trouble of the boot on you, friend
> your dentist fingers
> an orchard to mow
>   you also
> paint

Revised to the present text on MS dated Jan. 20, 1961; in *Origin* ser. 2, 2 (July 1961): 31; in "EIGHT POEMS," *Monks Pond* 1 (Spring 1968): 6; and in *The Voice That Is Great Within Us: American Poetry of the 20th Century,* ed. Hayden Carruth (New York: Bantam, 1970).

Come In   **Unpublished.**

Earliest MS dated "Xmas 1960" offers two alternative versions:

(i)

Thanksgiving, Glen Ellyn

Education, kindness
live here
whose dog does not impose
her long nose
and barks quietly.

Serious wags its tail
where green yard is exposed
by white tie-backs.
None here lacks
this outgoing.

(ii)

Education, kindness
live here
Whose grandfolk taught:
work hard,
whose dog does not impose
her long nose
and barks quietly.

Serious wags its tail
where white tie-backs expose
evergreen, green yard.
Hard
is lovely here.

LZ holograph on the above MS notes: "a later version r'cd on Jan. 12/61. Stanza 1 (same as above) and

Serious wags its tail
—little yard exposed
by white tie-backs—
at knick-knacks
like us knocking."

LZ's "stanza 1 (same as above)" most likely refers to the stanza beginning, "Whose grandfolk taught:"

Revised to the present text for MS dated Jan. 20, 1961.

LN to LZ, Nov. 27, 1960: "Harold took me to his brother Fred's in Glen Ellyn (suburb of Chicago) Thanksgiving day. . . . Nice house in a section of ranch type and colonial houses, . . . But show is not the usual thing with the Heins of Glen Ellyn. It's all education, science, teaching, family life. Quiet, well brought up family with three kids, the youngest just entering college. Even the big, beautiful Shepherd-collie barks quiet" (*NCZ* 270).

The men leave the car   *T&G, MLBW* **[EA].**

The experience this poem draws on is recorded on July 2, 1961 (*NCZ* 282).

Origin ser. 2, 6 (July 1962): 24.

LN to CC, Feb. 5, 1962: "It strikes me that an editor must wish fervently that his contributors head their poems so that he doesn't have to title all headless poems POEMS." She offers titles of "Calla of the Heart-Shaped Leaves" or simply "Calla" (*BYHM* 31).

The wild and wavy event   *T&G, MLBW* **[EA].**

LN to LZ, Dec. 31, 1961: "Trying to do a poem on Abigail Adams—what a gal" (*NCZ* 297).

Origin ser. 2, 6 (July 1962): 25. On Feb. 5, 1962, LN offered CC a title for this poem: "She watched the Battle of Bunker's Hill" (*BYHM* 31).

FLORIDA   **Unpublished in book form.**

MS dated Feb. 18, 1962, with the following variants:

part 1, line 3: his close proximity

part 4, line 5: the pink flamingo

Parts 1 and 4 in *Poor.Old.Tired.Horse.* 4 (undated, probably late 1962): n.p., where they are numbered 1 and 2.

My life is hung up   *T&G, MLBW.*

MS dated June 8, 1962.

In a group of "5 POEMS," *Origin* ser. 2, 8 (Jan. 1963): 26.

Easter   *T&G, MLBW.*

On the MS dated June 8, 1962, and in "5 POEMS," *Origin* ser. 2, 8 (Jan. 1963): 26, the first three lines read:

> Easter
>
> Land
> A robin stood by porch

LN's annotation alongside title on MS: "Shd. be: Easter After Flood".

Get a load   *T&G, MLBW.*

On the MS dated June 8, 1962, lines 2 and 3 merge into one. On the MS; in "5 POEMS," *Origin* ser. 2, 8 (Jan. 1963): 26; and in *T&G*, line 5 reads: like freight cars

Poet's work   *T&G, MLBW.*

MS dated June 8, 1962.

In "5 POEMS," *Origin* ser. 2, 8 (Jan. 1963): 27, there are periods at the end of each stanza.

In *T&G* the poem is untitled.

Property is poverty—   Unpublished in book form.

MS dated June 8, 1962. LN's annotation on MS: "(Don't confuse this with reality—I don't have to foreclose)"

In a numbered group of "THREE POEMS," *Poetry* 102.5 (Aug. 1963): 302–303, where the opening line mistakenly reads: Prosperity is poverty.

Now in one year   *T&G, MLBW* [EA].

MS version dated June 8, 1962, is a "five-liner":

> Now in one year a book
> published and plumbing—
> took a lifetime to weep
>   a deep
> trickle

Revised to the present text for a numbered group of "THREE POEMS," *Poetry* 102.5 (Aug. 1963): 303.

River-marsh-drowse   *T&G, MLBW* [EA].

MS dated June 8, 1962:

> The river ran off
> into marsh and in flood
>   moonlight
>   gave sight
> of no land.
>
> They fished, a man
> took his wife to town
> with his rowboat's 10-horse,
>   shipped his voice
> to the herons.
>
> Sure they'd drink—
> full foamy folk
>   till asleep
>   asleep
> on one leg in the weeds.

A second MS dated June 19, 1962, revises the poem to the present text for the numbered group of "THREE POEMS," *Poetry* 102.5 (Aug. 1963): 302.

Club 26   T&G, MLBW.

Titled "Place to Dine" in *Midwest* (Spring 1963): 54; variant lines 6–11:

> built white on a red carpet
> quiet
> for the massive steak
>
> the circular cool bar
> fingers caressing glass stems
>
> We stayed till the stamens trembled

An account of the experience related in the poem can be found in *NCZ*, July 29, 1962. LN submitted the poem to *Midwest* in August 1962 (*NCZ* 318).

To foreclose   *T&G, MLBW.*

Titled "O Catullus" in *Joglars* 1.1 (Spring 1964): 10, where it is the first of "THREE POEMS IN ONE YEAR, JONATHAN."

LN to LZ, Jan. 4, 1963: "Just wrote poem on foreclosing. Venom against property, the law, etc. I invoked Cat. 93 (Gregory's 2 lines for 93), the second line changed enough to suit what *I'm* talking about" (*NCZ* 327).

To my small / electric pump   T&G, MLBW **[EA].**

The second of "THREE POEMS IN ONE YEAR, JONATHAN," *Joglars* 1.1 (Spring 1964). Submitted to *Joglars* in late 1963 (*NCZ* 341).

T. E. Lawrence   MLBW **[EA].**

Origin ser. 3, 2 (July 1966): 32.

LN to LZ, Dec. 26, 1963: "Strange that the name Lawrence has such a fascination for me—D.H. and T.E., the latter overwhelmingly so. He was in the center of his own silence no matter how much action went on around him" (*NCZ* 337).

A ten-page typescript sent to Ron Ellis on Oct. 26, 1966, titles the poem, *"From T. E. Lawrence."*

As I paint the street   *T&G, MLBW.*

Origin ser. 3, 2 (July 1966): 18, and *T&G* add a final line: "from his neon home". The opening line is a title in its *Origin* appearance.

The language of the poem can be traced to her Dec. 13, 1963, letter to LZ (*NCZ* 338) and her March 12, 1964, letter to CC (*BYHM* 43).

Art Center   T&G, MLBW.

Paris Review 8.32 (1964): 198.

LN to LZ, Jan. 7, 1964: "My lovely husband . . . took me down to the Art Center. The building has box-like wings on the shore of the lake, gives impression of being all glass. If every human being took turns living there for only two days, we'd all come out a lovely new race" (*NCZ* 341–42).

In 1964, LN made three holograph collections of poems written into small, bound books and illustrated with watercolor paintings of her new home on Black Hawk Island. The first (8" × 5") was titled "HOMEMADE POEMS" (30 poems) and went to Cid Corman as a gift—"the product of the last year"—in Oct. 1964; the second two (6" × 4½"), titled "HANDMADE POEMS" (25 poems), went to LZ and to Jonathan Williams for Xmas 1964. The contents of the three are roughly equivalent—the collections have 22 poems in common although several are revised between "HOMEMADE" and "HANDMADE." At the end of the notes, the contents of each book are listed.

Consider at the outset: *T&G, MLBW.*
  "HOMEMADE POEMS" (Oct. 1964), variant line 8: A delicacy—the marrow.
  Revised to the present text for *Poetry* 106.5 (Aug. 1965): 342, where it appears in a numbered group of "FIVE POEMS."

Ah your face   *NC, MLBW.*
  Origin ser. 3, 2 (July 1966): 20.
  Included in "TRACES OF LIVING THINGS" (see p. 244).

Alcoholic dream   *T&G, MLBW* **[EA].**
  Paris Review 8.32 (Summer/Fall 1964): 198.

To my pres-/sure pump   *T&G, MLBW.*
  In a numbered group of "FIVE POEMS," *Poetry* 106.5 (Aug. 1965): 341.

Laundromat   **Unpublished in book form.**
  "HOMEMADE POEMS" (Oct. 1964), variant stanza 1:

>   Once again a public wedding
>   a casual, sudsy
>   social affair
>   at the tubs

  Copytext for posthumous publication in *BC* (1976).
  Revised to the present text for "HANDMADE POEMS" (Xmas 1964) and *Origin* ser. 3, 2 (July 1966): 21.

March   *T&G, MLBW.*
  In a numbered group of "FIVE POEMS," *Poetry* 106.5 (Aug. 1965): 342.

Something in the water   *T&G, MLBW* **[EA].**
  Combustion 15/*Island* 6 (n.d.): 31.

Santayana's   **Unpublished.**
  "HOMEMADE POEMS" (Oct. 1964), variant lines 2–3:

>   I don't know poetry?—
>   I like somewhat the putrid Petrarch

Copytext for posthumous publication in *BC* (1976).

Revised to the present text for "HANDMADE POEMS" (Xmas 1964). Both copies record her hesitation: "I might never use this—too much his own words."

If only my friend   *T&G, MLBW* **[EA].**

Very likely written in late 1962 when her friendship with Harold Hein was ending.

Frog noise/suddenly stops   **Unpublished.**

Published posthumously in *BC* (1976).

In the transcendence   **Unpublished.**

First stanza published posthumously in *BC* (1976).

To whom   **Unpublished in book form.**

"HOMEMADE POEMS" (Oct. 1964), variant lines 1–2:

> Is there someone
> I can leave

Copy text for posthumous publication in *BC* (1976).
"HANDMADE POEMS" (Xmas 1964), variant lines 1–2:

> Someone?—
> I can leave

variant line 7: copper-braced
variant line 9: when I leave
Revised to the present text for *Origin* ser. 3, 2 (July 1966): 26.

Margaret Fuller   **Unpublished in book form.**

Origin ser. 3, 2 (July 1966): 25 and posthumous publication in *BC* (1976).

Watching dan-/cers on skates   *T&G, MLBW.*

The present text follows "HOMEMADE/HANDMADE POEMS," *T&G,* and *Origin* ser. 3, 2 (July 1966): 27, which all break the title into two lines.

MLBW variant: unbroken title on single line.

Hospital Kitchen   **Unpublished in book form.**

Origin ser. 3, 2 (July 1966): 21, and posthumous publication in *BC* (1976).

Chicory flower/on campus   *T&G, MLBW.*

In "THREE POEMS," *Granta* 71.12456 (1964/5): 19, with variant line 5: in earth-evolved

Fall ("Early morning corn")   *T&G.*

"HOMEMADE POEMS" (Oct. 1964) adds an eighth line: tittle
Revised to the present text for "HANDMADE POEMS" (Xmas 1964).

LZ's   **Unpublished.**

LZ's copy of "HANDMADE POEMS" carries the note: "Never to be sent out if you say so." Copytext for posthumous publication in *BC* (1976).

Letter from Ian   T&G, MLBW.

In "HOMEMADE POEMS" (Oct. 1964), "HANDMADE POEMS" (Xmas 1964), and *Origin* ser. 3, 2 (July 1966): 23, the poem is titled *"Ian's"* with variant lines 2–3:

> middle of Edinburgh
> a castle on a rock—

LN to LZ, Sept. 11, 1961, includes transcribed extracts from letters from Ian Hamilton Finlay and Jessie McGuffie: "As for the castle, aye sure, there's a big castle on a rock in the middle of Edinburgh—we'll send you a postcard—and they floodlight it, and have a big show up there, with pipe bands and all. . . . Life is most hectic these days—you can't step outside without meeting a posse of poets from the Festival (*NCZ* 291 n.3).

Some float off on chocolate bars   *T&G, MLBW* [EA].

"HOMEMADE POEMS" (Oct. 1964), lines 7–10:

> and let the birds live
>
> Myself I gripped
> my melting container one night
> I heard the wild

Revised to the present text for "HANDMADE POEMS" (Xmas 1964).

EA inserts an extra line between lines 10 and 11: and the wood on the house

I knew a clean man   *T&G, MLBW.*

Combustion 15/*Island* 6 (n.d.): 33.

Scythe   T&G, MLBW.

So he said/on radio   Unpublished.

Published posthumously in *BC* (1976).

I visit/the graves   T&G, MLBW [EA].

The third of "THREE POEMS IN ONE YEAR, JONATHAN," *Joglars* 1.1 (Spring 1964). Submitted to *Joglars* in late 1963 (*NCZ* 341), but perhaps originating in a visit to her family gravesites recounted to LZ in Oct. 1960 (*NCZ* 269–70).

EA adds an apostrophe to "sons'" in line 2.

For best work   *NC, MLBW.*

Also included in "TRACES OF LIVING THINGS" (see p. 242).

Origin ser. 3, 2 (July 1966): 22, and *The Voice That Is Great Within Us: American Poetry of the 20th Century*, ed. Hayden Carruth (New York: Bantam, 1970).

The obliteration   Unpublished in book form.

In "HOMEMADE POEMS" (Oct. 1964):

> The radio talk this morning
> was of obliterating
> the world

> I notice fruit flies rise
> from the rind
> of the recommended
> melon

Copytext for posthumous publication in *BC* (1976).
In Jonathan Williams's "HANDMADE POEMS" (Xmas 1964), line 4 reads: Fruit flies rise
Revised to the present text for *Lines* 5 (May 1965): 33.

Spring   *T&G, MLBW.*

In a numbered group of "FIVE POEMS," *Poetry* 106.5 (Aug. 1965): 343.

LN's note on "HOMEMADE POEMS" (Oct. 1964): "Note—what happened to
Primavera, Florence, Italy and my visit to Grant Park beside L. Michigan, Milwaukee."

The park / "a darling walk / for the mind"   *T&G, MLBW* **[EA].**

In a numbered group of "FIVE POEMS," *Poetry* 106.5 (Aug. 1965): 344.

LN to Jonathan Williams, 19 Feb. 1964: "The one thing that's stark different
here—Saarinen's Art Center on the lake shore, huge glass mushroom transported from
some Walt Disney desert. Not far from it a park with (a comfortable) statue of Robert
Burns" (in *Truck* 16 [1975]: 46).

Who was Mary Shelley?   *T&G, MLBW* **[EA].**

In *Paris Review* 9.36 (Winter 1966): 144, but very likely one of three poems
accepted by the editor two years earlier in May 1964. However, only *"Art Center"* and
"Alcoholic dream" were published in the Summer-Fall 1964 issue while "Who was
Mary Shelley?" was delayed until Winter 1966. The following variant lines appear in
the *Paris Review* version:

line 4: She eloped with Shelley,

line 10: Created Frankenstein nights

line 14: She read Latin, Greek, Italian.

Meanwhile the poem was revised to the present text for "HOMEMADE POEMS" (Oct.
1964) and "HANDMADE POEMS" (Xmas 1964).

Wild strawberries   **Unpublished in book form.**

"HOMEMADE POEMS" (Oct. 1964):

> Ruskin found wild strawberries
> and they were a consolation
> poor man whose diaries
> were grey with instances of rose
>
> I think tonight we'll have the liver
> since tomorrow we go out
> tho not of course like him

to Metaphysical dinner
following Greco

Copytext for posthumous publication in *BC* (1976).
Revised for "HANDMADE POEMS" (Xmas 1964) with variant line 7: not like him
Revised to the present text for *Origin* ser. 3, 2 (July 1966): 24.

1965–1967

These years saw the start of her friendship with Gail Roub, a Black Hawk Islander and history teacher at Fort Atkinson High School.

In mid-1965 she prepared the typescript for *T&G*. She also began summer vacation car trips with Al Millen that would take them to the Black Hills in South Dakota in 1965, around Lake Superior in 1966, and to Copper Harbor, Mich., and Door County, Wis., in 1967. These travels provided impetus for major poems such as "LAKE SUPERIOR" and "WINTERGREEN RIDGE."

Autumn   Unpublished in book form.
Poor.Old.Tired.Horse. 9 (undated, possibly 1965): 1. The poem derives from the long version of the FPOP poem "Dear Paul," lines 188 and 191 (see p. 400).

Last night the trash barrel   Unpublished in book form.
Poor.Old.Tired.Horse. 9 (undated, possibly 1965): 1.

The boy tossed the news   Unpublished in book form.
Poor.Old.Tired.Horse. 9 (undated, possibly 1965): 1.

Popcorn-can cover   *T&G, MLBW* [EA].
Poor.Old.Tired.Horse. 9 (undated, possibly 1965): 1; variant line 3: over the hole

Truth   Unpublished in book form.
Poor.Old.Tired.Horse. 9 (undated, possibly 1965): 1.

Lights, lifts   *T&G, MLBW.*
Lines 5 (May 1965): 32.

O late fall   *T&G, MLBW* [EA].

CHURCHILL'S DEATH   *T&G, MLBW.*
Arts in Society 3.3 (Winter 1965): 429.
LN to CC, Feb. 11, 1965: "I did see Churchill's funeral, the Thames, St. Paul's, the solemn faces, Handel on the organ—I found it very moving. I didn't see the mechanical cranes along the Thames dip in salute as the body passed down, but the papers said they did. I hope it wasn't an order, an order from the top" (*BYHM* 54).

***The Badlands**   T&G, MLBW* [EA].

Origin ser. 3, 2 (July 1966): 14.

LN was visiting the Badlands of South Dakota when she heard of Adlai Stevenson's death (July 28, 1965, *BYHM* 68).

A student   *T&G, MLBW.*

An early version in *Poor.Old.Tired.Horse.* 13 (undated, possibly 1965): n.p., is composed as two five-line stanzas:

> A student
> my head always down
> of the grass as I mow
> and my low
> pillow
>
> I missed the cranes
> "These crayons fly
> in a circle ahead"
>   said
> a tall fellow

The same version appears in a June 20, 1967, letter to Gail Roub.

LN to LZ, Jan. 14, 1962: "Man here says 'these crayons' (cranes) 'fly in a circle but ahead'" (*NCZ* 298).

Bird singing   *T&G, MLBW* [EA].

Origin ser. 4, 16 (July 1981): 28–30, prints the three versions which LN sent to Gail Roub in 1965 after she had seen Gail's vivid acrylic painting. LN published the second version. Here are the other two plus her annotations:

Version I:

> *Prothonotary Warbler*
>
> Clerk of May Court
> singing ringing
> yellow green
>
> St. Francis image
> as perch—why judge—
> a niche in the wall
>
> and the man made green ring
> in his painting—grass
> the sweet bird flew in

and the friend took it
to testify: (Willa)
"they know how to live"

Version III:

Warbler

St. Francis' image
        —no grimace—
looks down
            past the nest in the niche
            and the yellow green
                        sound

    It is right
        to delight
    in this ringing
                bird-light
                from the emerald
                ground

I—Fairly conscious. II is the one I'll probably keep as the one *sleeping under* the other, in large part subconscious. I might have laid an egg (I) tho—?—in any event the egg out of the bird. In II the bird out of the egg and the song before that and the color—

Cather (last two lines of I—you remember she said that in Avignon they know how to live. (That was 1902—wonder what that place is now?)—

Version III—This might be *it*—or is it only fooling around, a kind of Mother Goose warbler?

Version II in *Combustion* 15/*Island* 6 (n.d.): 31, and in "EIGHT POEMS," *Monks Pond* 1 (Spring 1968): 7.

Easter Greeting   **Unpublished in book form.**
    Origin ser. 3, 2 (July 1966): 1, and posthumously in *BC* (1976).

CITY TALK   **Unpublished in book form.**
    Origin ser. 3, 2 (July 1966): 15, and posthumously in *BC* (1976).

As praiseworthy   *T&G, MLBW* [EA].
    Origin ser. 3, 2 (July 1966): 16; "EIGHT POEMS," *Monks Pond* 1 (Spring 1968): 8; and *The Voice That Is Great Within Us: American Poetry of the 20th Century*, ed. Hayden Carruth (New York: Bantam, 1970).

They've lost their leaves   *MLBW.*
Origin ser. 3, 2 (July 1966): 17.

My mother saw the green tree toad   *T&G, MLBW.*
Origin ser. 3, 2 (July 1966): 19, and *The Voice That Is Great Within Us: American Poetry of the 20th Century*, ed. Hayden Carruth (New York: Bantam, 1970).

TRADITION   **Unpublished in book form.**
Origin ser. 3, 2 (July 1966): 29, and posthumously in *BC* (1976).

Autumn Night   **Unpublished in book form.**
Origin ser. 3, 2 (July 1966): 31, and posthumously in *BC* (1976).
The poem refers to Aeneas McAllister, who was LN's neighbor and close friend from 1953 to 1960. He was a pianist, composer, and amateur astronomer.

Sky   *MLBW.*
Origin ser. 3, 2 (July 1966): 33.

Nothing to speak of   *MLBW.*
Origin ser. 3, 2 (July 1966): 34.

Swedenborg   *MLBW.*
Origin ser. 3, 2 (July 1966): 35.

I lost you to water, summer   *MLBW.*
Origin ser. 3, 2 (July 1966): 36.
Another poem addressed to Aeneas McAllister. See note for *"Autumn Night,"* above.

I married   **Unpublished in book form.**
Origin ser. 3, 9 (April 1968): 38, and posthumously in *BC* (1976).
LN to CC (letter plus poem), July 20, 1967: "Just a few minutes ago rather spontaneous from a folk conversation and I suppose some of my own dark forebodings. We shd. be true to our subconscious? Sorry it is another *I* poem. My god, I must try to get away from that" (*BYHM* 129).

You see here   **Unpublished in book form.**
In a group of eleven poems titled "HEAR & SEE," *Origin* ser. 3, 7 (Oct. 1967): 56, and posthumously in *BC* (1976).

Your erudition   **Unpublished in book form.**
In a group of eleven poems titled "HEAR & SEE," *Origin* ser. 3, 7 (Oct. 1967): 53, and posthumously in *BC* (1976).

Alone   *MLBW.*
In a group of eleven poems titled "HEAR & SEE," *Origin* ser. 3, 7 (Oct. 1967): 53.

Why can't I be happy   **Unpublished in book form.**
In a group of eleven poems titled "HEAR & SEE," *Origin* ser. 3, 7 (Oct. 1967): 54, and posthumously in *BC* (1976).

And what you liked   Unpublished in book form.

In a group of eleven poems titled "HEAR & SEE," *Origin* ser. 3, 7 (Oct. 1967): 54, and posthumously in *BC* (1976).

Cleaned all surfaces   Unpublished in book form.

In a group of eleven poems titled "HEAR & SEE," *Origin* ser. 3, 7 (Oct. 1967): 54, and posthumously in *BC* (1976).

Young in Fall I said: the birds   *MLBW* [EA].

In a numbered group of "FOUR POEMS," *Poetry* 111.3 (Dec. 1967): 159, and *The Voice That Is Great Within Us: American Poetry of the 20th Century*, ed. Hayden Carruth (New York: Bantam, 1970).

NORTH CENTRAL

This collection was published by Fulcrum Press in 1968. LN thought of the work as a long poem. She told CC on Oct. 13, 1967, "I'm mailing you today another envelope of poems that I think of as Part II of a long poem, the first section of which will be out this fall or winter in *Arts in Society*. Third section coming up (since Door Co. trip) . . ." (*BYHM* 131–32). The first section she refers to is "LAKE SUPERIOR," the second is what came to be known as "TRACES OF LIVING THINGS," and the third is "WINTERGREEN RIDGE." Between the first two sections she added the short poem "*My Life by Water*."

LAKE SUPERIOR   *NC, MLBW* [EA].

The poem arises in part from her 1966 summer car trip with Al Millen around Lake Superior. Her notes for the poem, now in the Roub Collection, number close to 300 pages. They include detailed research into the history and geology of the region. An Oct. 6, 1966, letter to Morgan Gibson refers to an early version of the poem called "CIR-CLE TOUR." However, the only surviving early version is "TRAVELERS/Lake Superior Region," in *Arts in Society* 4.3 (Fall/Winter 1967): 508–13:

TRAVELERS

Lake Superior Region

I
In every part of every living thing
is stuff that once was rock
    that turned to soil

In blood the minerals
    of the rock

II
Iron the common element of earth
in rocks and freighters

Sault Sainte Marie
the old day *pause* for *voyageurs,*
bosho (bon jour) sung out
by garrison men

Now locks, big boats
coal-black and iron-ore-red
topped with what white castlework

The waters working together
          internationally
Gulls playing both sides

III
Through all this granite land
the sign of the cross

Beauty: impurities in the rock

IV
Here we touch the polished
ruby of corundum
lapis lazuli
from changing limestone
glow-apricot red-brown
carnelian sard
from Uruguay
and silica-sand agate
from nearby shore

Greek-named, Exodus-antique
kicked up in America's
          Northwest
you have been in my mind
between my toes,
          agate

V
Let the English put sun
in the name Radisson
and make gooseberry jam

of Groseilliers
                (GrosaYAY)
river, falls, a whole country
gooseberry

"a laborinth of pleasure"
this new world of the lakes—
Radisson

Long hair, long gun,
no fingernails—
pulled off by the Mohawks
when they bound him to the stake
for slow killing

Forty years ago now
toward Rainy Lake
ospreys dived for fish
and eagles swooped to snatch
from ospreys as they did

when Radisson
Knife Lake-rendezvoused
with Chippewa, Huron,
Ottawa, Sioux for furs
this lake (State 65) named
for his gift to them
the first steel knife
they'd seen

VI
                The long canoes
"Birch Bark
    and white Seder
                for the ribs"

VII
Schoolcraft and party
left the Soo with canoes
US pennants, masts, sails,
chanting canoemen, barge,
soldiers
                for Minnesota
Their South Shore journey
            as if Life's—

The Chocolate River
      The Laughing Fish
and The River of the Dead

Peaks of volcanic thrust,
hornblende in massed granite
Wave-cut Cambrian rock
painted by soluble mineral oxides
washed by the waves and the rains
A green running as from copper

Sea-roaring caverns—
Chippewa threw deermeat
to the savage maws

Voyageurs crossed themselves
threw a twist of tobacco in

VIII
Of the wild pigeon

did not man

      maimed by no

         stone-fall

mash the cobalt

      and carnelian

         of that bird

IX
Into Minnesota
beside the great granite,
gneiss and the schists

to the redolent pondy lakes—
lilies, flag and Indian reed
"through which we successfully
         passed"

X
Came now to joy,
the shining lake-study-
pronouncement:
the primary source
of the Mississippi River

Itasca
(from *veritas caput*)

XI
The smooth black stone
I picked up in true source park
            the leaf beside it
was once stone

The sea went over
Calculate:
our coral bones

I caught myself faintly
in the glass of the museum's
glacier exhibit

XII
I'm sorry to have missed
            Sandy Lake
My dear one tells me
            we did not
We watched a gopher there

The segment beginning "And at the blue ice superior spot," was published in *Origin* ser. 3, 9 (April 1968) in an early grouping of "TRACES OF LIVING THINGS." It was later added to the final version of "LAKE SUPERIOR."

LN prepared an errata slip for copies of *NC*:
ERRATA
    The Lake Superior section:
    Beauty: impurities in the rock
    should be the 3rd line of the poem preceding.
    The Marquette poem then begins:
    And at the blue ice superior spot

EA excerpts three sections from "LAKE SUPERIOR": "And at the blue ice superior spot," "*Wild Pigeon*," and "The smooth black stone."

My Life by Water   *NC, MLBW* [EA].
    Untitled in *Origin* ser. 3, 7 (Oct. 1967): 55, and EA. In *Origin* it is part of a group of eleven poems titled "HEAR & SEE."
    Titled in *New Poetry Out of Wisconsin*, ed. August Derleth (Sauk City, Wis.: Stanton & Lee, 1969) 173.

TRACES OF LIVING THINGS
    The subtitle, "strange feeling of sequence," is Fulcrum Press publisher Stuart Montgomery's observation. An earlier group of "TRACES OF LIVING THINGS" in *Origin* ser. 3, 9 (April 1968): 39–42, included "Museum," "At the blue ice superior spot"

(subsequently moved into "ʟᴀᴋᴇ ꜱᴜᴘᴇʀɪᴏʀ"), "TV," "Far reach," "Years," "Unsurpassed in beauty," "Human bean," "High class human," "What cause have you," and "Stone."

Museum   *NC, MLBW.*

In an alternate group titled "ᴛʀᴀᴄᴇꜱ ᴏꜰ ʟɪᴠɪɴɢ ᴛʜɪɴɢꜱ," *Origin* ser. 3, 9 (April 1968): 39.

Far reach   *NC, MLBW.*

In an alternate group titled "ᴛʀᴀᴄᴇꜱ ᴏꜰ ʟɪᴠɪɴɢ ᴛʜɪɴɢꜱ," *Origin* ser. 3, 9 (April 1968): 40.

TV   *NC, MLBW.*

In an alternate group titled "ᴛʀᴀᴄᴇꜱ ᴏꜰ ʟɪᴠɪɴɢ ᴛʜɪɴɢꜱ," *Origin* ser. 3, 9 (April 1968): 40.

We are what the seas   *NC, MLBW* [EA, VV].

In a numbered group of "ꜰᴏᴜʀ ᴘᴏᴇᴍꜱ," *Poetry* 111.3 (Dec. 1967): 159.

What cause have you   *NC, MLBW* [EA].

In an alternate group titled "ᴛʀᴀᴄᴇꜱ ᴏꜰ ʟɪᴠɪɴɢ ᴛʜɪɴɢꜱ," *Origin* ser. 3, 9 (April 1968): 42.

Stone   *NC, MLBW.*

In an alternate group titled "ᴛʀᴀᴄᴇꜱ ᴏꜰ ʟɪᴠɪɴɢ ᴛʜɪɴɢꜱ," *Origin* ser. 3, 9 (April 1968): 42.

The eye   *NC, MLBW* [EA].

Origin ser. 3, 2 (July 1966): 37, with a second and third stanza:

> leaf feather
> fin fugue
> modify—
> renewed
>
> union of two
> in love—we—
> with the same
> sure thing
> to end
> when one sees
> new truething,
> Love

For best work   *NC, MLBW* [EA].

Included in "ʜᴏᴍᴇᴍᴀᴅᴇ ᴘᴏᴇᴍꜱ" and "ʜᴀɴᴅᴍᴀᴅᴇ ᴘᴏᴇᴍꜱ" (1964) (see p. 210).

Origin ser. 3, 2 (July 1966): 22, and *The Voice That Is Great Within Us: American Poetry of the 20th Century*, ed. Hayden Carruth (New York: Bantam, 1970).

Smile   *NC, MLBW* [EA].

In a numbered group of "FOUR POEMS," *Poetry* 111.3 (Dec. 1967): 160, and *The Voice That Is Great Within Us: American Poetry of the 20th Century*, ed. Hayden Carruth (New York: Bantam, 1970).

Fall ("We must pull")   *NC, MLBW.*

In a numbered group of "FOUR POEMS," *Poetry* 111.3 (Dec. 1967): 159.

Years   *NC, MLBW* [EA].

In an alternate group titled "TRACES OF LIVING THINGS," *Origin* ser. 3, 9 (April 1968): 40.

Unsurpassed in beauty   *NC, MLBW* [EA].

In an alternate group titled "TRACES OF LIVING THINGS," *Origin* ser. 3, 9 (April 1968): 41.

Human bean   *NC, MLBW.*

In an alternate group titled "TRACES OF LIVING THINGS," *Origin* ser. 3, 9 (April 1968): 41.

High class human   *NC, MLBW.*

In an alternate group titled "TRACES OF LIVING THINGS," *Origin* ser. 3, 9 (April 1968): 41.

Ah your face   *NC, MLBW* [EA, VV].

Included in "HOMEMADE POEMS" and "HANDMADE POEMS" (1964) (see p. 200). *Origin* ser. 3, 2 (July 1966): 20.

Sewing a dress   *NC, MLBW* [EA, VV].

Origin ser. 3, 2 (July 1966): 30.

I walked/on New Year's Day   *NC, MLBW* [EA].

In a group of eleven poems titled "HEAR & SEE," *Origin* ser. 3, 7 (Oct. 1967): 57, with a variant final stanza: Each spoke:/Peace

Titled "*I Walked*" in *New Poetry Out of Wisconsin*, ed. August Derleth (Sauk City, Wis.: Stanton & Lee, 1967) 172.

J. F. Kennedy after/the Bay of Pigs   *NC, MLBW* [EA].

An undated MS in the Roub Collection has variant lines 5–6:—and walk the South Lawn/By Sun

Revised to the present text for a group of eleven poems titled "HEAR & SEE," *Origin* ser. 3, 7 (Oct. 1967): 53.

LN to LZ, May 10, 1961: "I can't get over Cuba invasion and J. F. K. *with* the Republicans—that it turned out unsuccessful seems beside the point (*NCZ* 281).

Mergansers   *NC, MLBW.*

In a group of eleven poems titled "HEAR & SEE," *Origin* ser. 3, 7 (Oct. 1967): 54, with variant lines 4–5:

> Thoughts, things
> > fold, unfold

"Shelter"   *NC, MLBW* [EA].

In a group of eleven poems titled "HEAR & SEE," *Origin* ser. 3, 7 (Oct. 1967): 56.
Also in *New Poetry Out of Wisconsin*, ed. August Derleth (Sauk City, Wis.: Stanton
& Lee, 1967) 172.

WINTERGREEN RIDGE   *NC, MLBW* [EA, VV].

Caterpillar 3/4 (April–July 1968): 229–37, with the following variant stanzas:
stanza 67:

> (wintergreen)
> > grass of parnassus
> > And beyond:

stanza 73: "in a bathtub . . . in liver and head" is omitted.

stanza 86:

> which 'cannot be stopped'
> > the pollened ragweed
> > > sneezeweed

stanza 91:

> mourn the loss
> > of humans
> > > no wild bird does

VV uses the following excerpts: stanzas 1–2 ("Where the arrows . . . of matter"), stanzas
68–70 ("ferns . . . water lily"), and stanzas 84–end ("So far out of flowers . . . of Equinox").

1968–1970

T&G: The Collected Poems (1936–1966) was published by Jonathan Williams's The Jar-
gon Society in 1969. In June 1969, LN responded to CC's offer to publish a book by
preparing two typescripts: "The Earth and Its Atmosphere" and "The Very Veery." Al
Millen retired, and in Sept. 1969, LN and Al moved permanently to their Black Hawk
Island home. CC and his wife, Shizumi, visited LN and Al in Nov. 1970.

PAEAN TO PLACE   *MLBW* [EA, VV].

A draft dated August 1968 in the Roub Collection shows the following variants:
stanza 1, lines 1–3:

> F natural
> and the sensuous s
> Fish, fowl, flood

stanza 10, line 5: rail's

stanza 12, line 5: Knew duckweed

stanza 13, line 3: what lay

stanza 15, lines 4–5:

      Underneath he must net Run
Lonely

stanza 16:

    His bright new car—
    my mother—her house
       next his—queried:
      Can a hummingbird
haul?

stanza 25, line 4: while she piped

stanza 30, line 1: Effort in us

stanza 31, lines 2–4:

    that freely descend
      to oceans' black depths
    In us an impulse toward

stanza 33, lines 3–4:

      Saw no snake
in the house   Where were They?—

stanza 35, lines 3–4:

    Hope the long-stemmed blue
      speedwell renews

stanza 37, lines 3–5:

     Leave things unbought—
    all one in the end
Possession—

stanza 38, line 2: the word:

stanza 40, lines 3–5:

    It was not always
    so   In Fishes
    rose

stanza 41, lines 1–3:

> red Mars
> stream-imaged
>   in my mind

Stony Brook 3/4 (1969): 32–35. *Stony Brook* and *MLBW* omit the three bullets in the segment beginning "I grew in green" between "slime-/song" and "Grew riding the river." They are present in the two MS versions and in EA.

VV uses the following excerpts: "Fish/fowl/flood . . . to water," "Anchored here . . . of her hair,'" and "On this stream . . . on the edge."

Alliance   *MLBW* [EA, VV].

An undated MS in the Roub Collection has a variant line 6: in yukka
Revised to the present text for *Stony Brook* 3/4 (1969): 31, and all other appearances.

Bashō   Unpublished [VV].

Related to the poem above, *"Alliance."*

The man of law   Unpublished in book form [EA].

The second of four "POEMS AT THE PORTHOLE" in *Stony Brook* 3/4 (1969): 32.
Another version of the poem—an undated MS in the Roub Collection—published posthumously in *Origin* ser. 4, 16 (July 1981): 36:

> Jefferson—statesman
>   Hopkins—poet
>   on the uses
>   of grief
>
> Hopkins
>   Jefferson
>   on the law
>   of the oak leaf

Not all harsh sounds displease—   Unpublished in book form.

The third of four "POEMS AT THE PORTHOLE" in *Stony Brook* 3/4 (1969): 32.
Another version of the poem, an undated MS in the Roub Collection, was published posthumously in *Origin* ser. 4, 16 (July 1981): 36:

> Not all harsh sounds
>   displease—
> Yellowhead blackbirds cough
>   thru rushes
>   as thru pronged
>   bronze

JEFFERSON AND ADAMS   **Unpublished.**

MS dated Jan. 1970 in the Roub Collection, published posthumously in *Origin* ser. 4, 16 (July 1981): 26–27.

Katharine Anne   **Unpublished.**

MS dated March 1970 in the Roub Collection, published posthumously in *Origin* ser. 4, 16 (July 1981): 34.

A gift to Gail and Bonnie Roub on the birth of their first daughter.

War   **Unpublished in book form.**

Origin ser. 3, 19 (Oct. 1970): 53, and posthumously in *BC* (1976).

HARPSICHORD & SALT FISH

LN prepared the typescript of H&SF in 1970 and sent it to James Laughlin at New Directions without success. It was unpublished at the time of her death on Dec. 31, 1970. Cid Corman tape recorded her reading from the typescript in Nov. 1970; his transcriptions of the tape recording provide the text for many of the poems in *Blue Chicory*. H&SF was published posthumously by Pig Press in Durham, U.K., 1991.

THOMAS JEFFERSON   **Unpublished in book form [VV, H&SF].**

An early undated MS appears in the Roub Collection:

Latin and Greek
my tools
to understand
humanity

I rode horse
away from a monarch
to an enchanting
philosophy

1

Martha!
She's seen four
of our children buried

My wife is ill!
and I sit
waiting for a quorum

2

Fast ride
his horse collapsed
Now *he* saddled walked

Borrowed a farmer's
unbroken colt
to Richmond

Richmond How stop
Arnold's
redcoats there

3
Elk Hill destroyed—
Cornwallis
carried off 30 slaves

Jefferson:
Were it to give them freedom
he'd have done right

4
                    South of France
To gaze
alone through the whole

Speculate
on the causes of sea color

Here concur
air, earth and water

. . .

Men at Paris die
from great cold

as do our American cattle
reasons the same—

want of feed and housing
Ill-governed France

but its soil good
For America

I taste their glorious wine
note how they make

Parmesan cheese
Under penalty of law

slip rice out of Lombardy
Around Nantes the ragged people

eat rye
and the women smite the anvil
. . .

Roman temple
"simple and sublime"

Maria Cosway
on his mind

white column
and arch

of the truest
proportions

5

To daughter Patsy: Read—
read Livy

No person full of work
was ever hysterical

Learn music, drawing
dancing

(I calculate 14 to 1
in marriage

she will draw
a blockhead)

Science also
Patsy

6

I was confident
the French Revolution

would end well
Adams differed: What is freedom

to their thousands upon thousands
who cannot read or write—

"impracticable as for the Elephants Lions
Tigers Panthers Wolves and Bears

in the Royal Menagerie of Versailles"
I gave the Lafayette dinner

ten days before the fall
of the Bastille

Their cool argument
"disfigured by no tinsel"

worthy of Xenophon
Plato, Cicero

7

Agreed with Adams:
spermaceti oil to Portugal

(for their church candles)
and salt fish

U.S. salt fish preferred
above all other

8

Jefferson of Patrick Henry
backwoods fiddler statesman:

"He spoke as Homer wrote"
Henry eyed our minister at Paris—

the Bill of Rights hassel—
"he remembers . . .

in splendor and dissipation
He thinks yet of bills of rights"

9

True, French frills and lace
for Jefferson, sword and belt

but follow the Court to Fontainbleau
he could not—

house rent would have left him
nothing to eat

. . .

He bowed to those he met
and talked with arms folded

He could be trimmed
by a two-month migraine

and yet
            stand up

10

Dear Polly:
I said No—no frost

in Virginia
The strawberries were safe

I'd have heard—I'm in
that kind of correspondence

with a young daughter—
if they were not

Now I must retract
I shrink from it

11

On view in the capital
his invention

the moldboard plow
Robert Fulton's dynamometer

tested the amount of force
to pull it

On view—to turn the ground
of knowledge

12

Political honors "splendid torments"
"if one could establish an absolute

power of silence over oneself"

When I set out for Monticello—

My grandchildren, could they
        not   know   me?

a good housejoiner will go with me
How are my young chestnut trees?

13

What is my religion?
Don't pin me down on the mysteries—
three are one and one is three

and yet the one not three
and the three not one
Let us accept the precepts common

to all religions and let alone
the particular dogmas
in which all religions differ

14

The old grudge would always pop up
Adams: Where was you?
Dear Adams: I was there—I was a Stoic

but I longed for Tranquility
Horace, Epicurus
I value the passions

(the senses stimulate the mind)
though yours drew you away from me
Adams: I have no doubt you was "fast asleep

in philosophical Tranquility
when ten thousand People paraded
the streets of Philadelphia"

15

Hamilton and the bankers
would make my country Carthage

I am abandoning the rich—
their dinner parties

I shall eat my simlins
with the class of science

or not at all
Next year the last of labors

among conflicting parties
Then my family

we shall sow our cabbages
together

16

We must hope for a natural aristocracy
of philosophy and art

Remember—Adams again: the greengrocer's daughter
she walks the streets of London dayly

spinach on her head
The Painters see her lovely face

elegant figure, she sitts for them
"The scientific Sir Wm. Hamilton

outbids the Painters, sends her to Schools
for a genteel Education, marries her

The Lady not only causes the Triumphs of the Nile
of Copenhagen and Trafalgar

but separates Naples from France
and banishes the King and Queen of Sicily

Such is the aristocracy
of the natural Talent of Beauty"

17
The delicious flower
of the acacia

or Mimosa Nilotica
from Mr. Lomax

18
Polly Jefferson at 8 had crossed
to father and sister in Paris

by way of London—Abigail
embraced her—Adams said

"in all my life I never saw
more charming child"

Death of Polly, 25,
Monticello

19
My harpsichord
my alabaster vase
and bridle bit bound
for Alexandria, Virginia

The good sea weather
of retirement
The drift and suck
and die-down of life

20
These were my passions:
Monticello and the temples

of learning and of law
I passed on to carpenters

bricklayers what I knew
and to an Italian sculptor
how to turn a volute
on a pillar

Approach the campus rotunda
from lower to upper
terrace—Cicero
had levels

21

Adams envied him
his "Eyes, hand and Horse"
his own eyes dim

Ah one should not envy
Tom Jefferson's cantering
rheumatism

22

Body leaving, let mind leave
Let dome live, the spherical dome
and colonnade

Martha (Patsy) stay
The Committee of Safety
must be warned

Stay youth—Anne and Ellen
the telescope, the bantams
and the seeds of the senega root

Revised to the present text for *Origin* ser. 3, 19 (Oct. 1970): 57–64, with variant
Arabic numerals.
  BC uses Roman numerals and omits the final line of VI ("Patsy").
  VV excerpts only

My wife is ill!
And I sit
        waiting
for a quorum

The Ballad of Basil   **Unpublished in book form [H&SF].**
Stony Brook 3/4 (1969): 31, and posthumously in *BC* (1976).

Wilderness   **Unpublished [H&SF].**
On her tape recording, she titles the poem, "Wild Man," hence *BC*'s use of the same title. CC's transcription of "Wild Man" used posthumously in *Montemora* 2 (Summer 1976).

Consider   **Unpublished in book form [H&SF].**
Untitled in *Origin* ser. 3, 19 (Oct. 1970): 56, where the poem begins: Consider the alliance—
Copytext for posthumous publication in *BC* (1976).

Otherwise   **Unpublished [H&SF].**
In the 13-poem MS dated Jan. 1958, where the poem is titled *"Letter/of Gerard Manley Hopkins,"* a variant line 9 reads: By the way I've not found
Revised to the present text for H&SF.
For *BC*, CC transcribed LN's tape-recorded reading of the poem, hence the variant lineation and the title *"Gerard Manley Hopkins."*

Nursery Rhyme   **Unpublished [H&SF].**
On the tape recording, she omits both title and subtitle, hence its untitled appearance in *BC*. LN's "that" of her line 9 is easily mistaken on the tape recording for the "It" of CC's transcribed line 8 in *BC*.
LN to LZ, Nov. 18, 1962: "Mont[gomery] Ward man came and fixed pump—he cdn't have done better if he'd been 'the greatest plumber in all London' as Hunt's neighbors called the one that lived near em. A model now of silent perfection, that pump, between drawings of water. Greatest plumber poem finished . . ." (*NCZ* 325).

Three Americans   **Unpublished [H&SF].**
An early version dated July 23, 1970, forms part of the Roub Collection:

> I
> John Adams was our man
> but delicate beauty
> touched the other one—
>
> an architect
> and a woman artist
> walked beside Jefferson
>
> II
> Abigail
> (long face horse-name)
> of stony acre

cheesemaker, chickenraiser
spoke, wrote
for John and TJ to savour

III
The tragedies
The men in the boxes—
Jefferson mourned: to arrive

in Paris just too late
to see Diderot
alive

LN's annotation: "(I give three packages of gum and cattails in tall grass for a title) (But o my God what travail till this was completed) Abigail is Mrs. John Adams. The name Gail is wonderful but that terribly prosaic and kitchen-maid Abi preceding is horrible. But what a wonderful original woman."

Revised to the present text for H&SF: "savour" is LN's spelling.

On the tape recording, she omits the title, hence its untitled appearance in *BC*.

POEMS AT THE PORTHOLE

Blue and white   Unpublished in book form [EA, VV, H&SF].
A separate poem in *Origin* ser. 3, 19 (Oct. 1970): 54, and posthumously in *BC* (1976).

The soil is poor   Unpublished in book form [EA, H&SF].
The first of four "POEMS AT THE PORTHOLE" in *Stony Brook* 3/4 (1969): 32.

Michelangelo   Unpublished in book form [EA, H&SF].
The fourth of four "POEMS AT THE PORTHOLE" in *Stony Brook* 3/4 (1969): 32.

Wallace Stevens   Unpublished in book form [EA, VV, H&SF].
A separate poem in Origin ser. 3, 19 (Oct. 1970): 56, and in *BC* (1976). *Stony Brook*'s other two "POEMS AT THE PORTHOLE" are "The man of law" and "Not all harsh sounds displease" (see p. 271).

BC's "POEMS AT THE PORTHOLE" duplicate *Stony Brook*'s.

SUBLIMINAL   **The title is first used in H&SF.**

Sleep's dream   Unpublished in book form [H&SF].
A separate poem in *Origin* ser. 3, 19 (Oct. 1970): 55, with two additional lines at the end of the poem:

> and my sometimes
> happy fatherphosphor

Copytext for posthumous publication in *BC* (1976).

Waded, watched, warbled   Unpublished in book form [H&SF].

In *Origin* ser. 3, 19 (Oct. 1970): 55, this two-stanza poem is followed by three bullets and a further three stanzas:

> Faithful to the marsh
> of my childhood
> we camp on the dryest portion
>
> In April's flood-freeze
> crystals hang low on the bush
> all day
>
> Then green—we're en rapport
> with grass as once or twice
> with humans

Copytext for posthumous publication in *BC* (1976).
Revised to the present text for H&SF.

Illustrated night clock's; Honest; and Night   Unpublished [H&SF].

After seeing the H&SF typescript, CC published the complete five-poem sequence, "SUBLIMINAL," in *Origin* ser. 4, 16 (July 1981): 32–33.

LZ   **Unpublished in book form [H&SF].**

Origin ser. 3, 12 (Jan. 1969): 3:

> line 2: waved toward Peck Slip
>
> line 5: was "Test"

Copytext for posthumous publication in *BC* (1976).

LN to CC, Aug. 6, 1968: "Peck Slip—you know—it's the fish market area my father shipping carp from our lake in refrigerated cars to Peck Slip. We followed Jewish holidays—the buyers did—but LZ says his folks did not eat carp. LZ was at our place in '36 & my father spoke confidentially and kindly in his gentle fashion to him and LZ was touched" (*BYHM* 170).

Peace   **Unpublished in book form [H&SF].**

Origin ser. 3, 19 (Oct. 1970): 54, and *BC* (1976).

LN to LZ, April 1956: "AEn[eas McAllister] came over to show me two tiny music box movements—wound one up (Strauss waltzes) and went out into the dark night with it to go home—a kind of musical firefly" (*NCZ* 227).

Thomas Jefferson Inside   **Unpublished in book form [H&SF].**

Tuatara 2 (June 1970): 8, and posthumously in *BC* (1976).

Foreclosure   **Unpublished in book form [H&SF].**

Tuatara 2 (June 1970): 8, and posthumously in *BC* (1976).

HIS CARPETS FLOWERED   **Unpublished in book form [EA, H&SF].**

The first version of the poem appears in EA without the subtitle and with the following variants (listed by section numeral):

I, stanza 2, line 5: of society's

I, stanza 5, line 4: I'd be now a rich man

I, stanza 6, lines 2–4:

> Item—I work in—sabots
> and blouse
> in the dye-house

I, stanza 7, line 3: I enjoy the indigo vats

II, stanza 1, line 2: by religion—slow

III, stanza 2, line 1: *growing here—Please do not mow*

In *Origin* ser. 3, 19 (Oct. 1970): 51–53, with the following variants:

I, stanza 2, line 5: of society's

I, stanza 5, line 4: I'd be now a rich man

I, stanza 6, line 3: and blouse—

The *Origin* version serves as copytext for *BC* (1976).

LN to CC, May 7, 1969: "I'm absorbed in writing poems—sequence—on William Morris. I know how to evaluate—Ruskin, etc., their kind of socialism—paternalism—but the letters of William Morris have thrown me. Title will be His Carpets Flowered. I can't read his poems. I'd probably weary of all those flowery designs in carpets, wall papers, chintzes . . . but as a man, as a poet speaking to his daughters and his wife—o lovely" (*BYHM* 188).

DARWIN   **Unpublished [VV, H&SF].**

Completed Aug. 18–24, 1970 (*BYHM* 230–31). VV excerpts only the following:

> His holy
>   slowly
>   mulled over
>   matter

LN gave Gail and Bonnie Roub an undated draft of "DARWIN" (possibly in Aug. 1970) with the following variants (listed by section numeral):

III, stanza 3:

> the earthquake—
>   Talcahuana Bay drained out—
>   an all-water wall
>   thrown up from the ocean

III, stanza 4, lines 1–2:

> Six seconds
>> and the town demolished

III, stanza 8, lines 2–3:

> Penguins and seals
>> those cold-sea creatures

III, stanza 9, line 1: For FitzRoy it was Hell

IV, stanza 3, line 1: Brought Drosera home

IV, stanza 4, line 4: till he published it

V, stanza 2:

> Tierra del Fuego's
>> shining glaciers—
>>> translucent blue
>> clear down to the indigo sea

V, stanza 3, line 3: that anyone should care

V, stanza 6, line 4: with the details left

V, stanza 7, line 1: to the working out of chance

CC's transcription of the tape recording was published posthumously in *BC* (1976) and in *Montemora* 2 (Summer 1976). A collation of the Roub draft and the tape recording was subsequently published in *Origin* ser. 4, 1 (Oct. 1977): 54–58.

Prose and Radio Plays

1937

UNCLE   **Unpublished in book form.**

New Directions 2 (1937): n.p. Much of the story is autobiographical: the characters of Great Uncle Gotlieb and Great Aunt Riecky Beefelbein are based on LN's maternal grandparents, the Kunzes. The "two hundred acres owned by the family" is a reference to the property on Black Hawk Island that passed from the Kunzes to Henry and Daisy Niedecker at the time of their marriage. The character of Uncle John has some of Henry Niedecker in him: his ownership of the hotel, his carp fishing, his sale of the land, and his too-generous nature. The character of Matty is partly based on the neurasthenic Daisy Niedecker.

1951–1952

SWITCHBOARD GIRL   **Unpublished in book form.**

The first trace of this prose piece is the poem MS "Titillated flip Switchboard girl," dated Feb. 27, 1951.

Titillated flip switchboard girl
on the tide of the red-lit plug-in are you high
with those whose bag is full—"Get me a single"
"Good, I like to sleep close"—or low with those
who must be jazzed   Honeypot switchboard girl
hand em your line they'll slip you more nylons
than you can use   Yes   Go ahead   switchboard lust
takes love out of life   Lewd sings cuckoo

A second draft is dated March 5, 1951:

Are you high
with those whose bag is full—
"Get me a single"
"Good, I like to sleep close"—
or low
with those who must be jazzed
honeypot
switchboard girl
hand em your line
they'll slip you more
nylons
than you can use
yes
go ahead
lewd sings cuckoo

The prose MS "SWITCHBOARD GIRL," dated April 16, 1951, has the following variants: par. 3: "in America they gear civilization to the seventeen-year-old" replaces the present "in America . . . to the seventeen-year-old", and six lines from the end:

"Whom did they say they wanted? Somebody by the name of Christ."
"Human materiel obsolescing. Boy, pass the blood."

replaces the present "What was the name . . . obsolescing."
New Directions 13 (1951): 87–89.
The piece relates her search for a job when her poor eyesight made proofreading too difficult.

The evening's automobiles . . .   Unpublished.
MS dated June 15, 1951, with appended "Notes" addressed to LZ:

all about the virgin is out! Too pretentious—you saw that.
No title as yet—your "The Evening's Automobiles"—well, something like
that along line of *moving*, something that has to do with mind moving so as

to unite all time etc . . .

or: 'Brute Goodness' or Renaissance . . .

I feel queer too as a man! I could print it under a man's name! No.

1. "Why should we honour those that die upon the field of battle a man may show as reckless a courage in entering into the abyss of himself." (This is Yeats, but I wdn't credit him, I guess?) [Refers to p. 338, line 25.]

2. It was abrupt you said with just saying "and said"—I don't feel that's so—it wouldn't be in poetry necessarily. But maybe you like this better. [Refers to p. 339, line 12.]

3. Some things in life are not credible as fiction! She actually did carry milk bottles for that purpose, she said. A great many things about her I can't tell—just wouldn't be believed. [Refers to p. 340, lines 1–2.]

4. I've used spaces to give the eye the confusion in her mind. [Refers to p. 340, lines 20–25.]

5. Here's my "brute goodness," won't use it if I use it as title. [Refers to p. 341, line 4.]

6. This maybe I'd better omit—she was socially unacceptable, taking a laxative and then f—ting all afternoon. Or it could be interpreted differently and melt in with the rest of that paragraph's horror. [Refers to p. 341, lines 4–7.]

Nevermind spelling—my dictionary says dead line, two words—I always look [up] everything before I send em out [ ]

> Thanks—I know you're busy [ ]
>
> Lorine

This piece adopts a male persona but the content is thinly veiled autobiography. It begins as LN leaves her job at Hoard's and returns home to Black Hawk Island.

AS I LAY DYING   **Unpublished.**

A 17-page radio script of William Faulkner's *As I Lay Dying*.

MS dated Jan. 11, 1952. A page of revisions dated Jan. 28, 1952.

LN to LZ, Jan. 23, 1952: "I don't write a terribly conventional radio script (not good radio they'll say) because I like to take hunks from the printed page and plunk em down in radio" (*NCZ* 188–89).

from TASTE AND TENDERNESS   **Unpublished.**

A typescript of the complete two-act script for radio about the James family went to LZ for Valentine's Day in 1952.

Only Act 1, scene 3 survives in MS sent to Dahlberg on Aug. 30, 1955.

LN to LZ, Feb. 14, 1952: "Radio *should* be a good medium for poetry—speech without practical locale. Stage with all its costumes and place and humans tripping about too distracting sometimes. Poetry and poetic drama—suggestion—the private printed page plus sound and silence" (*NCZ* 191).

CONTENTS LISTS THAT DIFFER FROM ORDER IN THIS VOLUME

Listed here are the contents of those collections—published or unpublished—that are not represented in the text in their original sequence. Alternate titles and first lines are enclosed in brackets.

My Friend Tree (Edinburgh: *Wild Hawthorn Press, 1961*)

My friend tree
You are my friend—
The young ones go away to school
There's a better shine
Black Hawk held: In reason
I'm a sharecropper
Remember my little granite pail?
Paul / when the leaves
Along the river
Old man who seined
Don't shoot the rail!
He built four houses
Not feeling well, my wood uncut.
My man says the wind blows from the south,
Well, spring overflows the land,
The clothesline post is set

"HOMEMADE POEMS" (*Gift-book for Cid Corman, Oct. 1964*)

Consider at the outset:
Ah, your face—
Alcoholic dream
To my pres- / sure pump
March
Something in the water
Santayana's
If only my friend
Frog noise / suddenly stops
Laundromat
In the transcendence
Is there someone [To whom]
Margaret Fuller
Watching dan- / cers on skates
Hospital Kitchen
Chicory flower / on campus
Fall ("Early morning corn")
LZ's

459

Ian's [Letter from Ian]
Some float off on chocolate bars
I knew a clean man
Scythe
So he said / on radio
I visit / the graves
For best work
The radio talk this morning
    [The obliteration]
Spring
The park / "a darling walk / for the mind"
Who was Mary Shelley?
Ruskin found wild strawberries
    [Wild strawberries]

"*HANDMADE POEMS*"
(Gift-book for Jonathan Williams,
Xmas 1964)

Consider at the outset:
Ah, your face
Alcoholic dream
Something in the water
To my pres- / sure pump
Laundromat
Santayana's
If only my friend
Frog noise / suddenly stops
In the transcendence
Margaret Fuller
Watching dan- / cers on skates
Chicory flower / on campus
Fall ("Early morning corn")
LZ's
Ian's [Letter from Ian]
Some float off on chocolate bars

I knew a clean man
Spring
The park / "a darling walk / for the mind"
Who was Mary Shelley?
So he said / on radio
Scythe
The radio talk this morning
Wild strawberries

"*HANDMADE POEMS*"
(Gift-book for Louis Zukofsky,
Xmas 1964)

Consider at the outset:
Ah, your face
Alcoholic dream
To my pres- / sure pump
Laundromat
March
Something in the water
Santayana's
If only my friend
Frog noise / suddenly stops
In the transcendence
Someone?—[To whom]
Margaret Fuller
Watching dan- / cers on skates
Hospital Kitchen
Chicory flower / on campus
Fall ("Early morning corn")
LZ's
Ian's [Letter from Ian]
Some float off on chocolate bars
I knew a clean man
Spring
The park / "a darling walk / for the mind"

I knew a clean man
Jesse James and his brother Frank
Who was Mary Shelley?

THE YEARS GO BY

In the great snowfall before the bomb
Swept snow, Li Po,
March
Two old men—
My father said I remember
Dead
Mother is dead
The graves
He moved in light
Shut up in woods
To Aeneas who closed his piano
I am sick with the Time's buying sickness.
Hi, Hot-and-Humid
Horse, hello
Energy glows at the lips—
Happy New Year
I've been away from poetry
On hearing / the wood pewee
I rose from marsh mud,
February almost March bites the cold.

IN EXCHANGE FOR HAIKU

Hear
How white the gulls
New-sawed
Springtime's wide
Lights, lifts
Beautiful girl—
July, waxwings
If only my friend

Popcorn-can cover
O late fall
People, people—

HOME/WORLD

My life is hung up
Get a load
Easter
Dusk—
River-marsh-drowse
Linnaeus in Lapland
In Leonardo's light
Art Center
Club 26
My mother saw the green tree toad
The men leave the car
Something in the water
Now in one year
Watching dan- / cers on skates
Letter from Ian
As I paint the street
Grandfather *[Poet's work]*
The Badlands
To foreclose
To my small / electric pump
I visit / the graves
Scythe
Fall ("Early morning corn")
Chicory flower / on campus
The wild and wavy event
Bird singing
CHURCHILL'S DEATH
To my pres- / sure pump
Consider at the outset:
Alcoholic dream
Some float off on chocolate bars

"The Very Veery" MS
(*June 1969*)

Designer: Janet Wood
Compositor: Westchester Book/Rainsford Type
Text: 10/14 Janson
Display: Franklin Gothic Heavy, Janson+ Expert
Printer and Binder: Edwards Brothers, Inc.